AVOIDING UNFAIR DISMISSAL CLAIMS

AVOIDING UNFAIR DISMISSAL CLAIMS

Daniel Barnett

Barrister, Lincoln's Inn

JOHN WILEY & SONS, LTD
Chichester • New York • Weinheim • Brisbane • Toronto • Singapore

Published by John Wiley & Sons Ltd,
Baffins Lane, Chichester,
West Sussex PO19 1UD, England

National   01243 779777
International   (+44) 1243 779777
e-mail (for orders and customer service enquiries): cs-books@wiley.co.uk
Visit our Home Page on http://www.wiley.co.uk
                 or http://www.wiley.com

Other Wiley Editorial Offices

John Wiley & Sons, Inc., 605 Third Avenue,
New York, NY 10158-0012, USA

WILEY-VCH GmbH, Pappelallee 3,
D-69469 Weinheim, Germany

Jacaranda Wiley Ltd, 33 Park Road, Milton,
Queensland 4064, Australia

John Wiley & Sons (Asia) Pte Ltd, 2 Clementi Loop #02-01,
Jin Xing Distripark, Singapore 129809

John Wiley & Sons (Canada) Ltd, 22 Worcester Road,
Rexdale, Ontario M9W 1L1, Canada

British Library Cataloguing in Publication Data

A catalogue record for this book is available from the British Library

ISBN 0-471-96564-2

Typeset in 11/13pt Times New Roman by The Midlands Book Typesetting Company, Loughborough, Leicestershire.
Printed and bound in Great Britain by Biddles Ltd, Guildford and King's Lynn.
This book is printed on acid-free paper responsibly manufactured from sustainable forestry, in which at least two trees are planted for each one used for paper production.

To Miranda

For agreeing to become my wife

ACKNOWLEDGMENTS

One of the most frequent comments I hear when representing employers and employees is 'I wish someone had told me that six months ago'. Employers are increasingly conscious of the need to ensure that the correct procedure is followed when dismissing employees, but the only way to learn the correct procedure is through painful, and often expensive, experience.

I would like to thank, without naming them, the many solicitors and employers who encouraged me to write this book as a basic guide to the procedures employers must follow when dismissing employees. Many of the suggestions in this book arise from the practical experiences of people whom I have represented.

I would also like to thank my parents, Garry and Lynne Barnett, for their support and assistance over many years. They spent many hours proof-reading the various drafts of this book, ensuring that it was easy to understand and could be followed by people who were unfamiliar with a traditional legal style. Thank you both.

Finally, I would like to thank Miranda. As a fellow member of the Bar, she is fully aware of the temptation to switch off after a day in court. She helped me remain motivated during the many months it took to write this book.

CONTENTS

PREFACE

Unfair dismissal claims are won or lost according to the behaviour of an employer *before* the dismissal. If you act in an unfair or arbitrary manner before you dismiss an employee, almost nothing you do after the dismissal will be able to rectify this.

This is a book about how to carry out dismissals in a way which employment tribunals (previously known as industrial tribunals) will consider to be fair. The bulk of this book is directed at steps you should take to ensure that all relevant procedures, no matter how trivial or inconvenient, are complied with. If you follow the advice in this book, your dismissed employees will be left with little ground to argue that you acted unfairly, either in the decision that you took or in the way you reached that decision.

The remainder of this book deals with how to prepare for and conduct hearings before employment tribunals, should you choose to represent yourself and not engage the services of a lawyer.

An important point to bear in mind is this: if a resentful employee decides to claim against you for unfair dismissal, nothing in the world can stop him. You will lose at least one working day when attending the tribunal to defend the claim. You may have to call other employees as witnesses, and will therefore lose their day's productivity. You may choose to be represented by a lawyer and therefore incur legal costs. However, if you follow the advice in this book, there is a good chance that you will *not* have to pay your employee compensation at the end of the day.

Before the various steps you should take are addressed, it will be useful to give a very brief overview of how the law relating to unfair dismissal works. For convenience the name 'Alf' has been adopted throughout this book for the employee who is claiming unfair dismissal.

The law is stated as of 30th September 1998, although some changes have been made to reflect developments up to 31st January 1999.

1. THE LAW OF UNFAIR DISMISSAL: AN OVERVIEW

1.1   Can Alf get his claim off the ground?

There are several hurdles which Alf will have to overcome before an employment tribunal can even hear his claim. They are as follows:

a   Is Alf employed? Alf cannot claim unfair dismissal if he is not actually employed by you. The law recognises a distinction between the employed and the self-employed. If Alf is self-employed (as, for example, a window-cleaner might be) and you terminate his services, he cannot claim unfair dismissal. The main indicators are whether you supply equipment and materials to Alf (employed) or he supplies his own (self-employed); whether you deduct tax and national insurance at source (employed); whether you pay holiday and sick pay (employed) or whether Alf fends for himself (self-employed); whether Alf works exclusively for you (employed) or whether he works for a number of different clients (self-employed). It can sometimes be quite difficult to determine Alf's status, although it is crucial in determining his right to claim unfair dismissal.

b   Length of employment: Alf must have worked for at least two years before he is allowed to claim unfair dismissal. If he has not worked for two years, he cannot claim unfair dismissal. There are a number of exceptions to this rule, which are discussed at 18.15. Moreover, the government is presently considering reducing this two-year qualifying period to one year.

c   Age: If Alf is over the normal retirement age for his job, he may not be able to claim unfair dismissal. A word of caution – the normal retirement age is not necessarily the state pension age. This is discussed further at 10.9.

1.2   Was Alf dismissed?

Unless Alf is actually *dismissed*, he cannot claim unfair dismissal!
An employment tribunal will take a fairly robust attitude as
to what constitutes a dismissal. A dismissal can occur without
the use of phrases such as 'you are sacked' – the central question will be whether it was you or Alf who, in reality, terminated
his employment. Indeed an employment tribunal can even
deem there to have been a dismissal when Alf appears to have
resigned.

Generally it will be obvious when Alf has been dismissed,
and so this should not be an issue in the case. For example, if
he has been dismissed for theft, or for persistent absence or
incompetence, then you will admit that he was dismissed. The
only real issue for an employment tribunal will be whether the
dismissal was fair or unfair.

Sometimes, however, the situation is not quite that
straightforward. Complications arise, for example, if Alf has
simply stopped turning up to work – has he resigned? What if
you tell him 'if you don't resign, you'll be sacked!' and he resigns
as a result. Is that a resignation or dismissal? What if you have
been reducing his pay or making life difficult for him with a
view to forcing his resignation? Or if you told him 'go home
and don't come back', meaning 'don't come back today', but
Alf interpreted that as being dismissed?

If you think that there might have been a resignation
rather than a dismissal (thus preventing Alf from claiming
unfair dismissal), you should have a look at the categories
set out in Chapter 17 to see if the situation falls within one of
the bands of resignation that the law interprets as being a
dismissal.

1.3   Was the dismissal fair or unfair?

To show that a dismissal was fair it is, in general, necessary to
show that the dismissal was for one of four reasons. It is then
also necessary to show that the dismissal was reasonable in all
the circumstances.

The reasons are:

a   Capability or qualifications: If Alf is unable to do his job properly or lacks the appropriate qualifications then this will be a potentially valid ground for dismissing him. Examples include if Alf is unable to work due to ill-health, if his quality of work decreases and it is decided that he is no longer capable of doing the job properly, or if he has misled you over the qualifications he possesses.

b   Conduct: Conduct at work is probably the most common reason for dismissal. This can be one incident of serious misconduct (such as theft) or the accumulation of less serious incidents of misconduct (such as aggressive or offensive behaviour, persistent absenteeism or refusal to obey your instructions).

c   Redundancy: Many people do not realise that redundancy is a form of dismissal and that if the correct procedures are not complied with then it will be an unfair dismissal. Redundancy has a different meaning to a lawyer than to a layman, and unless the situation clearly falls within the lawyer's definition of redundancy then you run the risk of an employment tribunal finding that the dismissal was unfair.

d   Contravention of an enactment: If a law prohibits an employee doing something for which he is employed (e.g. a lorry driver who loses his driving licence) then it will be potentially fair to dismiss him.

It should be noted that the four headings above are not exhaustive. The tribunal has the right, if it considers that there is some other substantial reason for the dismissal that does not fall within the list above, to decide that the dismissal was fair. Each of these categories is considered in full in the following chapters.

1.4   Even if a reason for dismissal falls into one of the above categories that is not, of itself, enough to make the dismissal fair. It must be shown that the dismissal was reasonable in the circumstances. There is a three-stage test that an employer should adopt before dismissing someone. You must:

i   Be absolutely clear in your own mind what the reason (or, if more than one, the principal reason) for the potential dismissal is.

ii   Investigate the matter fully. If Alf is suspected of theft, tell him who the witnesses against him are and give him the opportunity to defend himself. If he is absent through illness, investigate the nature of the illness, whether work can be done from home, and how long he is likely to be absent.

iii   Decide what disciplinary sanction is appropriate. It would not be reasonable to dismiss someone for carelessly damaging a piece of equipment worth £50, although a warning might be appropriate. Alf should be invited to comment on the proposed sanction, and any explanation he offers for his conduct should be taken into account when deciding on the appropriate penalty.

If any of these three stages is omitted then a dismissal is likely to be unfair. If an employer comes to a clearly unreasonable decision (or a decision taken in bad faith) when considering stages (ii) or (iii) then the dismissal is also likely to be unfair.

2. HOW TO DISMISS SOMEONE FOR INCAPABILITY

Introduction

2.1   There is sometimes a degree of overlap between incapability and misconduct. If Alf is failing to sell a sufficient number of products or is making too many mistakes in the ordinary course of his work this may be due either to incompetence or to laziness/ indifference, which would qualify as misconduct. Accordingly the procedures for this sort of incapability/misconduct are very similar.

This chapter will address how to dismiss somebody in the following situations:

a   where Alf is simply incompetent – i.e. he is not up to the job;

b   where Alf is ill and therefore continuously absent from work (either for a long period or a series of regular short absences);

c   where Alf lacks the proper qualifications to do the job.

(a) Dismissing Alf for incompetence

Introduction

2.2   It may be difficult to show that Alf is incompetent if he has been doing the same job for a long time. It will be almost impossible if he has recently received a good report or a pay rise (unless the pay rise was across the board). Incompetence is more commonly a reason for dismissal if Alf has been transferred to a new job and it transpires that he is not up to it, or if he is employed for a trial period to see if he is suitable. In the latter situation Alf will be unlikely to have the required two years' service and therefore would not be entitled to claim unfair dismissal in any event.

Before dismissing Alf for incompetence you must generally be sure of four things:

i   that he *is* incompetent,

ii   that he has been given the opportunity to improve,

iii   that he has not improved, and is not likely to do so; and,

iv   that it is not reasonable to give him an alternative job.

Step 1: You must be sure that Alf is incompetent

2.3   Sometimes this step is fairly easy to satisfy, for example if there has been a clear fall-off in sales due to Alf's work (or lack of it). Sometimes, however, incompetence is simply a matter of impression rather than hard, objective evidence (such as a diminution in production). Given that you will be concerned about not making a mistake, and also be concerned about preventing (or winning) an unfair dismissal claim being brought against you, you should see if there is any more concrete evidence than simple 'impression'. Such evidence might be:

- in a larger organisation, statements from people who are in daily contact with Alf;

- a comparison of Alf's daily output figures (for example, number of contracts negotiated, letters typed or customers served) with those of other employees;

- frequency of complaints received from customers.

At the end of the day you have to be able to form a genuine belief (i.e. not motivated by dislike of the individual concerned) that it is more likely than not that he is incapable of doing the job.

2.4   If you know that *one* of your employees is not competent, but do not know exactly who, it is generally not justifiable to dismiss all (or both) possible employees. This is because employment tribunals will always view any arbitrary action as extremely serious; it will almost always be arbitrary to dismiss an employee when you cannot be more certain than not that he is the incompetent one.

There is an exception to the above rule. If the nature of the job is such that it is imperative that there can be no risk of future mistakes then it may be justifiable (under the general catch-all 'some other substantial reason') to dismiss more than one person when you cannot be sure that he is the culprit. An example might be where one of two mechanics in a factory makes a fundamental error resulting in a serious risk to other workers, being an error which may re-occur. It may be, in the employer's view, imperative that the incompetent employee be dismissed. If each mechanic blames the other for the error, and the employer (after extensive investigation) cannot tell who is telling the truth, he would be justified in dismissing both of them. This is because of the possible dire consequences of continuing to let the incompetent mechanic work outweighing the unfairness involved when dismissing someone who is not personally culpable.

This exception, however, will only be appropriate to rely upon in the rarest of circumstances. Unless it is absolutely imperative that a mistake should not re-occur (and mere financial loss is unlikely to be sufficient) then you must be satisfied that you have correctly identified Alf as being the person responsible for the mistakes when administering disciplinary sanctions.

2.5　　At the end of the day, however, the important thing is that you have to have a genuine belief that Alf is incompetent. If you do not genuinely believe that, or if an employment tribunal forms the view that you did not believe that, then you will be found to have dismissed Alf unfairly. It is the need to prove to a tribunal that, at the time of dismissal you genuinely believed that Alf was incompetent, which makes it desirable to have the sort of objective evidence referred to above.

Step 2: You must have given Alf the opportunity to improve

2.6　　If you do not think that Alf is capable of doing the job properly you must tell him before you dismiss him. He may think that he is doing the job properly, or it may even transpire that he was incorrectly shown how to do his job.

It is never pleasant to tell someone that they are not up to scratch and many employers are reluctant to do so through embarrassment. It is, however, obvious that from Alf's point of view he would prefer to be given a chance to improve than be dismissed without warning or notice.

2.7　　You must explain to Alf precisely what it is that he is doing wrong. If his work involves a degree of technical skill then demonstrations of that skill must be provided.

2.8 You should put a warning as to his competence in a letter. This is for two reasons:

- Alf will take a written warning more seriously than mere verbal guidance. It has a higher chance of encouraging him to do the job properly and therefore a higher chance of resolving the problem without recourse to dismissal; and,

- in the event that dismissal does become necessary and Alf claims against you then you will have clear evidence to put before the tribunal showing that you did warn him as to his competence and that you did give him the opportunity to improve.

2.9 The letter should contain the following points:

- Full details of the faults being complained of. If there are a very large number of small matters it is sufficient to refer to them in passing (i.e. 'You will recall our conversation yesterday when we discussed the ways in which your work required improvement').

- A warning that you consider the problem to be serious enough to justify dismissal if Alf does not improve.

- A minimum time period during which Alf has the chance to improve before you review his performance (see 2.10 below).

- An invitation to Alf to discuss the matter further with you.

2.10 The minimum time period should be sufficient to allow Alf to improve. It is unlikely that a period of less than four weeks will be adequate. A long-standing employee who is being required to perform new tasks can expect to receive a longer period to adjust than a new employee who has no track record of efficiency and who gives no indication of being capable of improvement.

During the period for improvement you should monitor Alf's performance carefully. Beware, however, of being seen to be breathing down his neck – this might be seen by him (and by an employment tribunal) as a way of deliberately putting pressure on him to encourage him to resign. In those circumstances a resignation would be viewed by a tribunal as a dismissal and you would almost certainly be found to have acted unfairly (see Chapter 17).

2.11 Sometimes it is not necessary to allow a period for improvement. This may be the case when the consequences of Alf's mistakes are so serious, or so potentially serious, that you simply cannot take the risk of another mistake.

Example

A pilot was dismissed after making a faulty landing (for which he was to blame), which caused considerable damage to the airplane. The Court of Appeal held that some jobs, such as flying an airplane, require such a high standard of professional skill that even the slightest departure from the norm is enough to justify dismissal – *Alidair v Taylor [1978] IRLR 82*

Step 3: You must have formed the view that Alf is not likely to improve

2.12 After the monitoring period has expired you should re-evaluate Alf's performance. Clearly if he is now achieving the goals you set the problem will be solved. If he is only a little way short of the goals then you should extend the monitoring period and inform him of what you have decided. It will *not* be reasonable at this point to dismiss someone who has significantly improved, albeit not to the level that you hoped.

2.13 If Alf has not improved at all, or has failed to improve sufficiently to warrant giving him a longer period, you will need to hold a meeting with him at which the options can be explored. You will need to inform him in writing, prior to the meeting, of the following points:

- that in your view his performance has not improved and that you are considering dismissal as a result;

- that you wish to have a meeting with him to discuss (a) whether you are correct in your assessment that he has not improved, and (b) if you are correct, whether there are any reasons why he should not be dismissed;

- that he may bring a friend/representative to the meeting

together with any colleagues who may be able to attest to his ability and effort.

The letter should also state the date (and place) of the meeting. If it is inconvenient for Alf to attend you must reschedule it to a more convenient time.

2.14   Before the meeting you must investigate whether there are any alternative positions within the company which could be offered to Alf. This is considered below at 2.16.

2.15   At the meeting you must permit Alf to make any representations that he considers appropriate. See the advice on how to hold a disciplinary/dismissal meeting in Section 4.40.

Step 4: You must be sure it is not reasonable to offer Alf another job

2.16   It is necessary for you to consider whether it is possible to redeploy Alf in a position where he will be able to cope. In a small or medium company the answer will usually be obvious – either there is a position available or there is not.

In a larger company (60+ employees) or a company which is associated with (or linked to) others, you will need to make slightly more extensive enquiries. This can be done by various means, for example:

- sending Alf's details to the personnel department;

- contacting other managers directly with a view to seeing if they have any appropriate vacancies;

- circulating a memo to department heads;

- contacting any associated employers to enquire whether they have any suitable positions.

It is also well worth asking Alf, during the dismissal meeting, whether there are any areas in which he would particularly like to work. It may be that he knows (through the employee grapevine) of vacancies that may soon become available through resignations or otherwise.

Keep a thorough record of all steps you have taken when considering alternative employment – this is the type of evidence which impresses employment tribunals and encourages them to view you with favour.

2.17 If you form the view that there is another job which Alf might be capable of doing, you should ask him, either at the dismissal meeting or preferably before, whether he wants to do it. Put this enquiry in writing so that you can prove to an employment tribunal that you did make the offer.

If he wishes time to consider his options you must allow him a reasonable amount of time. A week will usually be sufficient unless the new job involves major considerations such as moving house.

It is justifiable to offer Alf a new position which involves a certain reduction in wages. An employee might prefer a lower paid job to no job at all. Therefore a reasonable employer will offer his employee the lower paid job if it is available. Failure to offer suitable alternative employment can render an otherwise fair dismissal unfair.

(b) Dismissing Alf for absence due to illness or injury

Introduction

2.18 There is a distinction between illness or injury caused by the employment and illness or injury arising that is unconnected to the employment. The former situation might arise if Alf has an allergy to substances found in your factory, or if he sustains a back injury when lifting. In that sort of case it will be justifiable to dismiss Alf, provided you have made appropriate attempts to find him alternative employment within the company (see 2.16).

2.19 The two situations when you will be considering dismissal are where Alf is frequently absent for short periods and where Alf is absent for one long, continuous period. As you will see the procedure adopted is slightly different depending on which case it is.

2.20 This heading covers absence due to sickness. It should not be confused with absence due to lethargy or indifference (i.e. taking the day off). If Alf is simply taking days off for no particular reason then you should use the 'conduct' section of this book (see Chapter 4).

Investigating the illness

2.21   Short, frequent absences will usually be due either to a recurring illness (or injury), due to a heightened susceptibility to infection or simply due to hypochondria! The basic question that a tribunal will ask, if Alf claims against you, is 'should you have waited any longer to see what happens, and if so, for how long?'

There are three steps you must take in this situation before you dismiss Alf.

Step 1: Establish the reason for Alf's absence

2.22   This may appear obvious: however, you should discuss with Alf (and preferably obtain in writing) precise details of his ill-health. If he is persistently absent for short periods, you can discuss this at work. If he has been continually absent for a long period, you should write to him and ask him for exact details of his illness and when he thinks he will be ready to return to work.

Step 2: Consider whether improvement is likely

2.23   The second step is to consider, with the aid of medical advice, whether Alf's attendance record is likely to improve in the future. To this purpose you should ask Alf to provide you with a brief letter to his GP authorising the GP to provide a short medical report (see 2.25 below if Alf does not give permission). If Alf has been examined by a company doctor then legally you do not require his consent; the company doctor, however, may be reluctant to divulge confidential information due to medical ethics. You should then write to the GP, enclosing a letter of authority from Alf, asking him to advise you on the following points:

- the nature of the illness;

- if Alf has been absent for one long continuous period, how long he is likely to remain off work;

- if Alf has been persistently absent for short periods, the likelihood of recurrence or of some other illness arising; and,

- how any recurrence will affect Alf's ability to work in the future.

Some GPs will require a small payment for such a report – you should check first and offer to pay this if necessary.

2.24   It may be wise, if the GP's response is tentative or unclear, to ask Alf to consent to being examined by a consultant. Although this may cost you a few hundred pounds it is clearly preferable to losing an unfair dismissal claim. Consider it an investment – a medium to large company (over, say, 40 employees) could be seen as acting unreasonably in failing to obtain a consultant's report when the GP's report is unclear.

The reason for obtaining medical advice is that neither you nor Alf are qualified to determine the prospects of his ability to work in the future. Accordingly you are not in a proper position to judge whether dismissal is an appropriate course.

2.25   If Alf refuses to undergo a medical examination at your request or refuses to authorise his GP to provide a report then you will have to act on the facts currently within your knowledge. Legally, Alf is not obliged to provide you with medical information unless there is a term in his contract of employment to that effect.

If you dismiss Alf as a result of the facts within your knowledge, but without the benefit of medical advice due to his refusal to authorise it, then you cannot be criticised if non-disclosed medical evidence suggests at a later stage that you acted incorrectly.

You are not entitled to infer any sinister reason behind Alf's refusal to authorise the release of medical records. He may be reluctant to disclose them for a reason entirely unconnected with his absence from work. If you assume the worst because of Alf's failure to divulge all the details of his personal medical history then you will be acting unfairly in dismissing him. You must only act based on the information that he allows you to have. It is, however, legitimate to assume in the absence of evidence to the contrary, that the current state of affairs (i.e. absence from work) will be ongoing provided that you have tried to investigate the situation, kept Alf informed of your enquiries and invited his comments at all stages.

Step 3: Is dismissal justified?

2.26   The third step is to consider, in view of the medical information as to Alf's ability to work in the future, whether it is reasonable to dismiss him. In doing so you must remember that Alf has a legal right not to be unfairly dismissed which he can enforce in the tribunals. The decision to dismiss him, which is obviously a draconian remedy from his point of view, must be justifiable in the terms of the cost or lost revenue if you continue to employ him (albeit at a lower level of efficiency).

2.27   In deciding whether dismissal is necessary you should consider the following facts:

- the length of the various absences and the spaces of good health between them;

- your need for the work to be done by that particular employee;

- the impact of Alf's absence on those who work with him;

- any considerations personal to Alf which place an additional obligation on you to retain him (e.g. length of service).

Dismissal

2.28   By the time you have gone through the above steps you would have formed a preliminary view as to whether it is justifiable to dismiss Alf. In addition Alf will be aware that you are considering dismissal.

You will come to one of three conclusions:

i   That it is necessary to dismiss Alf. This will often be the conclusion reached in cases of one long, ongoing period of absence. It will be less common to reach this conclusion when Alf is frequently absent for short periods.

ii   That Alf is likely to carry on being absent in the future; however, it cannot be guaranteed and therefore he should be given a final chance. A tribunal would usually expect a reasonable employer to offer Alf a final chance even when he has taken long periods of absence in the past – remember, you are dismissing him due to the risk of future absences, not past.

iii Alternatively, that Alf is likely to return to work soon and is unlikely to continue being absent in the future – in this case it will be unfair to dismiss him.

2.29 If you have decided that it is necessary to dismiss Alf with immediate effect, then you should write to Alf informing him that he is dismissed. The letter should contain the following points:

- a brief description of the length and frequency of Alf's absences.

- a synopsis of your investigation into his illness (this is important because it might be the only proof before a tribunal that you have made efforts to determine whether Alf's illness is likely to be ongoing).

- that you have formed the view that his illness prevents him carrying out his duties as an employee.

- that, after consultation with him (and, if appropriate, medical advisers – name them) there does not seem to be a reasonable chance of improvement.

- (if appropriate) that you have considered other options such as Alf working from home, having a part-time job or working flexitime, but those options would not work.

- in the circumstances you have no option but to dismiss him with notice. See Chapter 12 for any payments (such as notice pay) that you must make to him upon dismissal.

- that he has the right to appeal against your decision. If he wishes to appeal, he should put his reasons in writing to you within, say, seven days (note: the manner of requesting an appeal should be appropriate to the nature of Alf's incapacity). See Chapter 11 for appeal procedures.

You should attach a cheque representing any accrued wages/ holiday pay/notice period.

2.30 If, by contrast, you have decided that Alf should be given a final chance, then you will need to set out the position in writing. The letter should contain the following points:

- the first two points mentioned above (2.29), i.e. description of illness and your investigation;

- your concern that, at present, he seems unlikely to be able to continue fulfilling his role as an employee;

- a warning that unless he is able to resume normal attendance within a reasonable period (four weeks is suggested) then you will have no other option but to dismiss him and seek a replacement.

2.31   If Alf does not reply to your letter, and if he fails to resume his work within the allotted period, then you will be entitled to dismiss him. The dismissal letter should take the same form as the one set out above. If he responds that he did not receive the first letter, you will need to re-offer the final chance as set out above.

(c) Dismissing Alf due to lack of proper qualifications

2.32   It is not easy to claim that your principal reason for dismissing Alf is his lack of appropriate qualifications. This is for the simple reason that by the time an unfair dismissal action can be brought Alf will have been working for you for at least two years (one year if the government's recent proposals become law). Accordingly an employment tribunal will view with some scepticism a claim that Alf turned out to be improperly qualified.

2.33   As a matter of reality there are only two situations when it might be possible to dismiss Alf for reasons relating to his qualifications. The first situation is if the law relating to required qualifications changed. Thus if Alf was an electrical engineer, and a law came into being requiring all electrical engineers to gain a new qualification, then you (as a responsible employer) would encourage Alf to take the appropriate exam. If, however, he kept failing the exam (or refused to take it) then you would be justified in dismissing him for lacking the necessary qualification. Note that there is an overlap between the incapability reason in this example and the 'failure to comply with an enactment' reason for dismissing an employee (see 10.3) – the most common example being a driver who loses his driving licence.

2.34   Secondly, you might be entitled to dismiss Alf if he misled you when he applied for a job. Thus if Alf was employed as a printer and it transpired that he did not possess the Guild qualifications that he had claimed to have, you might be entitled to dismiss him (provided you followed the appropriate procedure). This would be very closely linked to a dismissal for misconduct. You should be careful, however, that you are not perceived as acting disproportionately. Unless the fact of having the qualification is important to the continued performance of the job, if Alf can do the job you should allow him to continue with it (albeit, perhaps after issuing a written warning for misconduct).

3. HOW TO DISMISS SOMEONE FOR CRIMINAL ACTS OUTSIDE OF WORK

Introduction

3.1 Crimes outside of employment which affect employment will usually take the form of a violent or dishonest act. It will be unusual to fairly dismiss Alf simply because of a criminal act that he has committed outside of work. It may be that the criminal act is the icing on the cake, or it may be that it makes you think that he is an undesirable person to have as an employee. It is only in certain circumstances, however, that a criminal act occurring outside of work justifies immediate dismissal, namely when it means that Alf becomes unsuitable to continue working, or other employees refuse to work with him.

3.2 It is important to note that for Alf's actions to qualify as a crime, he does not need to have been arrested by the police or convicted by a court. You are entitled to act on the basis that Alf has committed a violent or dishonest act if you have investigated the circumstances of the alleged act and formed a reasonable belief that Alf is guilty of it. If, with hindsight, it transpires that he was *not* responsible for the violent or dishonest act that you had blamed him for, you will not be criticised by an employment tribunal for acting unfairly provided you had investigated the matter fully at the time.

If Alf has been convicted and is in prison, or if he is in custody awaiting trial, then it may be that his contract of employment has been 'frustrated' and he is not allowed to claim unfair dismissal (in which case you need not be concerned about the mechanics of dismissal). This means that Alf's contract of employment is prevented from operating normally due to circumstances beyond your control – i.e. the fact that Alf is in prison. The courts have not laid down clear guidance as to how long Alf must be imprisoned for before the contract of employment becomes frustrated: however, a rule of thumb is that imprisonment of more than three to six months is likely to 'frustrate' the contract (and thus prevent Alf claiming unfair dismissal).

3.3   Throughout this chapter the words 'crime' or 'criminal' may be used as a convenient way of describing acts of violence or dishonesty. If Alf is referred to as a criminal, or his acts referred to as crimes, it does *not* mean that has been arrested by the police and prosecuted. It simply means that you suspect him of having committed an act which is technically illegal and involves elements of violence or dishonesty.

3.4   You will have to convince an employment tribunal on three points before it will declare a dismissal for criminal conduct outside of work to be fair:

a   that you had a genuine and reasonable belief that Alf *had* committed the criminal act (see 3.5);

b   that the criminal conduct makes it difficult for you to continue employing Alf, due to its adverse affect on your business or the risk to your business of continuing to employ him (see 3.12);

c   that dismissal is a reasonable sanction in the circumstances (rather than, for example, issuing a written warning or suspending Alf for a period) (see 3.20).

(a) A genuine and reasonable belief that Alf had committed the criminal act

3.5   If Alf has been convicted of a criminal offence, then this step will clearly be satisfied. No reasonable employer could believe anything other than that Alf has committed a crime if he either pleaded guilty or a court found him guilty. If this has not occurred, you will have to conduct your own investigation into whether you believe he is guilty.

If he is in custody, it may be that his contract of employment has become impossible to perform. If so, the law regards his employment as automatically terminated and Alf cannot claim unfair dismissal (see 3.2).

If he has been charged and is awaiting trial, you may be justified in suspending him pending the result of the trial. Any suspension should be on full pay unless Alf's contract of employment expressly provides that he can be suspended without pay. Suspension, however, may not be ideal (you may be short-staffed and still have to pay Alf his wages). In addition, an unreasonably long period of suspension (maybe as little as four weeks), particularly without pay, may entitle Alf to resign and claim that he has been constructively dismissed (see 17.2).

The best approach, therefore, is not to await the result of the trial but to conduct your own investigation so as to enable you to form a view as to whether he may be guilty.

Step 1

3.6   When conducting your own investigation, the first stage is to consider what made you *suspect* that Alf had committed a criminal act. He may have come and told you about it, in which case it is clearly reasonable to believe that he had done it. You may have heard others gossiping, in which case you must speak to them to confirm that you had not misunderstood the allegations. Ideally, you should obtain signed statements from these people, but if they are reluctant to cooperate (and you should not press them too hard for fear of being accused of concocting evidence) you should make a written note of what they have told you whilst it is still fresh in your mind. Ensure that this note is dated and keep it safe – this is in case Alf later persuades them to retract what they have said.

Another reason for suspecting Alf of a criminal act is if you see his name in the newspaper being linked with a crime, or if you happen to know that Alf was in a particular place at a particular time and may be the culprit. In the absence of more concrete evidence it will be difficult to persuade an employment tribunal that your belief that Alf was guilty is reasonable. Accordingly you should be extremely wary of proceeding on the basis of speculation alone.

3.7   If you have sufficient information to believe that Alf may be guilty of a crime, then you should write to him, stating the following:

- That you believe he may have committed an offence of dishonesty, violence, etc. Specify the crime that you believe he may have committed, and set out the date(s) on which he is thought to have committed it.

- Your reasons for believing that he has committed the crime. If the reason is gossip, state the names of the people from whom you heard the gossip. This is important because the informant might dislike Alf and have fabricated the allegations. Although you might be unaware of any grudges between employees, Alf might be able to explain the allegations if you tell him who the informant was. An employment tribunal is unlikely to condone your failure to tell Alf who was making allegations against him (except in exceptional circumstances – see 4.8).

- That this might have an effect on his continued employment with you.

- A request to discuss the accusations with you. Include a date for the discussion in the letter, but make it clear that the date can be rearranged if inconvenient to him.

- That he is entitled to bring people, whether witnesses or a representative, with him to the meeting.

3.8 At the meeting, you must explain to Alf the precise nature of the allegations being made against him. Allow him to make any representations he thinks fit, and if he wishes more time to investigate the matter you should allow him extra time (unless there is a compelling reason not to, such as extreme urgency). Do not hesitate to question him on inconsistencies in his explanation – if he cannot explain away inconsistencies then you will be better able to justify your belief in his guilt.

3.9 As with all interviews, what is said is less important when it comes to a tribunal hearing than what you can *prove* was said. Even if Alf admits a crime, if he later denies that he admitted it and a tribunal believes him then you are worse off than if he had not admitted it to start with (because the tribunal will think that *you* are lying). Accordingly you should have a witness in the room with you who should take a detailed note of the proceedings. If the note is legible at the end of the interview, invite Alf to read and sign it. If the note is not legible, type up a legible version immediately after the meeting and ask him to sign the typed version. If he refuses to sign the note, do not let him have a copy since his refusal to sign it can only be based on a belief that it is inaccurate and, if inaccurate, a copy would be of no use to him. If he signs it, you should offer him a copy immediately.

It is not necessary to get him to sign a receipt for the copy.

Do not make a decision during the meeting as to whether Alf committed the crime. In particular, you must *not* inform Alf of your decision at the conclusion of the meeting, no matter how much he may ask you. A tribunal might think that an immediate decision is either arbitrary or predetermined. You should put your decision in writing to him if and when you reach stage (c) (see 3.20).

Step 2

3.10   After interviewing Alf, you should consider the information that you have received from different sources and make up your mind whether you think Alf is guilty of the acts that have been alleged against him. You do not have to be certain beyond a reasonable doubt, but you must reasonably believe that he has committed the crime. Although a decision will not necessarily be easy, you simply have to make up your mind which version of facts you accept. If Alf has given an alibi or some other defence, you should take reasonable steps to investigate his story (making sure you keep a full record of all steps you take).

Step 3

3.11   If your conclusion is that you think Alf is guilty then this will not be criticised by an employment tribunal even if it later turns out that Alf is innocent. Provided that you can prove to a tribunal that you have investigated the matter properly, have a genuine belief that Alf is guilty and that there are reasonable grounds for your belief, then any action you take as a result will not be unfair just because there was an incorrect assumption of guilt.

(b) The criminal conduct must make it difficult for you to continue employing Alf

3.12   The ACAS Code of Practice on Disciplinary Practice and Procedures, which is viewed by tribunals very much as the 'highway code' of employment law, sets out the general test for dismissing somebody for criminal conduct outside of work. It provides that such offences:

'. . .should not be treated as automatic reasons for dismissal regardless of whether the offence has any relevance to the duties of the individual as an employee. The main considerations should be whether the offence is one that makes the individual unsuitable for his or her type of work or unacceptable to other employees.'

Thus in order to fairly dismiss Alf for criminal conduct outside of work, you must be able to persuade a tribunal that you decided one of the following:

i   that as a result of the criminal conduct, Alf has become unsuitable for his type of work, or

ii that as a result of the criminal conduct, other employees will no longer work with Alf and so either his work (or their work) cannot be performed properly.

3.13   Offences of dishonesty: These will usually fall under the first test, namely that Alf has become unsuitable for his type of work. This is often the case if Alf occupies a position involving a degree of trust (such as the handling of cash). If, however, you are going to use this as a ground for dismissal, do *not* delay in dismissing Alf – it is no use trying to dismiss Alf for an offence of dishonesty which you discovered a month ago. This is because a tribunal may decide that your continued employment of him during the month is inconsistent with a genuine belief that he has become unsuitable for the work.

Example

A shop assistant at Heathrow Airport was accused of stealing £100 from the till. However, the employer allowed nine days to elapse between reconciling the till (when it discovered the discrepancy) and accusing the employee. Although the decision is not particularly clear, the Employment Appeal Tribunal's grounds for finding the dismissal unfair would have been, in part, the nine day gap whilst the employee remained on the till being inconsistent with a genuine belief or suspicion that she was dishonest – *Allders International v Parkins [1981] IRLR 68*

A tribunal is more likely to support the dismissal of Alf if he is a high-ranking employee. This is on the basis that he should be all the more aware of the potential consequences of his dishonest acts.

Example

A manager who had worked at C&A for 20 years was believed to be shoplifting at a shop down the road. It was held that the dismissal was fair because the employee, when knowing of the harm to a retailer that shoplifting can do, had nonetheless committed such an act, must therefore have been indifferent to the needs of his employer, and it was therefore risky to retain her in employment – *Moore v C & A Modes [1981] IRLR 71*

3.14   It may also be possible to dismiss somebody for offences of dishonesty because of the adverse effect that the retaining of employees believed to be dishonest would have on your business. Examples include where Alf is engaged as a security guard, handles other people's money or deals with clients' confidential information.

> ### Example
>
> A shipwright who handled cargo onboard a ship was dismissed because of theft away from work. It was held that the dismissal was fair because it would adversely affect his employer's business if clients discovered that they employed a man convicted of theft to handle their goods – **Robb v. Mersey Insulation Co. Ltd [1972] IRLR 18**

3.15   You must, however, ensure that you can show a tribunal that Alf's dishonesty means that he is unsuitable for his job. Some offences of dishonesty will not necessarily satisfy this test. For example, if Alf was convicted of receiving stolen goods, then it would not necessarily mean that he had become unsuitable for his job as, say, a secretary or a builder.

3.16   Offences of violence (other than sexual misconduct): Offences of violence will usually fall under the second test set out in paragraph 3.12, i.e. that other employees will no longer work with Alf or find it difficult to do so. It will be comparatively unusual to find that, as a result of violence away from the workplace, Alf is no longer a suitable person to perform the type of job which he does (i.e. the first test) unless Alf is engaged in a position where physical restraint is particularly important (for example, a security guard or a nightclub bouncer).

3.17   You must guard against deciding on your own that other employees will find it difficult to continue working with Alf. A tribunal will need to be satisfied that your belief is reasonable. You will need to be approached by employees who say that they are uncomfortable working with Alf. If you suspect that they will find it difficult to work with Alf, but they have not approached you, you should be wary of how you approach them.

Do *not* put any such approaches in writing – if Alf obtains a copy, or if a tribunal orders you to produce a copy, it could be argued at the tribunal that you were looking to dismiss Alf arbitrarily and seizing on the offence of violence as an excuse (on the basis that you had engaged in a witch-hunt in an effort to find evidence against Alf). Keep your enquiries low key, and ask employees whom you feel comfortable approaching for their views and the views of their colleagues.

It is only if the other employees confirm to you that they feel it to be difficult to continue working with Alf that you may be able to dismiss him. You will still, however, have to satisfy a tribunal that dismissal was a reasonable sanction in the circumstances (see paragraphs 3.20).

3.18   Offences of sexual misconduct: Offences involving sexual misconduct committed away from the workplace will *sometimes* be capable of justifying dismissal, but will by no means invariably justify dismissal. Dismissal may be justified under both tests set out at paragraph 3.12, namely that it may mean that Alf can no longer perform his job properly or it may mean that other employees will no longer work with Alf.

Example

A college lecturer, who taught mixed-sex teenagers between the ages of 16 and 18, was dismissed following a conviction for gross indecency with other men in a public toilet. The tribunal held that the dismissal was fair under both tests. Under the first test, the college was reasonable in deciding that a man who could not control himself in public ought not to be trusted with young persons. Under a slightly varied form of the second test, it decided that the school was justified in taking account of the views of parents who did not want the lecturer to continue teaching their children – *Gardiner v Newport County Borough Council [1974] IRLR 262, IT*

Example

A BBC cameraman was dismissed following a conviction for indecently assaulting a 13-year-old girl. The BBC argued that it would have to be selective in the assignments on which it could send him in the future (i.e. avoiding assignments where he would come into contact with young children) and it would be unreasonable to expect it to do that. The tribunal accepted that the BBC's views were reasonable, and held the dismissal to be fair – *Creffield v BBC [1975] IRLR 23, IT*

3.19   However, sometimes Alf's sexual misconduct will clearly not affect his ability to do the job or render his workmates reluctant to work with him. If you dismiss Alf in such a case and Alf claims unfair dismissal against you, he will succeed.

Example

A male employee was convicted of incest and dismissed as a result. A tribunal held that his employers acted unreasonably in dismissing him. The incest was an isolated incident and had nothing to do with the employee's work. He did not work with women, and the gang of men with whom he worked did not seem to mind. There was no suggestion of any of his workmates being exposed to physical or moral danger. Accordingly the dismissal was unfair – *Bradshaw v Rugby Portland Cement Co. Ltd [1972] IRLR 46*

(c) Dismissal must be a reasonable sanction in the circumstances

3.20   By this stage you will have decided that Alf has committed an offence which either makes him unsuitable for his job or makes it difficult for his colleagues to work with him. Accordingly dismissal may seem like the most sensible course.

However a tribunal will want evidence that you have specifically considered whether dismissal is an appropriate sanction. In an extremely large company, it may be possible to transfer Alf to another department. Thus if he sexually molests a woman outside work, and his female colleagues are apprehensive about continuing to work with him, dismissal will be unfair if he could easily be asked to work from home or be transferred to a male-only environment.

3.21   The best view to obtain as to whether there is a reasonable alternative to dismissal is Alf's. It he is unable to suggest any alternatives to dismissal or explain why dismissal is not justified, then you will have gone a long way towards establishing that the dismissal was fair.

You should ask Alf, in writing, to come to a meeting with you to discuss his future position in the company. The letter should state the following:

- The offence which you believe Alf to have committed, the fact that you are considering dismissal and the reason that you are considering dismissal. If you had a meeting with Alf to establish whether he had committed the offence, briefly summarise the reasons for your decision from that meeting.

- An invitation to Alf to discuss the situation with you. You should state that the purpose of the meeting is to see if there are any reasons why Alf's conduct should not give rise to dismissal, and whether there are any alternatives to dismissal that can be adopted.

- An invitation to Alf to bring a representative to the meeting if he so desires.

3.22   At the meeting you should ensure that a full note is taken (see paragraph 3.9). You must consider any alternative proposals to dismissal that Alf puts forward. Do not forget that he will have a different perspective on events and that his views, as the person who is most directly affected, should not be dismissed out of hand. If, however, after having considered his proposals you are not satisfied that they are feasible (and, more importantly, you are satisfied that it is reasonable to reject his proposals) then you will be justified in dismissing him.

Again, do not tell Alf the result whilst you are actually in the meeting. This is to avoid an accusation of having prejudged the situation, and so that your reasons can be set out in writing after having been properly drafted. This is particularly important because your reasons for dismissal should be in written form to be seen by the tribunal (if necessary). If you state your reasons orally in the heat of a meeting, then they may not come out in precisely the way that, upon reflection, you would want them to come out. This might prejudice your position in tribunal proceedings.

3.23   If, after the meeting, you are of the view that dismissal is a proper course to take, you will need to write a letter of dismissal. You must ensure that the letter contains the following points:

- That you write following your meeting, stating the date, with your decision.

- The act of violence or dishonesty that you believe Alf has committed. If he has been convicted, refer to the conviction. If your decision that he has committed an offence followed an investigative meeting with him, refer to the date of the meeting and your findings.

- That Alf's continued employment is not possible, and your reasons for concluding this. Identify whether you rely on criterion 1 (i.e. that Alf is no longer suitable to undertake his job) or criterion 2 (i.e. that other employees find it difficult to continue working with Alf). Set out the reasons for your conclusions.

- That you have considered the matters put forward by Alf at your recent meeting, but that you remain of the view that dismissal is the only appropriate action. If Alf suggested alternatives, set them out and explain why they are not appropriate.

- That Alf has a right of appeal from your decision. See Chapter 11 on appeals.

The letter of dismissal should contain any monies that Alf is owed – see Chapter 12 for what you must pay. You should not permit Alf to work out his notice period since a tribunal would view this as being inconsistent with a belief that Alf could not continue in his job, and thus your credibility at the hearing would be severely undermined.

References

3.24   Treat any requests for references that come in within the next three months with suspicion. It is common practice for employee's advisors to try to obtain a reference from an employer in the hope that the employer will not refer to the reason for dismissal within the reference. This will then be used against you at a tribunal hearing as evidence that your stated reason for dismissal was a fabrication.

You are under no legal obligation to provide references for ex-employees. Indeed, many large employers nowadays refuse to give any substantive reference due to concerns about being sued for negligence. Accordingly, if you are concerned about giving a reference but do not want to prejudice Alf's chance of obtaining alternative employment, it may be appropriate to give a reference in the form:

> 'Alf worked for this firm as a sales assistant between June 1992 and April 1997. It is this company's policy not to give any information on the capability or conduct of any employee. This should not be seen as an adverse reflection on Alf.'

If Alf is going to claim unfair dismissal against you, he must do so within three months of the termination of his employment (but see paragraph 18.9). If he was dismissed with notice then the three month period begins running from the expiry of the notice period. Accordingly, if you have not received an unfair dismissal claim form within three months, you are highly likely to be safe from a claim and can give such references as you please.

Note that if you give an unjustified bad reference through mistake or malice, Alf may have a claim against you for negligence or defamation.

4. HOW TO DISMISS SOMEONE FOR BREACHES OF DISCIPLINE AT WORK

Introduction

4.1   Breach of discipline at work is probably the most common reason for immediate dismissal, as contrasted with dismissing Alf with notice. An immediate dismissal is often referred to by its legal description as a 'summary' dismissal. As you will see, however, you will not always be able to justify summary dismissal to a tribunal, and you must guard against over-reacting to Alf's breach of disciplinary standards. Although a tribunal will take account of the size and resources of your business when judging whether or not you have acted fairly, even the smallest business needs to follow a proper procedure when dismissing somebody for what may seem, on the face of it, a manifestly dismissable offence.

Breaches of discipline can cover all sorts of behaviour. It is apparent that behaviour such as violence or theft at work will fall within this heading. Breach of discipline will also cover less serious offences such as smoking in breach of company policy, swearing, mild intoxication or personal use of the telephone. It can also cover more unusual conduct such as divulging confidential company information or harassing fellow employees.

The principal test which an employment tribunal will apply is to see whether your action was something which 'no reasonable management would have done'. If the tribunal decides that no reasonable management would have acted in the way that you did, then the dismissal will be unfair. It is important to note that this does *not* mean simply that you need to arrive at a conclusion (i.e. to dismiss) and be able to show that the conclusion was reasonable. Even if your conclusion is reasonable, but a tribunal decides that you *reached* that conclusion in a way which no reasonable management would have done (for example, if you failed to hold a disciplinary hearing) then it will hold the dismissal to be unfair.

4.2   In deciding whether you have acted fairly, a tribunal will look at whether your actions fall within a band of reasonable responses which a reasonable employer could make. The tribunal will not criticise you for failing to act in a perfect or ideal way, provided your actions bring you within the band of reasonable responses. In other words, a tribunal should not find that a dismissal is unfair simply because the members of the tribunal might have acted differently in the same situation. They will, however, find the dismissal to be unfair if they conclude that your actions were such that no reasonable employer would have acted in that way.

Example

A company dismissed an employee under its policy not to employ drug addicts. The Employment Appeal Tribunal held that although a more lenient employer might not have dismissed him, it was within the range of reasonable responses to have a policy against the employment of drug addicts, and thus the dismissal was fair – **Walton v TAC Construction Materials Ltd [1981] IRLR 357**

Ideally, you should have a clear disciplinary code setting out the type of conduct which you consider would warrant disciplinary action, and the potential consequences if the code is breached. If such a code has been brought to Alf's attention, and he then commits an act which is prohibited by the code, you will have gone a long way towards showing that you have acted fairly in dismissing him. If your company does not have a disciplinary code, one should be issued to all employees to cover yourself in future situations (indeed, it is a legal requirement that a disciplinary code should be given to employees within two months of commencing employment). An example of a disciplinary code can be found in the sample written statement of particulars of employment in Appendix I.

The benefit of a clear disciplinary code is such that you can often dismiss somebody for breach of disciplinary rules without any prior warning if the offence and the consequence is spelled out clearly enough in the code. This will be examined in more detail at 4.31 below.

4.3   There are three stages as to which you must satisfy a tribunal
before it will declare that your dismissal of Alf was fair. They
are:

i   that you had a genuine and reasonable belief that Alf had
breached good discipline;

ii   that you had given Alf the opportunity to defend himself
and to raise any matters that he feels to be material; and,

iii   that dismissal is a reasonable response to Alf's actions (taking into consideration any mitigation or representations made
by Alf).

As with dismissals for incapability, it is just as important to be
able to *prove* that you have gone through each of these stages as
it is that you have actually gone through them!

One exception must be mentioned. If Alf is a trade union
official, you *must not* dismiss him (or issue written warnings)
unless you have discussed the case with a senior trade union
representative or a full-time trade union official. If you fail to
liaise with a senior representative throughout the disciplinary
process, it is highly likely that a tribunal will find the dismissal
to be unfair. The reason for this requirement is to make it harder
for an employer to dismiss someone who is involved in trade
union activities by dressing up the dismissal as being for
misconduct.

There is a certain degree of overlap with dismissals for criminal
acts outside of the workplace (see Chapter 3). As before, each
step needs to be addressed separately by you and thus will be
discussed separately below.

Suspending Alf pending dismissal

4.4   Whilst you are going through the dismissal procedure, you will
need to decide whether to suspend Alf pending the completion
of your investigations. If the breach of discipline is so serious
that you are considering dismissing him summarily, you will
usually need to suspend him. If you fail to suspend him in such
circumstances, you leave yourself open to the argument that,
given you permitted Alf to remain at work whilst investigating
the breach, it could not have been serious enough to warrant
removal from the workplace and thus could not have justified
dismissal. Avoid this argument by suspending Alf.

You must not suspend Alf without pay unless his contract of employment expressly provides that you can do so. If his contract does not set out your right to suspend him without pay, you will be in breach of your obligation to pay him wages if you do so. This would entitle him to resign and claim that he was constructively dismissed (before you have even got around to dismissing him properly).

If you have suspended him with pay, you can take as long as you like with the investigation. If you have suspended him without pay, you must act reasonably diligently. If you take longer than, say, three weeks, or if you drag your heels (even within a shorter period), Alf may be able to resign and claim constructive dismissal – all it takes is a visit to his local Citizens' Advice Bureau and Alf will rapidly become aware of his employment rights.

Stage (i): A genuine and reasonable belief that Alf has breached discipline

4.5   You can be convinced, to different degrees, that Alf has committed a particular breach of discipline. The clearest example will be when Alf has admitted it after being caught in the act, for example if he is discovered removing money from the till or in the middle of a fight. If he admits the act, you should obtain some form of corroborating evidence (since there is always the risk that he will deny his admission at a tribunal).

Ideally, you should obtain a statement from Alf, but it is important to avoid intimidating him with procedure at this stage. The easiest way to obtain a statement is to ask Alf to set out, in writing, the circumstances surrounding the offence. If he declines to do so, on the basis that there are no mitigating circumstances and so nothing is served by setting out his acts in writing, invite him to sign a statement confirming that he has not committed any similar breach of discipline before. Do *not* tell him that if he signs such a statement, he will not be dismissed: this would be misleading and you would be found to have acted unfairly.

Alf may refuse to sign anything admitting his act if it is likely to give rise to a criminal prosecution (e.g. theft). If this is the case, you should make a full note as soon after his admission as possible, date it, and ensure it is kept safely.

There will also be situations where you have not actually caught Alf in the act, but where evidence is discovered which makes it almost inconceivable that he has *not* committed the breach of discipline. Thus, for example, stolen company property might be discovered at his house, or a letter may be discovered addressed to a competitor which he has signed. You should remember, however, that such strong evidence is *not* the same as proof, and it will not avoid the need to perform an investigation into the allegations and give Alf an opportunity to put his case. The scope of the investigation is, however, flexible, and you will not be criticised for undertaking a smaller scale investigation than in a situation where Alf's involvement is based on circumstantial evidence only.

Finally, you will encounter situations where there is very little to go on, and you either suspect Alf simply because you have eliminated everyone else, or you know it must be one of a group of people who have been in breach of discipline, but you do not know which one. In the latter situation, as will be seen in paragraph 4.9, it may sometimes be fair if you dismiss *all* of the employees who are under suspicion and do not pick arbitrarily between them.

4.6   If Alf pleads guilty to a criminal offence in connection with the breach of discipline, or is found guilty by a court, then you will be entirely justified in treating this first step as fulfilled and moving on to the second stage. As set out above, where his guilt is clear you will not need to expend too many resources in investigating the breach of discipline. You must, however, still investigate the surrounding circumstances insofar as they may be material to stage iii, since there may be circumstances which cast a very different complexion upon the appropriate sanction even if Alf has pleaded guilty.

Example

A miner, during the miners' strike, was charged with assaulting a fellow employee. The NCB decided to dismiss him if he was convicted. The miner pleaded guilty on a technicality, namely that he had threatened violence (which is technically an assault) but maintained that there had been no physical contact. His dismissal was held to be unfair since the NCB failed to give him an opportunity to explain his conviction and, if he had been allowed to explain his guilty plea on a technicality, they might not have dismissed him – ***McLaren v National Coal Board [1988] ICR 370***

4.7   What evidence should you obtain? The ideal evidence would be a signed admission by Alf that he had committed the breach of discipline in question. However, this will rarely be forthcoming.

As long as you can prove that you had a genuine and reasonable belief in Alf's guilt, you will satisfy the first step of the dismissal. Accordingly any evidence showing that Alf committed the breach of discipline in question should be sought, whatever its form. It is not necessary for the evidence to be technically admissible in ordinary courts, since all you are seeking to show is that *you*, not a court, had grounds to suspect Alf. Thus hearsay evidence, which is not admissible in a criminal court, would be perfectly acceptable so as to show you had reasonable grounds for believing Alf to have committed a disciplinary offence.

Common forms of evidence are as follows:

- Statements from other employees setting out that they saw Alf committing the disciplinary breaches, heard him admitting to it or saw him in the relevant area at the relevant time. This will frequently be the case if Alf has used violence in the workplace and a complaint is made by the victim. You should obtain statements in writing (rather than by word of mouth) so that if the employee leaves your company before a tribunal hearing, you will still be able to prove that the statement was made. Such statements should be obtained as soon as possible so as to avoid the suggestion at a tribunal that memory has faded due to lapse of time.

- Complaints by customers. This will often be the case if Alf has been acting in an offensive manner. Ideally the complaints will be in writing, but often they will simply be comments over the telephone on an informal basis. Often you may be reluctant, for reasons of your company image, to ask the customer to confirm the complaint in writing. You should, therefore, ensure that the customer's complaint is carefully noted by you immediately after it is made. If you delay noting the complaint for several days, you open yourself to cross-examination on the grounds of diminished recollection.

- Video surveillance: If you have video evidence from a security camera, this will be very compelling evidence to put before a tribunal. Make sure that it is easy to identify Alf on the video – you do not want a tribunal deciding that you acted hastily in concluding Alf to be guilty because his face was not clear on the screen. You should allow Alf to watch the video and make a note of any comments or admissions that he makes as a result of the viewing.

- Till mismatches: The fact the money is missing from the till does not necessarily indicate dishonesty – it could instead be indicative of incompetence (see Chapter 2). Assuming, however, that you suspect something sinister, the first task will be to identify who is responsible for the discrepancies. If only one person has used the till at the time that the discrepancies arose, then this will be clear. If, however, a number of employees use the till then you will have to revise your system so as to allocate one employee to each till or, alternatively, to count the cash whenever there is a change of personnel. You should keep careful records of cash in the till, and ensure that this is clearly checked against the till rolls. If you have to prove your case in front of a tribunal, it would be useful to have graphs or charts plotting the expected amount in the till against the real amount over a period.

- Arrest/conviction by police: This is addressed at 4.6 above. Remember – the mere fact that the police arrest Alf does *not* mean that you have reasonable grounds for believing him to have committed the act in question. You still need to carry out your own independent investigation.

The problem of anonymous informers

4.8   Sometimes an employee may have given you information, but
on condition that you do not disclose his/her identity to Alf.
This can create a problem, since Alf is entitled to know who is
making accusations against him so that he can explain away
any grudges or improper motives on the part of the accuser.
Provided the informer has a genuine reason for wishing to remain
anonymous, such as fear of retaliation, the law permits you to
conceal his/her identity providing the following steps have been
taken:

a   You must produce a statement from the informer setting
out all material information. The statement should be in a
complete form, including names and other identifying items
(such as the informer being in the same room as Alf at a
particular date and time). It should include information relating to:

i   the date and time of any observation or incident;
ii   the opportunity and ability of the informer to observe
clearly and with accuracy;
iii any circumstantial evidence, such as knowledge of a
system or arrangement, or the reason for the presence
of the informer and why certain small details are
memorable; and,
iv   whether the informer has suffered at Alf's hands previously or has any other reason to fabricate his evidence,
whether because of a personal grudge or otherwise.

b   You must then undertake an independent investigation looking for evidence to corroborate or undermine the informer's
evidence. In particular, you must be able to demonstrate to
a tribunal that you have sought to establish, independently,
whether the informer has a grudge against Alf. This can
include tactful enquiries to other employees.

c   You will then need to decide how vital the informer's evidence
is. If the evidence is non-essential, less objection will be taken
to preserving the informer's anonymity. If the evidence is
central, and without it you cannot reasonably conclude that

Alf is guilty of misconduct, you must make a choice. Some tribunals will be sympathetic to the problem of an anonymous informer, and will permit you to rely on his/her evidence. Others will not be so sympathetic, and will take the view that if your case cannot stand without such doubtful evidence, you cannot reasonably conclude that Alf is guilty. At the end of the day, you have to perform a balancing act between judging the informer's credibility (both in terms of the evidence he/she gives and in terms of his/her reasons for wishing to remain anonymous) and your desire to proceed with the disciplinary process.

What if it might be one of a number of people?

4.9   If you cannot tell whether it was Alf or another person who has been acting improperly, you may sometimes be justified in dismissing both or all of them. You will need to prove the following to a tribunal:

a   that a breach of discipline has been committed which, if committed by an individual, would justify dismissal;

b   that you had thoroughly investigated the situation so as to try to identify a culprit;

c   that, after your investigations, it remained the case that there was more than one person who could have committed the offence;

d   that you had identified the possible culprits, and that there were no circumstances distinguishing any of them so as to make it more or less likely that (s)he had committed the offence.

You will usually be able to dismiss two people if you cannot work out which one committed the breach (provided you have gone thorough a full process of interviewing both persons). As the number of suspects increases, however, you will find yourself harder pressed to justify dismissing all of them. This is on the basis that a failure to narrow the group down is indicative of a failure to investigate thoroughly.

Example

Money had disappeared from an employer's safe. The employer believed that the culprit was one of two people, but could not establish which one had committed the theft. The Court of Appeal held that it was fair to dismiss both in these circumstances because the employer had to take action to protect its financial position and it had done everything it could to identify one or other of the employees as the thief – *Monie v Coral Racing Ltd [1980] IRLR 464*

Stage (ii): Giving Alf the opportunity to make representations

4.10   By this stage you ought to be able to prove that you have formed a genuine and reasonable belief as to Alf's guilt. You should have evidence to back this up, whether taking the form of statements, your own notes of conversations or documentary evidence such as altered invoices (proving theft).

Before you can dismiss Alf, however, you need to give him the opportunity to explain the relevant events. It may be the case that the evidence against him has been concocted by other employees, in which case he may be able to point out discrepancies that you had not appreciated. It may equally be that there is a perfectly innocent explanation for the evidence, for example he might have removed £50 from the cash register at the request of another manager.

Accordingly it is necessary to put these allegations to Alf and see whether he can provide an adequate explanation or show that he cannot have been guilty of the offences of which he has been accused.

4.11   Failure to allow Alf an opportunity to defend himself will almost inevitably render a dismissal unfair, as your decision to dismiss will be regarded as hasty and premature. You will not persuade a tribunal that you have acted reasonably if you have ignored matters which Alf might have brought to your attention.

Example

An employee took two packets of pork chops from her employer without paying for them. She was not permitted to explain, and she was dismissed immediately for theft. The dismissal was held to be unfair on the basis that a fuller investigation might have supported her claim that she had the intention to pay for them – *Wm Low & Co. v MacCuish [1979] IRLR 458*

You must guard against taking the view that Alf's guilt is so obvious that there is nothing he can say which will cause you to change your mind. Apart from the fact that such an arrogant attitude will irritate a tribunal, it is extremely rare for an employer to be justified in deciding that there can be no explanation or mitigation which would have a bearing on his decision. A tribunal will decide that you have acted unfairly if you have reached a conclusion which it would have been reasonable to postpone until you have discussed the matter with Alf. It is worth remembering that some of the greatest miscarriages of justice appeared at the time to be clearcut cases. Do not fall into the trap of assuming that Alf cannot possibly answer your allegations or explain his actions.

There is one exception to the requirement to hold an investigative meeting. This is where Alf has already admitted to you that he committed the offence in question. In such a situation, you are entitled to forgo the rest of the investigative stages and turn to the final stage, namely whether Alf's conduct justifies dismissal. If, however, Alf's admission to you is not in writing, it may be best to have the meeting in any event so that somebody else can hear, and take a note of, Alf's admission.

The investigative meeting

4.12   Whether or not he is suspended, you will need to invite Alf to an investigative meeting. It is at this meeting that he will be able to put forward his representations or explanations. Prior to the meeting, you should inform him of the nature of the allegations being made against him. He will probably be fully aware of the allegations, particularly if you have already suspended him. However, you should still set out all relevant information in one document so as to prove to a tribunal, some months down the line, that you were addressing your mind to the proper matters.

You should write to Alf, stating the following:

- Matters have come to your attention which lead you to suspect that he has committed a breach of discipline (stating in full the breach or breaches).

- You would like to give him the opportunity of putting forward any explanation or representations.

- Your reasons for believing that he had committed the breach (in outline). You should enclose copies of any statements in support of the allegation (unless anonymity or confidentiality is an issue – this is addressed at 4.8). This is important because it gives Alf the opportunity to comment on any bad blood between him and those offering evidence against him.

- Invite Alf to meet with you at a convenient date. Include a date, place and time, but be prepared to change it to suit Alf's reasonable convenience (particularly if he has been suspended and thus is not present at the workplace).

- He is entitled to bring a representative should he so desire, and any witnesses whom he thinks would be of help. You should not seek to limit the class of person from whom he can select his representative (i.e. do not bar trade union officials, non-employee friends, or even lawyers).

In exceptional cases, tribunals have held that it is fair to have the entire investigative stage conducted in writing. In other words, you would not hold a meeting, but would simply invite Alf's written representations on the evidence against him. This is a risky way of approaching disciplinary matters – tribunals do not like it for three reasons. First, written representations are not interactive, i.e. Alf cannot respond to new matters raised. Secondly, Alf may not be as articulate in writing as he would be face to face. Thirdly, you are less able to judge credibility when something is said to you in writing than when it is said face to face. You should only refuse to have an oral hearing if you have a very good reason for doing so, for example, you have strong grounds for believing that Alf may be violent in such a meeting.

It is perfectly legitimate to hold the meeting off your premises or after normal hours, so as to avoid disturbing other employees.

4.13   You should prepare carefully for the meeting. You must not allow yourself to become emotionally aroused or appear to be personally critical of Alf at this meeting. The purpose of the meeting is investigative, not disciplinary. The disciplinary meeting comes later.

A person should be present to take notes. This is important so that the tribunal can see, when it reviews the circumstances of the dismissal months down the line, that you permitted Alf to make full representations. It is equally important so that the tribunal can see whether Alf was able to come up with a proper explanation at the time, in case he claims at the hearing that he said something which he did not, in fact, say. If you have the administrative resources available, a secretary should take full shorthand notes and thereafter produce a transcript. If you do not have such resources available, you should take as thorough a note yourself as you are able – in particular, record any admissions that Alf makes or any explanations that he puts forward in respect of the allegations.

There is no need to use a cassette recorder. Although it may appear prudent to have a incontrovertible record of what was said, in practice it is unusual to hear tape-recorded evidence and it is unwise to have any aspect of the dismissal as being something out of the ordinary. Furthermore, Alf may argue at the tribunal that the fact you recorded the conversation indicates that you expected him to dispute the facts, and this therefore indicates that you had already partially made up your mind.

If you are not the person who will be taking the final decision on dismissal, he or she should, ideally, be present. Tribunals sometimes criticise employers when the decision-maker has not personally interviewed the employee being dismissed. However, if you are part of a large organisation with clearly defined procedures, or if your dismissal procedure has been agreed with a trade union, then this is unlikely to present any real difficulty.

4.14   What if Alf fails to attend the investigative meeting? If Alf does not attend the investigative meeting, you should write to him pointing out that he missed the appointment and asking him to contact you within, say, three days to rearrange the meeting. If he fails to contact you, or if he does not attend the rescheduled meeting, a tribunal will say you are justified in assuming that he is refusing to co-operate in the investigative procedure.

Once you have given Alf the chance to attend the investigative meeting, but he has not done so, you will be in a stronger position when it comes to deciding whether or not he has committed the breach of discipline concerned. If he has had a reasonable opportunity to explain, but has not taken it, you are entitled to assume that there is no reasonable explanation and that your understanding of events is correct.

4.15   At the beginning of the meeting, you should formally introduce everyone in the room (unless to do so would be ridiculous) and explain their role in the hearing. If Alf is not represented, confirm that he does not want to have a representative present. If he states that he does want a representative, ask him who he wants and why the representative is not attending at that meeting (NB you would have said, in your letter, that representatives are permitted – see 4.12). Provided he comes up with a reasonable explanation, you should permit *one* adjournment of the hearing so as to allow him to obtain a representative. Remember – a tribunal will be concerned to see if you have allowed him a proper opportunity to explain his case, and if you have unreasonably denied him access to a representative then you may be found to have acted unfairly.

Explain the purpose and format of the meeting to Alf (or his representative). Emphasise that the hearing is investigative and is *not* to determine what sanction should be applied. Also state that you will not be giving a decision at the end of the meeting, but will take your time to consider what Alf has said.

The exact procedure to be followed is up to you. However, there are three essential elements to the hearing:

a   Alf should know exactly what disciplinary rules he is alleged to have breached, and what evidence exists against him;

b   he should be given a full opportunity to state his case; and

c   you must act, and must be seen to act, in good faith.

If your company has agreed a disciplinary procedure with a trade union, then the procedure set out in the agreement must be followed. Although deviation from an agreed procedure will not automatically mean that a dismissal is unfair, it does give Alf the basis of a case and makes it much more likely that a lawyer or Citizens' Advice Bureau worker will advise Alf to take you to the employment tribunal. If you *do* follow an agreed procedure without any deviation, a tribunal will not find that you have acted unfairly unless you are regarded as having taken any decisions in bad faith.

(a) Evidence against Alf

4.16   If you have been following the procedure set out in this book, you will have satisfied the requirement that Alf knows exactly what rules he is alleged to have breached. He will also, if you sent him copies of witness statements, know the evidence which exists against him.

If you do not have statements (or did not send him copies), tell Alf the gist of any evidence coming from other employees, customers, etc. If Alf keeps interrupting, stop him and explain that he will have the opportunity to comment later. Do not let him cause you to lose the flow of what you are putting across.

If you rely on an informer's statement (see 4.8), you must show Alf a copy (with any identifying elements omitted or blanked out). If Alf, or his representative, has any questions which they wish to put to the informer, you should adjourn the hearing in order for you to put such matters to him/her. This is an exception to the rule that Alf is not usually permitted to cross-examine witnesses – see 4.17.

You should also show Alf any documentary evidence (such as till rolls, letters of complaint from customers, or a copy of your company's no-smoking policy). If Alf tries to destroy any incriminating evidence then, provided both you and your witness will attest to that before the tribunal, you will have gone a long way towards justifying any dismissal (on the grounds that you cannot continue employing someone who deliberately destroys company documents for his own advantage).

If you are relying on a rule in Alf's contract of employment which he has breached, or on a rule contained in a notice or a memo, show Alf a copy of the contract or memo and ask him if he received a copy. If he says yes, you are entitled to regard his conduct as all the more serious (since he has deliberately, or, at best, indifferently, ignored a company rule). If he denies having received the memo, you may need to investigate whether he did receive a copy (e.g. check the circulation list).

(b) Alf's opportunity to put his case

4.17   Once you have told Alf the nature of the case against him, you must allow him (or his representative) to explain the evidence or state his version of events. If Alf's version of events is radically different, and raises fresh issues which have not been considered (for example, if Alf says that he removed money from the till because he was instructed to do so by a supervisor) then you must investigate these new issues after the hearing by talking to (and, if appropriate, obtaining statements from) anyone who may be able to assist.

Alf may wish to challenge the truth of other people's statements. He could allege that evidence has been fabricated due to a grudge or to move suspicion away from the real perpetrator. If, of course, Alf has been caught red-handed then you may feel that no further investigation is necessary before making up your mind. However, if Alf's explanation is plausible, a tribunal will want to see that you have performed such further investigation as is necessary in order for you to be able to take an informed decision as to which version of events is correct.

Legally, you do not have to allow Alf (or his representative) to cross-examine the witnesses who are making allegations against him. However, a tribunal might be better disposed in your favour if you have permitted Alf to cross-examine a witness where there is a crucial conflict of evidence. If you allow such a cross-examination, it will show to a tribunal that you are taking steps over and above what is actually necessary to secure a fair hearing for Alf. This may help you in case you have made any mistakes in your procedure. If, however, you do not want cross-examination of the witnesses, you should not be criticised for refusing to let it take place.

(c) Acting in good faith

4.18   You must act, and be seen to act, in good faith. There are two elements to this. First, you must not have made up your mind before hearing Alf's version of events. Just as importantly, you must not be perceived by others as having made up your mind! Do not tell Alf you do not believe what he is saying (although it is legitimate, and indeed good practice, to point out to Alf inconsistencies in his representations and invite him to explain them). Do not be overly critical or judgmental during the investigative meeting – the time for criticism and discipline is during the disciplinary meeting (see 4.40).

Secondly, and ideally, you should not be both witness and decision-maker. If you are the principal witness, let someone else conduct the investigative meeting and take the decision as to whether Alf has committed the breach of discipline. In a very small company, it may not be possible to separate yourself from the proceedings – if so, a tribunal will not criticise you on this basis. However, if your company has sufficient management resources, you should not allow the same person to be both witness and judge.

Example

An employee was dismissed following allegations of sexual harassment. The chairman and club secretary saw one of the incidents of harassment, and were witnesses during the investigation. The entire committee of the club, including the chairman and club secretary, voted to dismiss him. It was held that the dismissal was unfair because there was no good reason why they had to act in dual capacities and their position as witnesses must have affected their impartiality as decision makers – *Moyes v Hylton Castle Working Men's Social Club and Institute Ltd [1986] IRLR 482*

You will see that the separation of witnesses and decision-makers is described as an 'ideal'. Tribunals have not been consistent in the way that they approach this point, and there are a number of cases where the courts have said that tribunals should take a practical view and realise that employers are capable of both witnessing events and judging them impartially. However, given that you wish to make any dismissal as watertight as possible, it is prudent to avoid this type of dual role unless you are a small company and lack the resources to do otherwise.

4.19 After you have permitted Alf to put his case, you should summarise his explanations. Ensure that a full note is taken of your summary so that you can demonstrate that you are taking into account everything that Alf has said. You should then tell Alf that you will consider his representations, make any further enquiries that are necessary, and give him a decision within the next few days. Do *not* tell Alf at that stage what your decision is, or even give an indication of the likely decision. If you do so, you run the risk of being accused of having already made up your mind.

4.20 Following the meeting, you should check the note that was taken and ensure that it is legible. If you have the administrative resources, have a transcript typed up. Do not give a copy to Alf – he is not entitled to a copy unless he commences a claim against you and there is no need to let him think that you are acting defensively.

If Alf has raised any fresh issues during the hearing (such as evidence coming from someone with a grudge, or suggesting an alternative culprit) you must undertake further investigation. The degree of investigation will depend on the nature of the new issues raised. If you do *not* investigate further, a tribunal is likely to decide that you have acted unfairly because you would have pre-judged the situation without being in possession of all the relevant facts. Make sure that you keep notes of the further investigations.

Once any additional investigation is complete, you need to decide whether you consider Alf to have committed the breach which is alleged. You must weigh up the statements and the evidence which go against Alf together with Alf's explanation, and decide what you think happened. You do not have to be *sure* that Alf committed the breach of discipline – you simply have to decide whether it is more likely than not that Alf *did* commit the breach of discipline.

If Alf takes you to an employment tribunal, you will not need to show a tribunal that you were right in deciding that Alf had committed the breach of discipline. You simply need to show that your decision was a reasonable one. This is a very important distinction from your point of view since, if further evidence appears after (and if) you have dismissed Alf showing that he could *not* have done what you thought, it will not affect whether Alf's dismissal was fair or unfair. Provided you have conducted a proper investigation, and provided that your conclusion was one which a reasonable employer might reach, a dismissal will be fair (provided that the other requirements set out in this chapter have been complied with).

4.21   If you decide that Alf probably did not commit the breach of discipline complained of, or if you feel that you will not be able to justify such a decision to an employment tribunal and do not want to take the risk of a claim being made, you should confirm this in writing to Alf. State that you accept his explanation, that you will not be taking these disciplinary proceedings any further and that although the investigation will be kept on file for administrative purposes it will not be held against him in any way. Be gracious – if you write a letter stating that 'we think you did it but cannot prove it' you are placing yourself at risk of allegations of bias if you need to bring other disciplinary proceedings against Alf in the future.

4.22   If you have decided that Alf *did* commit the breach of discipline complained of, and you wish to proceed with the disciplinary procedure, you will need to arrange a formal disciplinary hearing. You should put your decision to Alf in writing. Your letter should contain the following:

- A statement that, on weighing up the evidence/statements and considering Alf's explanations, you find that he committed the breach of discipline in question. If you feel confident justifying the reasons for your decision, set them out *briefly*. If you put too much in writing, you may find yourself a hostage to fortune. If you do not feel as confident as you should be that your reasons will stand close scrutiny, do not give reasons.

- That you want to hold a disciplinary meeting. Inform him that the purpose of the meeting is to consider what

disciplinary sanction is to be imposed. If you are considering dismissal (see 4.23 for whether dismissal is an appropriate or a possible sanction) you must specifically state this
and tell Alf that he should be prepared to put forward any
reasons why dismissal is not appropriate.

● A statement of the time and place and, as before, tell Alf
that if the date is inconvenient it can be rearranged. Tell him
that he is entitled to have a representative of his choice present.

● A statement that he is entitled to appeal against your finding that he committed the breach of discipline in question,
but that the appeal procedure will not come into operation
until after the disciplinary meeting. Inform him that you
will set out the mechanics of appealing at that time.

Stage (iii): Dismissal must be a reasonable response to Alf's actions

4.23   You are normally not entitled to dismiss Alf for a first offence
unless the breach of discipline is severe (often referred to as
'gross' misconduct). Offences involving theft or other forms of
dishonesty will usually justify immediate dismissal. Offences
involving violence may do so, depending on the degree of violence
used – if you dismiss an employee with 20 years' service with
your company because of a single lapse involving a minor fracas,
a tribunal will probably find that 'the punishment exceeds the
crime' and that you have acted unfairly. By contrast, if a perpetu-
ally troublesome employee becomes aggressive and engages in
violence, you may well be justified in dismissing him for a similar
lapse.

   The distinction between a first breach of discipline and
subsequent breaches is a fundamental one for the purpose of
deciding whether dismissal is an appropriate sanction. Accordingly the two scenarios are examined separately.

First offences

4.24   The ACAS Code of Practice on Disciplinary Practice and
Procedures in Employment states that employees should not be
dismissed for a first offence except in cases of gross misconduct.

However, tribunals tend to be a little more relaxed in deciding whether a dismissal for a first offence is fair or unfair. As with determining whether Alf actually *committed* the breach of discipline, a tribunal is not concerned with whether *it* would have dismissed Alf for an offence, but whether the decision to dismiss was a reasonable one in all the circumstances. The law states that if some employers *would* have dismissed in a particular set of circumstances, but other employers would have only issued a warning, you should not be held liable for unfair dismissal simply because some employers *might* have acted less stringently.

In general, you should issue a warning (rather than dismiss) for first offences. You can, however, dismiss Alf for a first offence in three situations:

i   where he has committed an act of gross misconduct;

ii   where you have good reason to believe that warnings will be ineffective; or,

iii where Alf has been made aware, in advance, that the breach of discipline in question would lead to his dismissal.

The above three situations are discussed in turn below.

(i) Gross misconduct

4.25   This is not as straightforward as it sounds. Gross misconduct usually describes conduct which is so serious that immediate dismissal is warranted. This is, of course, a circular definition. One of the advantages in dismissing an employee for gross misconduct is that you do not need to pay him/her any pay in lieu of notice (as you are obliged to do when dismissing for other reasons – see Chapter 12).

The courts have always refused to lay down a definition of gross misconduct or to set out categories of offences which amount to gross misconduct. This is because each case has to be considered on its own facts, and a tribunal simply has to decide whether an employer has acted reasonably in dismissing for a particular offence. Laying down firm categories would limit a tribunal's ability to consider each case on its own facts, and accordingly the courts have avoided doing so.

However, if you dismiss Alf for one of the following reasons, tribunals are generally sympathetic to employers' claims that the acts amounted to gross misconduct and thus warranted dismissal for a first offence:

- Violence: violence in the workplace will usually justify immediate dismissal. However, the three factors which a tribunal will take into account (in addition to the fact that violence has occurred) are:

  (i)   Whose fault was the violence? If Alf was acting in self-defence (albeit that he struck the first blow) or was so strongly provoked that violence is understandable, then a tribunal may find that a reasonable employer would have issued a warning, and that your dismissal of Alf was unfair. You should have come to a view on whose fault the violence was during the investigative stage, and a tribunal will have little sympathy for you if you say that you did not know or were not interested in who was at fault.

  (ii) How long has Alf been employed? If Alf has been a good employee for many years, you run the risk of a tribunal finding that you acted unreasonably in dismissing Alf. This is because the hypothetical reasonable employer would have realised that the violence was a one-off incident and issued a warning rather than resort to dismissal.

  (iii) The nature of the workplace. Any degree of violence may be unacceptable in an office environment, whereas a certain degree of physical banter would be accepted as the norm on a building site. Your reasonable response, as an employer, has to take into account whether Alf's behaviour has crossed the line from inappropriate to unacceptable.

  If you have considered the above factors, and think that there are no extenuating circumstances, then dismissal may well be an appropriate sanction (subject to representations made by Alf at the disciplinary hearing).

- Theft: This will almost always justify dismissal, other than in first offences of petty theft (such as stealing a few stamps). The dishonest removal of cash, even if only a small sum, will almost always amount to gross misconduct.

- Entering into competition with employer: A tribunal will not regard *preparatory* steps for setting up in competition with an employer as being gross misconduct unless there is a clear prohibition on such conduct in Alf's contract of employment. It is not sufficient to say that Alf should have known that competition is not permitted if it does not appear in his contract. However, if matters go further than mere preparation and Alf actively engages in conduct which is detrimental to your business, you will be justified in treating such actions as gross misconduct. Note that applying for jobs with your competitors is *not* gross misconduct, or indeed misconduct at all, since an employee is under no legal obligation to remain employed by you. An exception to this rule is if Alf's contract contains a clear clause prohibiting him from working for other employers in a particular area, or from using confidential company information. Such clauses are subject to very complex legal checks to determine whether they are enforceable, and if you are contemplating dismissal on grounds of Alf entering into competition you should seek proper legal advice.

- Intoxication: Unless alcoholic intoxication is accompanied by aggravating factors, such as extreme rudeness to customers or violence, it is unlikely to be regarded as gross misconduct by tribunals. If, however, your company has a clear rule prohibiting alcohol then Alf's intoxication may fall within category (iii) below (see 4.31 onwards). If the intoxication is as the result of, or linked to, the use of illegal drugs then Alf's conduct will usually amount to gross misconduct and you can readily dismiss him for a first offence.

- Matters particular to your business: Some businesses may have particular standards which, if breached, will justify dismissal without warning even though they do not fall within conduct usually regarded as gross misconduct. At the end of the day, a tribunal has to decide whether you acted reasonably in dismissing for a first offence in the absence of express, prior warnings or notices. The disciplinary breach must be fairly substantial to satisfy this test. They will often relate to conduct affecting health and safety, as shown by the following example:

Example

An employee tied down a lever on an automatic lathe in a factory, thereby removing an important safety device. Although the employment tribunal was not certain that this breached any of the employer's rules, it decided that the employer had acted fairly in dismissing him because the conduct endangered the health and safety of all other workers and it was fair to dismiss for a first breach – *Martin v Yorkshire Imperial Metals Ltd [1978] IRLR 440*

4.26 Note that the decision as to whether something amounts to gross misconduct is an objective one – i.e. the tribunal will decide whether the hypothetical reasonable employer, in the same situation, would regard Alf's actions as gross misconduct. The fact that you have labelled Alf's actions as being gross misconduct will not assist if, as a matter of reality, they did not amount to gross misconduct.

Example

An employee failed to use the correct procedure when ringing up a £1.46 purchase on the till. This fell within the employer's definition of gross misconduct and she was dismissed as a result. The tribunal held that the employer had not acted reasonably because this was a one-off lapse, and the fact that an act was labelled as gross misconduct did not necessarily mean that the dismissal was justified – *Laws Stores Ltd v Oliphant [1978] IRLR 251*

4.27   It is vital that you are consistent in treating particular acts as gross misconduct. In other words, if someone else has committed the same breach of discipline on an earlier occasion and you did not dismiss him, a tribunal will find that you have acted unreasonably and arbitrarily in dismissing Alf for the same breach. Any such dismissal is almost certain to be found unfair.

It was, however, you can show that the earlier person *would* have been dismissed were it not for particular exceptional circumstances that do not exist in Alf's case, then you will not be acting arbitrarily and will be able to justify your different treatment of the two employees.

4.28   If you can establish that Alf's act amounts to gross misconduct, you are justified in dismissing him for a first offence unless he can produce extenuating or mitigating circumstances sufficient to displace the presumption that dismissal is a reasonable response. The disciplinary hearing, and your actions subsequent to that, are considered below at 4.40.

(ii) Where warnings will be ineffective

4.29   If a first offence does not amount to gross misconduct, then you cannot dismiss Alf for it unless he has specifically been made aware that such conduct might lead to dismissal. The appropriate course of action is to issue a warning to Alf that if he continues to act in that way then he will be facing dismissal.

Occasionally, however, it is clear that any such warning will be futile, for example from Alf's employment history.

Example

A college lecturer was dismissed, following a reorganisation of teaching duties, because he had objected to the reorganisation, become uncooperative and argumentative with the head of the college and tried to involve students in the dispute. The college argued that a warning would have been futile. Although the lecturer said that he would have ceased being disruptive if he had received a warning, the tribunal held that a warning would have made no difference to his conduct and found that dismissal was an appropriate sanction – *Farnborough v Governors of Edinburgh College of Art [1974] IRLR 245*

4.30   Note that your belief and assertion that a warning will be futile does not necessarily mean it *would* be futile. You may need to be able to justify your position to a tribunal. If you are unsure, and do not want to risk paying compensation to Alf, take the safe route and issue a warning for a first offence.

It is important to be able to show that you considered whether a warning would be effective *before* coming to the conclusion that dismissal is appropriate. It is *not* a defence to say, at the tribunal hearing, that you did not think about it at the time but upon reflection you do not think a warning would have made any difference (although such an argument, if proven, may have some effect on the level of compensation – see Chapter 13).

Bear in mind, however, that if Alf has a history of such action, he should have received warnings before (in which case you should be considering dismissal for subsequent offences – see 4.36). If you have failed to give him warnings in the past he has a legitimate expectation that his ongoing breaches of discipline will be overlooked by you. If that is the case, a tribunal will view a dismissal as arbitrary (because it is contrary to past practice) and thus unfair.

Example

An experienced machine operator was dismissed for disobeying an instruction to help a new, inexperienced assistant. She had similarly refused in the past. However, in the past the employer had taken a more relaxed attitude and had not issued warnings. The tribunal held that the dismissal was unfair because the employee had a legitimate expectation that her conduct would not lead to dismissal, and that the employer should have first warned her that he would no longer tolerate her attitude – *Hackwood v Seal (Marine) Ltd [1973] IRLR 17*

(iii) Where Alf is aware that the breach of discipline in question will lead to dismissal

4.31   The presumption a tribunal adopts is that it is unfair to dismiss an employee for a first offence unless he has committed an act of gross misconduct. Instead, a reasonable employer should give a clear warning that dismissal is likely if the employee does not cease acting in the way that he has been doing.

The rationale behind requiring an employer to give a warning is so that the employee is made fully aware that the employer views his conduct as serious enough to warrant dismissal. Tribunals take the view that in the absence of such a warning, it is unfair to dismiss an employee for minor matters. However, once such a warning has been given and the employee is aware of the weight which the employer attributes to his conduct, it becomes reasonable to dismiss him if he continues to act in a way which he knows is contrary to the employer's instructions.

It follows that if the employee is aware, even on a first offence, of the weight that an employer attaches to particular matters, yet nevertheless disregards rules prohibiting him from acting in that way, it may be reasonable to dismiss him for such a first offence. In essence, the rule will act as a substitute for a formal disciplinary warning.

4.32   The rule must have been brought to the attention of the employee before his wrongful act took place. It is no good trying to persuade a tribunal that a dismissal is justified because of a rule that Alf was unaware of, since he cannot be at fault for disregarding something he does not know about.

Example

An employee missed a morning's work as a result of a hangover brought on by excess drinking at his firm's Christmas party. Because the same thing had happened (with different employees) the year before, the employer had agreed with the trade union that such misconduct would lead to instant dismissal. However, this was not communicated to the employee. The tribunal found that the dismissal was unfair because the employee had not received any notice or warning that such conduct would lead to dismissal – *W Brooks & Son v Skinner [1984] IRLR 379*

Ideally, the rule should be contained in Alf's contract of employment. If he does not have a written contract, or if the contract does not contain such a rule, it will be sufficient if you can show that Alf was *aware* of the rule. Ideally, he should have seen the rule in writing (for example, in a memo or a notice pinned to a notice board). It is dangerous to try to persuade a tribunal that someone had informed Alf orally of the rule, since a tribunal may not accept such evidence, if it is contested by Alf, or may conclude that insufficient weight was given to the rule if it was simply mentioned in conversation.

Needless to say, if such a rule does not exist then you will not be able to rely on it for the purpose of dismissing Alf for a first offence. You may, however, wish to consider imposing such a rule for future occasions. This can easily be done in a memo circulated to all staff. Ensure, however, that the new rule is not contrary to any of the current terms of employment (e.g. a unilateral change in working hours) since this would entitle your employees to resign and claim constructive dismissal.

You will need to be able to *prove* that Alf was familiar with the rule. It is irrelevant whether he was thinking about the rule at the time he committed the offence; all you need to prove is that the rule had been brought to his attention. If the rule is contained in Alf's contract, which he (presumably) would have signed, then you will have no difficulty showing a tribunal that Alf was aware of the existence of the rule.

If the rule was contained in a memo, or a notice, you should ask Alf during the disciplinary meeting (see 4.16) if he was aware of it. If he denies having been made aware of it, or denies having received the memo, you will have to take a calculated risk as to whether you want to proceed with the dismissal, and risk a tribunal finding that Alf was not familiar with the rule and thus that dismissal was a disproportionate sanction for a first offence. The alternative is to issue a formal warning to Alf in respect of his conduct and dismiss him should he offend a second time.

4.33   The rule must be clear and unambiguous. It must state exactly what conduct is prohibited in a clear and concise fashion. A tribunal is unlikely to find that it is reasonable to dismiss for a first offence of breaching a rule when the rule is not, itself, clear. Accordingly a rule saying that 'any employee who is guilty of misconduct will be dismissed' will be disregarded by a tribunal because it is so wide as to be meaningless. The conduct which is warned against must be spelled out in the rule with precision and clarity.

Furthermore, the rule must explicitly state that breach *will* lead to dismissal. In the past tribunals have shown a tendency to find that a rule which simply says that breach 'may' lead to dismissal is not sufficient to place the employee on notice that breach will result in their dismissal. This is a peculiar approach, since any reasonably intelligent employee understands the meaning of the phrase 'breach of this rule may lead to your dismissal'. Nevertheless, there have been a number of cases where tribunals have said that this is inadequate and that an absolute form of wording is required before the employer can rely on the rule to justify dismissal for a first offence. Although tribunals are becoming more realistic about the precise wording of the sanction to the rule, there remains a slight risk in dismissing somebody in reliance on a rule which is not written in absolute terms.

4.34   The rule must have been rigidly enforced in the past. If you have ever waived the rule or sanction for other employees, a tribunal will say that Alf could not have been certain that his conduct would lead to dismissal, since it had not led to dismissal for others, and thus it is unreasonable for you to arbitrarily impose a heavier sanction for a first offence that you have done in the past.

Example

A company had a no-smoking policy due to high fire risks. The employees were aware of this rule: however, in practice employees who were caught smoking were simply given casual warnings. The employee in this case was dismissed following being caught smoking. The tribunal held that the dismissal was unfair because he had been lulled into a false sense of security due to the more casual approach taken by the employers in the past both with himself and with other employees – *Bendall v Paine & Betteridge [1973] IRLR 44*

If, however, you can point to particular mitigating circumstances in the prior case where you did not dismiss, you can probably explain your previous failure to dismiss and thus show that your conduct is not inconsistent or unreasonable.

4.35   Even if the rule is clear and it has been rigidly enforced in the past, you must still form the view that dismissal is a reasonable sanction in all the circumstances of the case. Even when rules justifying dismissal exist, tribunals will regard rigid adherence to them as unfair if the hypothetical reasonable employer would have formed the view that dismissal was not warranted due to the particular circumstances of the case. You therefore have to be sure that you can justify your adherence to the rule to a tribunal.

Subsequent offences

4.36   If Alf has committed disciplinary offences in the past, which have resulted in warnings rather than dismissal, you will usually be justified in dismissing him for further breaches which would not, on their own, warrant dismissal.

The ACAS Code of Practice on Disciplinary Practice and Procedures in Employment states:

'Often supervisors will give informal oral warnings for the purpose of improving conduct when employees commit minor infringements of the established standards of conduct. However, where the facts of a case appear to call for disciplinary action, other than summary dismissal, the following procedure should normally be observed:

a   in the case of minor offences, the individual should be given a formal oral warning or if the issue is more serious, there should be a written warning setting out the nature of the offence and the likely consequences of further offences. In either case the individual should be advised that the warning constitutes the first formal stage of the procedure;

b   further misconduct might warrant a final written warning which should contain a statement that any recurrence would lead to suspension or dismissal or some other penalty, as the case may be;

c   the final step might be disciplinary transfer, or disciplinary suspension without pay (but only if these are allowed for by an express or implied condition of the contract of employment), or dismissal, according to the nature of the misconduct. Special consideration should be given before imposing disciplinary suspension without pay and it should not normally be for a prolonged period.'

This sets out what the courts regard as ideal personnel management, namely an oral warning, then a written warning, and only then moving to dismissal. However, the law does not require employers to act in an ideal fashion, but only to act fairly and reasonably. There are three situations to be considered, as set out below:

i   where the previous episode of misconduct resulted in a formal warning;

ii   where the previous episode of misconduct did not result in a formal warning; and,

iii where the previous misconduct is of a different nature to the present misconduct (for example, where Alf's earlier misconduct concerned timekeeping whereas the present misconduct concerns rudeness to customers).

(i) Where a formal warning exists

4.37   Notwithstanding the provisions of the ACAS Code of Conduct (above), tribunals do not generally require employers to have gone through an oral warning and a written warning prior to dismissal. Likewise, you may have heard about the need for a first written warning and a final written warning. There is no legal basis for these requirements; the purpose of a multitude of warnings is to encourage better industrial relations. If you are concerned as to whether or not you are entitled to dismiss Alf, it is the legal 'bottom-line' which is important and not developing better industrial relations.

As with dismissals in all circumstances, the essential requirement is that your decision to dismiss must be reasonable. It will not be reasonable to dismiss Alf for a first offence unless it falls into one of the categories described above. However, once Alf has received a formal written warning in respect of his conduct, yet nevertheless continues to act in a way which you have forbidden, it will only be in the rarest of circumstances that a tribunal will say that you have acted unreasonably in dismissing him.

The formal warning must have made it clear that dismissal was a likely, or a possible consequence if Alf erred again. The courts are not concerned with whether the prior warning was oral or in writing, provided it was clear and made the consequences of repeat performance obvious. However, you should be wary of relying on an oral warning (unless you made a note of the warning in Alf's personnel file at the time) since Alf may deny ever having received the warning. It is always best to put these things in writing.

Do not rely on very old warnings as justifying dismissal. An employee who commits a minor offence when he starts employment, works well for ten years and then slips up again is entitled to different treatment to that received by an employee who has committed the same offence twice within six months. The general rule of thumb is that warnings should be disregarded after two years when deciding an appropriate sanction.

Provided that the offence which Alf has repeated is not trivial (trivial offences being such as making personal telephone calls, using vulgar language away from customers or smoking in a non-smoking area) then a tribunal is unlikely to say that your decision to dismiss Alf falls outside the band of reasonable responses which you could make. Accordingly, if you have performed a full investigation and held a proper disciplinary hearing, your decision to dismiss Alf will be upheld if he takes you to an employment tribunal.

If the offence *was* trivial, you will not be entitled to dismiss Alf after just two offences. A tribunal would consider that a reasonable employer would, in such circumstances, issue a stern final written warning (see 4.45) and that dismissal at this stage would be excessive. You should, therefore, issue one more warning and only dismiss Alf if he breaches your rules once again.

(ii) Where a formal warning does not exist

4.38   Even if Alf has committed the offence before, if you did not formally warn him that his conduct breached good discipline then you cannot dismiss him for repeating the offence. If you issued a verbal rebuke, this may be sufficient to be a formal warning if you made it clear at the time that a repeat of the offence was likely to result in dismissal – see 4.37.

The reason for not being able to dismiss Alf is that a tribunal will say that, by not warning him on the prior occasion, you lulled him into a false sense of security and thereby his conduct must be viewed as *less*, not more, culpable than the last time. Accordingly, since you did not dismiss him after the first offence, it can hardly be reasonable to dismiss him following the second offence in respect of which he is less blameworthy.

Since you are not able to dismiss Alf, you should use the opportunity to protect your position so that if he offends a third time, you will be able to dismiss him lawfully. This will involve issuing a stern formal letter warning him that you regard his conduct as extremely serious and that, although you waived disciplinary proceedings the first time, you are not prepared to carry on doing so and that if he repeats his actions again he will be dismissed. See 4.45 for more details on the contents of formal written warnings.

(iii) Where the misconduct is of a different nature

4.39   You are entitled to dismiss Alf due to his conduct even if his previous misconduct has been of a different type. Thus, for example, if Alf receives a warning for ignoring safety procedures and then, one month later, commits a completely unrelated offence, you may still rely on the first warning to justify dismissal. This is because it will, subject to it being otherwise reasonable on the facts of each individual case, be within the band of reasonable responses to dismiss an employee who has engaged in more than one act of misconduct even though they are of a different nature.

However, if the two acts are completely dissimilar, and are not closely linked in time (within, say, six months of each other), then a tribunal may find that on the facts of the individual case it would not be reasonable to rely on the warning for the first offence as justifying dismissal for the second offence. You may be safer issuing another warning. Should Alf then offend again, you will be in a much stronger position to justify his dismissal to a tribunal (given that there will be *two* warnings on record and he will therefore have a well-documented history of misconduct).

The disciplinary meeting

4.40   Tribunals tend to be more concerned about going through the correct procedure during the investigative, rather than the disciplinary, stage of effecting a dismissal. Nevertheless, it is important that you adhere to the various procedural requirements for three reasons. First, you will want to ensure that the sanction you impose is a proper one and is proportionate to the offence. Second, you do not want to leave any holes for Alf to exploit during a tribunal hearing. Third, and perhaps more practically, you do not want any advisor to seize on a procedural omission and recommend to Alf that he has a potential claim against you.

Unlike the investigative meeting, if Alf fails to attend without explanation you can regard his first non-attendance as disinterest or non-cooperation. If he does not attend but asks for the meeting to be rescheduled, you should agree to do so.

It is important that you have somebody present at the meeting to take notes, or take as full a note yourself as is possible.

There are two approaches to adopt, depending on whether you are contemplating dismissal. If, having considered the matters set out above, you are of the view that dismissal is likely to be an unreasonable response then you should *not* follow the same approach as you would do if dismissal were contemplated. At the end of the day, however, you must take a commercial decision as to the best way forward for your business, bearing in mind the risk and the sum of money involved if Alf succeeds in proving unfair dismissal to a tribunal (see Chapter 13).

(i) Dismissal *is* being contemplated

4.41   If dismissal *is* being contemplated, you must state at the outset of the meeting that you are considering dismissal. Ask Alf if there are any extenuating or mitigating circumstances that he wishes to put forward.

It Alf asserts that he did not commit the act of misconduct, tell him that you have already decided that he *did*, that he had the chance to make representations on his guilt during the investigative stage, and that this meeting is solely concerned with the disciplinary sanction. If you are anything other than a very small business, you should also tell him that he will have a future opportunity to appeal against your decision that he has committed the act of misconduct (see Chapter 11 on appeals).

Allow Alf to put forward any matters that he considers to be relevant. Even if you think that his submissions are immaterial, allow him to have his say.

It is often useful to ask questions like 'if you were me, what would you do?' or 'do you understand that the company cannot continue employing people who verbally abuse customers?' It is surprising how many employees capitulate in the face of questions like this, and agree that dismissal is appropriate. This has a powerful psychological effect, since it may inhibit them from claiming against you once they have admitted that dismissal was reasonable. Further, if you have taken a proper note of their responses, it will go down well with a tribunal that Alf did not challenge your proposed actions during the disciplinary meeting.

Once Alf has put his point of view forward, you should tell him that you will consider his comments and put your decision to him in writing. Do not give him any indication of your likely decision at this stage.

(ii) Dismissal is *not* being contemplated

4.42   You may *not* be contemplating dismissing Alf, and prefer to issue a warning, or you may simply have decided to issue a warning due to the risk of a tribunal finding a dismissal to be unfair. If this is the case, you should tell Alf at the beginning of the meeting that you do not intend to dismiss him but are considering issuing a formal warning. Ask him if he has any representations to make. If he denies having committed the offence, tell him that the question of guilt has been decided, is a matter for appeal and it is not why you are holding the meeting.

It is unlikely that Alf will want to prolong a meeting which he will find very embarrassing. Once he realises that you do not wish to dismiss him, he will probably want to finish the meeting as quickly as possible and may well agree that a warning is appropriate. It is for *this* reason that holding a formal disciplinary hearing is useful – it will mean that you are in a stronger position to dismiss Alf should he re-offend if he agreed to a formal warning in respect of the present offence.

Deciding on an appropriate disciplinary sanction

4.43   There are a number of sanctions you can impose. They are as follows:

- Dismissal: If you decide to dismiss, you will need to be certain of your reasons and certain that you can justify the decision to dismiss as reasonable in the circumstances. If you have followed the guidelines set out in this book and considered all the relevant factors, you should be confident that you can justify a dismissal.

- Demotion/transfer: Be very careful if the demotion or transfer involves a reduction in salary or prestige (as will inevitably be the case). It will entitle Alf to resign and claim constructive dismissal (although he will not succeed if you could have reasonably dismissed him for the offence). If his offence does *not* justify dismissal, you run as much risk in reducing his salary as you do in dismissing him.

- Suspension *without* pay: This is only permissible if Alf's contract of employment specifically authorises it. If you suspend without pay when the contract of employment does *not* authorise you to do so, Alf can claim constructive dismissal on the ground that you are in breach of your contractual obligation to pay him wages.

- Suspension *with* pay: On first thought, this may appear more of a reward than a disciplinary sanction. It may have a use, however, if Alf is denied the opportunity of earning commission or overtime, or where the suspension itself would embarrass Alf amongst his colleagues.

- Formal warning: This will be the most common sanction imposed when you are not resorting to dismissal.

- Fine: You are not permitted to fine Alf, except in very specific circumstances where his fault has led to a discernible financial loss for your company and he has agreed to your right to make deductions from his wages in writing before he started employment. Avoid this – if you fine him when you are not entitled to do so he can resign and claim constructive dismissal (see Chapter 17).

- Informal warning: An unlikely sanction since this will be a simple reprimand of the type which may occur during the ordinary course of a working day. If you have been through the full investigative and disciplinary procedure, it is likely that the offence warrants something more than an informal warning.

4.44   Although you will have formed a view as to the appropriate sanction, if it is dismissal you should specifically consider other options and think about why they are not appropriate. Thus in a case of aggression towards customers, you may think that demotion is not appropriate because Alf would still come into contact with customers, that suspension without pay is not appropriate because his contract does not authorise you to do that, and that you had already issued a formal warning and thus a further warning is unlikely to be of any effect.

Do take into account Alf's explanations. If he says that the reason he was late for work was because of a death in the family, a tribunal is not going to agree that dismissal was a reasonable sanction. However, it will often be the case that Alf's mitigation is immaterial to your reasons for dismissal. Thus if he seeks to justify 'borrowing' money from the petty cash box on the basis that he was temporarily short of money, you may think that this is not relevant since you are dismissing him for dishonesty and the reason for his dishonesty has no bearing on your decision.

The purpose in considering other options is one of justification at a later date – if you tell a tribunal that you actively considered alternate sanctions then they are more likely to condone your decision to dismiss as reasonable than if you admit that you had not considered other options at all.

If you are a very large employer, it may be worthwhile having a form printed listing alternative sanctions and containing space for you to fill in why they are not appropriate. This will be useful from an evidential point of view at any tribunal hearing. If you are not a large employer, having such a form will appear artificial and peculiar to the tribunal and thus it would be unwise to use one.

The necessary elements of both a formal warning letter and a dismissal letter are set out below.

Warning letter

4.45 It is important that the warning letter is clear and to the point. It should state that continued misconduct, or a repetition of the offence, is likely to lead to dismissal. The letter should contain the following points:

- You write further to your meeting on March 13, 1999, at which you discussed the appropriate sanction for the offence. Identify the offence in a few words, but do not go into detail – this will have been done in your previous letter following the investigative meeting.

- If Alf agreed that a formal warning was appropriate, reference should be made to this in the letter. In any event, state that the letter constitutes a formal warning that, if there is a repetition of the offence or continued misconduct, Alf is likely to be dismissed unless there are exceptional extenuating circumstances.

- State that he has a right of appeal from the warning, and that his appeal should be sent to the appropriate person in writing within, say, seven days. See Chapter 11 for more details on appeals.

- If Alf has been on suspension, inform him of the date that you expect him to resume work.

It does not matter whether you hand the letter to Alf or post it to him. You should, however, ask him to sign a copy of the letter as an acknowledgment of receipt and return it to you. This is important because, should you dismiss Alf in the future, you will need to prove that he had received the formal warning.

Dismissal letter

4.46   If Alf is suspended, you can justify sending a letter to him at home. However, if he has continued working during your investigations, a tribunal will regard it as callous (and thus evidence of an unreasonable attitude) if you simply send him a letter of dismissal by post. Accordingly you should inform him verbally that he is being dismissed and either hand him the letter or tell him that you will confirm the dismissal in writing within 24 hours.

If you are dismissing Alf for gross misconduct, you do not need to give him any notice pay. Indeed, for various legal reasons (which fall outside the scope of this book) it is actually detrimental to your case to give any notice period. Accordingly the dismissal should be instant (or, to use the legal word, summary).

If the dismissal is not for gross misconduct, you need to give an appropriate notice period. Chapter 12 deals with the number of weeks' notice that you are legally obliged to give to Alf. You have three options as to how to deal with Alf's notice period:

i   require him to continue working during the notice period;

ii   require him to remain on your company's books, but to remain at home and not work for any other persons (this is known as 'garden leave'); or,

iii pay a lump sum in lieu of notice. Note, however, that this option may sometimes prevent you relying on restraint of trade or confidentiality clauses in Alf's contract. If such clauses exist, and you wish to rely on them, you should seek specific legal advice.

4.47   Your letter should state the following:

- That you write further to your meeting on March 13, 1999, which you called in order to determine whether dismissal was justified as a result of Alf's conduct. Identify the conduct in one or two sentences.

- If you are dismissing Alf as a result of gross misconduct, state that his actions amount to gross misconduct. If you are dismissing him following breach of a rule or a warning, identify the source and/or date of the rule or the warning and state that your decision has been taken against the background of the rule or the warning.

- If appropriate, that you have considered suspension or demotion, but that you are of the view that they would not be appropriate. State that your business interests prevent the continued employment of Alf and give a reason (such as you are losing customers as the result of Alf's conduct, or that his drinking problem is affecting the quality of his work).

- If the dismissal is for gross misconduct, that Alf is summarily dismissed and that he is not entitled to notice pay. Otherwise, state which one of the options in paragraph 4.46 applies and, if appropriate, enclose a cheque or say that a cheque will follow.

- Unless you are a very small company, tell Alf that he is entitled to appeal within, say, seven days. If he wishes to appeal, he should set out his reasons in writing in a letter to the appropriate person. See Chapter 11 for more details on appeals.

4.48   If Alf contacts you after receiving the letter, be firm but polite. Do not say anything that might prejudice your case at the tribunal (such as you were not sure that it was him who was stealing, but you had to sack someone to protect your own job).

References

4.49   See the discussion of references at 3.24.

5. HOW TO DISMISS SOMEONE FOR CONCEALING CRIMINAL OFFENCES

Introduction

5.1   Chapter 3 dealt with situations where Alf committed a criminal offence away from work. Chapter 4 dealt with situations where Alf may have committed a criminal act at work. Sometimes, however, you may discover that Alf has prior criminal convictions that he failed to disclose when you first employed him. If it is a very minor conviction (such as a driving offence) you would be unwise to dismiss him, since a tribunal would almost certainly find that your action is disproportionate (unless a clean driving licence is an essential element of Alf's employment).

Can you dismiss Alf?

5.2   In order to dismiss Alf for concealing a conviction, it is essential that he must have actively misled you. If there is a space on your application form for criminal convictions, and he has failed to disclose the offence, this will clearly suffice. If, however, you did not ask him about convictions during the selection process, he will not have concealed the offence and you cannot dismiss him on that basis.

Unless the offence is trivial, a tribunal will uphold your decision to dismiss Alf for deliberate concealment of a criminal offence before starting work. This is particularly so if Alf is employed in a position of trust.

Example

Mr Torr was a guard for British Rail. When he applied for the job, he stated that he had not been convicted of any criminal offences. In fact, he had been convicted of two offences; the first involving a prison sentence of three years (16 years before his job application) and the second involving a prison sentence of nine months (six years before his application). Eighteen months into his employment, the first conviction was discovered and he was dismissed. The Employment Appeal Tribunal decided that the dismissal was fair, even though the conviction was 16 years old, since the job of a guard involved supervision over a train, its passengers and freight and it could not be entrusted to a person who dishonestly concealed a criminal conviction – *Torr v British Railways Board [1977] IRLR 184*

There are three steps which you must go through before you can dismiss Alf:

a   ensure that there actually is a conviction;

b   ensure that the conviction was not 'spent' at the time Alf applied for employment;

c   give Alf the opportunity to explain why he failed to disclose the conviction.

(a) Ensure that there actually is a conviction

5.3   This sounds self-evident. However, if Alf claims unfair dismissal and then denies the conviction, you will have to prove that he had been convicted of an offence. Presumably you would have been told by someone about Alf's conviction – thus the easiest way to verify it is to ask your informant about his source.

As a matter of reality, most employees will admit to a conviction if confronted with it (since they believe that the conviction can be verified with the police). This is a misapprehension – the police will not disclose details of convictions to the public, or even to an employer. Accordingly you may place yourself at risk if you dismiss Alf on the basis of unsubstantiated or unconfirmed allegations of concealing a conviction.

If Alf admits the conviction, make sure that his admission is recorded in writing (so that a later denial to a tribunal will carry little weight). The best place to do this is in a letter inviting Alf to explain why he failed to disclose the conviction.

(b) Ensure that the conviction is not spent

5.4   Under the *Rehabilitation of Offenders Act 1974*, convictions become 'spent' after a certain period of time. If a conviction is spent at the time he applied for his job, Alf is regarded as a 'rehabilitated person' and is entitled, by law, to withhold details about the conviction from you. If you dismiss Alf because of a concealed spent offence, the dismissal will be unfair and you may have to pay considerable compensation to him.

The rehabilitation periods are as follows:

- Over 30 months' imprisonment – No rehabilitation period – the conviction will never become spent;

- Imprisonment between 6 and 30 months – 10 years;

- Imprisonment for less than 6 months – 7 years;

- Fine or probation – 5 years;

- Conditional discharge or binding over – 1 year or, if longer, the duration of the order.

The above periods should be halved if Alf was under 18 when he committed the offence.

(c) Give Alf the opportunity to explain his failure to disclose the conviction

5.5   Once you have established that Alf has an undisclosed, unspent conviction, you must give him the opportunity to explain why he failed to disclose it. You can also use this occasion to allow him to put forward reasons as to why he should not be dismissed.

You should write to Alf, making the following points:

- You have discovered that he concealed a conviction at the time he applied for his job. Set out what the conviction was and, if you know it, the sentence he received. If Alf has admitted the conviction to you, make reference to his admission in the letter.

- You consider the deliberate concealing of a conviction to be a very serious matter.

- You would like him to come to a meeting to explain why he failed to disclose the conviction. State the date, time and place of the meeting. Inform him that he can have a representative present if he wishes.

- In view of the seriousness of his actions, you are considering dismissal and he should use the meeting as an opportunity to put forward reasons why dismissal would not be an appropriate response.

5.6 At the meeting, you should follow the same procedure as for investigative meetings when dismissing someone for breaches of discipline (see paragraph 4.12). Do not forget to invite Alf's comments on whether dismissal is an appropriate response – see 4.41. Do *not* tell Alf your decision during, or immediately after, the meeting.

The decision to dismiss

5.7 Once the meeting has concluded, you will need to decide whether Alf has produced a reasonable excuse for failing to disclose his conviction. There are a number of excuses regularly used. These range from 'oh – I didn't realise it included convictions for shoplifting – I thought it was just for violence' to the unlikely 'I forgot about the conviction'.

A tribunal is unlikely to criticise you for disbelieving Alf's excuse that he forgot about a conviction. A conviction for a criminal offence is not the sort of thing that slips people's minds, particularly if their focus has been triggered by the question 'do you have any convictions?'

If, however, the question asked at the selection stage was 'do you have any criminal convictions which might affect your suitability for the job', rather than the wider 'do you have any criminal convictions?', you may have to accept an excuse from Alf that he did not think a particular conviction relevant. This is a question of fact and degree – if the job is a security guard and Alf has been convicted of theft, it is clearly relevant and you will be justified in rejecting his excuse. It is important therefore that your application form includes such a question.

Most frequently, you will simply face a lack of cooperation from Alf. If he fails to put forward an excuse for concealing the conviction, you should have little difficulty justifying his dismissal to a tribunal, subject to the following point.

5.8 Once you have satisfied yourself that Alf lacks a valid reason for concealing the conviction, you need to decide whether dismissal is an appropriate sanction. Provided your view is reasonable, a tribunal will uphold the dismissal if Alf later complains of unfair dismissal.

Dismissal will usually be appropriate if Alf has deliberately concealed an unspent offence. The fact that an offence was near, but not quite at, its rehabilitation date when you employed Alf will not assist him. The courts have made it clear that there is no obligation on an employer to extend the social policy behind the *Rehabilitation of Offenders Act 1974* by discounting offences which are not yet spent under the Act.

If, however, the offence was a very minor one then a tribunal may say that dismissal was an unreasonable response. Usually, minor offences will become spent fairly quickly and thus the fact that it is not spent means it is likely to be a more serious offence. If Alf has had warnings for incompetence or misconduct, you will be on stronger ground even if the offence is minor, since it is more reasonable to dismiss a 'bad' employee for concealing a minor offence than it is to dismiss an able, trusted employee.

You will not be able, in these circumstances, to dismiss Alf without notice. Therefore you can either require him to work out his notice period, or pay him money in lieu of notice – see 4.46 for further details.

5.9 If you decide that dismissal is reasonable, you should write to Alf setting out the following:

- Further to your meeting on January 28, 1999, you have considered the reasons he gave for failing to disclose his conviction. State, briefly, his explanation and explain why you do not accept it.

- Although you have taken into account his comments about

dismissal and (if appropriate) his long/good working record, you are of the view that his continued employment is not possible because he secured the employment only by deliberately concealing details of his past conviction.

- You are dismissing him. State whether you are requiring him to work out his notice period or paying him in lieu of notice.

- Alf is entitled to appeal within, say, three working days. If he wishes to appeal, he should set out his reasons in writing in a letter to the appropriate person. See Chapter 11 for further details on appeals.

The letter can either be handed to Alf or posted to him at home.

6. HOW TO DISMISS SOMEONE FOR REFUSING TO OBEY INSTRUCTIONS

Introduction

6.1 Although Alf may not have committed any disciplinary offences, and may be perfectly capable of doing his job properly, you may wish to dismiss him for failing to obey instructions. Such instructions can include telling Alf to enter credit card transactions in a certain manner, or imposing a 'no-smoking' policy on the whole office. It will only be in the rarest circumstances that you can dismiss somebody for a one-off failure to obey instructions; more usually, you will need to give them at least one clear warning.

As with all dismissals, it is necessary to follow a careful procedure or you risk a tribunal finding that you have acted unfairly.

Alf's refusal to obey instructions can arise in two different ways, namely:

a   a refusal to carry out tasks which Alf ordinarily does; and,

b   a refusal to carry out new tasks which did not form part of his ordinary working day.

There are also more fundamental instructions which Alf may be reluctant to follow, such as changing job locations (which may or may not require a move of home) or changing from a day-shift to a night-shift. Each of these will be considered in turn.

(a) Refusal to carry out tasks which are usually undertaken

6.2 This will usually be a valid reason for imposing disciplinary sanctions. If Alf is refusing to complete tasks which fall within his usual remit, you are entitled to take action to compel him to do so. If he continues to refuse, dismissal may become an appropriate sanction.

Common examples of this may be where Alf refuses to work

with a particular colleague because of friction or a grudge, or where he decides that he does not wish to use safety equipment. You must be in a position to show that your instruction is both lawful and reasonable. It will be lawful if it is a task which Alf is required to do under his contract of employment. This is usually a matter of inference and practice; however, if you have a job description sheet (of which Alf has a copy) then any task appearing on that sheet will fall within those which he is contractually obliged to do.

If there is no job description sheet, or if the task is not included on that sheet, then a tribunal will almost always find that an instruction falls within Alf's contract of employment if it is something that he has been required to do (and has done) in the past or if it is something that employees of his job description in other companies are asked to do.

The instruction must also be reasonable. Although you may be contractually entitled to insist that Alf operates a particular piece of machinery, it will not be reasonable to require him to operate it if the safety mechanisms are broken. If you dismiss him for disobeying an unreasonable order, even if it is technically lawful, a tribunal is likely to find that the dismissal was unfair.

(b) Refusal to carry out new tasks

6.3   Again, the central issue, in determining whether or not you can discipline Alf, is whether the instruction was a lawful and reasonable one. If the task is one which you have not required Alf to carry out before then you may have greater difficulty showing that Alf is contractually obliged to do it (unless it is contained within a job description).

Are the new instructions lawful? The law recognises that an employer's requirements change (for example, you may need Alf to work in a different department or use new safety equipment). Accordingly, you are allowed to alter Alf's job description (for unfair dismissal purposes) if you can show that there is a 'sound, good business reason' for doing so. Note that you must establish a 'sound, good business reason' – if it is simply 'desirable' it may not be enough.

What is meant by a 'sound, good business reason'? There is no straightforward answer to this question, and thus you should

be confident that you can justify to a tribunal that you are acting reasonably. If the new instructions do not affect Alf's financial
circumstances (such as requiring him to work additional hours
but giving him a *pro rata* pay increase so that it does not
detrimentally affect his pay) and you can show that the changes
are good for your business then a tribunal is likely to say that
you are entitled to make the changes to Alf's job description.

Sometimes issuing Alf with new tasks will be as the result of
a general, widespread business reorganisation. Dismissing as
the result of a business reorganisation are dealt with in Chapter
8.

6.4   Is the new instruction reasonable? This is a question to be decided
in each case. It would probably not be reasonable to instruct a
senior employee to clear the dustbins, even though it is in your
business's interests that *someone* empty them. If your instruction is unreasonable, then Alf will have a claim for unfair dismissal
if you dismiss him following his non-compliance with it.

(c) Fundamental instructions

6.5   Fundamental changes, such as changing shifts or moving work
locations, can sometimes justify dismissal if Alf refuses to comply.
Unlike the above two scenarios, however, if the change is
fundamental then you are more likely to be able to dismiss Alf
for his initial non-compliance (rather than having to go through
a warning stage before dismissal).

The first point to consider is whether Alf's contract of employment entitles you to give the relevant instructions. It is necessary to have an express clause; you will not be able to imply one
should it not have been specifically agreed or set out in writing.
Many contracts of employment contain a 'mobility clause', allowing you to require Alf to move to anywhere within the United
Kingdom. Such a clause will entitle you to dismiss Alf if he
refuses to move.

If there is no express right to issue the fundamental instruction in Alf's contract, you will need to show that it is reasonably
necessary for your business interests to make the change to his
contract. This is discussed further in Chapter 8. Note that if
you want Alf to move his place of work, you may have a
redundancy situation – see Chapter 7 for further details.

Tribunals will be more sympathetic to you if you dismiss Alf for his refusal to comply with a fundamental instruction than if he is dismissed for failing to comply with a mundane, everyday instruction. This is because fundamental instructions are, by their nature, usually far more central to the business's interest and thus a tribunal will be more inclined to find that you were justified in taking the action that you did.

The first failure to obey instructions

6.6   Usually, you will not be entitled to dismiss Alf following his first failure to obey instructions (unless it is a fundamental instruction). Your approach should therefore be different depending on the type of instruction in question.

Non-fundamental instructions

6.7   In this situation, you should issue Alf with a formal warning. Write to him, and state the following:

- That you are concerned about his failure to comply with your instruction(s) on January 28, 1999. Set out what the instruction was, and briefly refer to the circumstances surrounding Alf's refusal.

- If Alf's conduct had an effect on health and safety, on customer relations or on the profitability of your company, say so. It will justify the weight that you place on compliance with instructions.

- Give the reason, if not covered by the above, why it is important that Alf comply with the instruction.

- State that your company requires its employees to comply with reasonable instructions, and that in failing to do so Alf is in breach of his contract of employment.

- In the circumstances, you are giving Alf a formal warning that continued disobedience, whether of this or any other instruction, may lead to his dismissal.

- That he has a right of appeal against the warning. If he wishes to exercise the right, he should do so in writing within, say, seven days (see Chapter 11 on appeals).

You should ask Alf to sign a copy of the letter as evidence that he received it – it is not uncommon for employees to claim, at tribunal hearings, that warning letters had been concocted and were never sent.

Fundamental instructions

6.8   You should write to Alf, stating the following:

- The actual instruction and the fact that he has failed to comply with it. If you have discussed the matter with him, and he has indicated an ongoing disinclination to comply, state the date and gist of the conversation.

- *Either* that he is obliged to comply with the instruction under his contract of employment (and, if appropriate, quote the relevant section).

- *Or* that it is necessary, in the interests of your business, that he comply with the instruction. Give a brief (one sentence) explanation of why it is in the business's interests to require Alf to act in this way. Do *not* concede in correspondence that it is a change to his contract of employment.

- Give a time limit within which Alf will have to comply with the instruction. Often, in this type of situation, it is better to give a time limit within which Alf will have to confirm that he will comply. The time limit must be a reasonable one – it would be unreasonable to insist, for example, that Alf agrees to move to a new place of work 200 miles away within twenty-four hours.

- State that if Alf does not comply with the instruction he will be dismissed.

6.9   If Alf complies with your instruction, or indicates that he will do so, then your goal will have been achieved. If he states, after having received the letter, that he has no intention of complying you should still allow the time limit to elapse, but can then miss out the next stage and proceed to the dismissal (see 6.14).

If the time limit elapses and Alf has not responded positively, you should write one further letter to him setting out the following:

- you write further to your previous letter, and note that Alf has failed to comply with the instruction by the date set;

- you are giving him one final chance to comply (or to agree that he will comply); if he does not do so within, say, 48 hours then he will be dismissed.

Again, if Alf complies with this final letter you will have achieved your goal. If not, you can proceed to dismissing him (see 6.14).

Subsequent failures to obey instructions

6.10   If, after having received *one* warning for failing to obey instructions, Alf continues to disobey your orders then you may be able to dismiss him at this stage. It will depend on the type of instruction he has disobeyed, the time gap between the two incidents and whether his subsequent refusal is related to the first one. If you cannot justify dismissal (and this is addressed in more detail below), you should give a second warning.

If, after having received *two* warnings for failing to obey instructions, Alf continues to disobey your orders then you will be able to dismiss him (except in exceptional circumstances).

Can you dismiss after just one warning?

6.11   If Alf's second refusal to obey instructions is in connection with a fundamental instruction going to the basis of his work (such as changing working hours, as above) you should follow the same procedure as in 6.7 above.

If neither instruction has been a fundamental instruction, you need to satisfy yourself that it would be reasonable to dismiss Alf in the light of just one prior warning. In general, for it to be reasonable *all three* of the following tests must be satisfied:

a   The instructions must have been important ones or, more accurately, not trivial ones. They must be related to the way in which he performs his work (or the type of work which he undertakes). An example of a trivial instruction, which would not justify dismissal at this stage, would be not wanting to take a lunch break at a particular time.

b   There must not have been a long time gap between the two refusals. As a rule of thumb, if the two refusals occur within one month of each other you can probably justify dismissal. If the time gap is longer you should issue a second warning before dismissing.

c The two refusals must be connected. This can be satisfied either by Alf refusing to obey the same instruction after having received a written warning, or by him refusing to obey instruction 'B' *because* he had received a warning for refusing to obey instruction 'A' – in essence, if he is objecting through spite over the first warning.

In the absence of all three tests being satisfied, it would be dangerous to dismiss Alf based on one warning only. You should issue a second warning (see 6.7) and then re-consider dismissal if he offends a third time.

6.12 *Smoking: a special case:* A common situation where Alf refuses to obey instructions is where you have brought in a 'no-smoking' policy. In such circumstances, assuming Alf has been made aware of the policy, you should issue him with a formal warning (as above) if he is caught smoking.

If he re-offends, you will need to consider relocating him to a suitable environment where smoking is permitted. If there is no appropriate place where he can continue working as a smoker, or if he refuses to be relocated, you will be justified in dismissing him. Your dismissal letter should follow the format set out below at 6.19.

Can you dismiss after two or more warnings?

6.13 You will rarely be criticised for dismissing Alf after two warnings. There are only two scenarios where a dismissal might be found to be unfair:

a If there has been a long time gap between the warnings. In general, any warning over two years old should be disregarded. If, however, almost two years have elapsed since the last warnings (and thus Alf has been on 'good behaviour' for a long time) you are much better off issuing another warning since a tribunal might find that you are acting unreasonably in relying on old warnings for comparatively minor matters.

b   If the instructions in question have been very trivial ones, such as refusing to bring the milk in or make coffee, a tribunal may find that you are using Alf's refusal to comply as a sham to hide the real reason for dismissal. If it forms this view, the dismissal will be unfair. If you genuinely want to dismiss Alf for failing to make the coffee, this is likely to be symptomatic of a more general breakdown of the relationship between Alf and other members of staff. Consider dismissal because of personality clashes – see 10.4

Dismissing Alf

6.14   Since a failure to obey instructions is a form of misconduct, you need to follow a similar procedure to that involved in dismissals for misconduct. You should write to Alf, stating the following:

- That you are concerned about his failure to obey instructions. Set out the incident in question and refer (briefly) to any discussions you have had about it.

- That this is not the first time that he has failed to obey instructions. Refer to the previous warning letter(s) and state that he was warned on that occasion that repeated failure to comply might lead to his dismissal.

- That you cannot justify continuing to employ somebody who persistently refuses to obey reasonable instructions.

- You would like him to meet you to discuss reasons why he should not be dismissed. State a date, time and place for the meeting, but say that it can be changed if it is not convenient for Alf. Tell him he can bring a friend or representative to the meeting.

If Alf fails to attend the meeting, you should reschedule it *once*. If he fails to attend a second time, you can dismiss him without further enquiry (unless he provides a good reason for the second failure to attend). Use the dismissal letter set out at paragraph 6.19 below, but amend it so that it refers to Alf missing the meetings.

6.15   At the meeting, you should have someone present to take notes.

If you are a small company, you can take notes yourself (although it is never ideal to do so since it is difficult to think, talk and write at the same time).

Explain the purpose of the meeting to Alf. Tell him that you are not happy about his failures to obey your instructions, and that you find it difficult to see how you can continue employing someone who disregards instructions. Ask him whether he understands your position, and whether he understands that it goes against the interests of your business to carry on employing him. If he agrees with you, it will place you in a strong position should he then turn around and claim unfair dismissal.

If he does not agree, ask him *why* he failed to obey the most recent instruction. If he tries to discuss an earlier warning for disobeying a previous instruction, explain to him that he had the right to appeal against that warning when it was first issued and it is too late to challenge it now.

Unless he has a very good reason for refusing to obey the instruction, you can continue with the dismissal process. His belief that your instruction was bad for the business, or detrimental to customer relations, will *not* be a good reason – you are the manager and it is for you, not him, to decide policy. He cannot substitute his decision for yours and then disregard instructions to do what he is employed to do.

Safety of customers or other employees will, if justified, usually be a good reason and will prevent you from dismissing Alf (indeed, sometimes dismissing Alf in connection with him taking steps during a health and safety emergency will mean the dismissal is automatically unfair – see 18.2). Likewise, if Alf has received conflicting instructions from two managers, and he is not at fault in failing to clarify those instructions, he cannot be dismissed for failing to comply with one of the two sets of inconsistent instructions.

6.16   If you decide that he has a good reason for not obeying your instruction, or are concerned that a tribunal might perceive him as having had a good reason, tell him that you accept his explanation and that you will take no further action. Write a letter to him confirming your decision.

6.17   If he does not have a good reason for non-compliance, you move on to consider the sanction. Do not inform Alf at this stage that you do not accept his excuse – it is better to do so in writing when you can choose your words with care.

Tell him again that you are considering dismissal. Ask him if there are any facts of which you are not aware which might influence your decision. Feel free to question him on anything he puts forward – if his excuses contain inconsistencies it will assist with justifying a decision to dismiss to a tribunal.

Conclude the meeting by telling him that you will consider what he has said and put your decision in writing. Do not give an answer, or even a preliminary indication, at that stage (otherwise you may face the allegation at a tribunal that you had already made up your mind).

6.18 You then need to consider whether or not it is reasonable to dismiss Alf. If he refuses to comply with a fundamental obligation, or if he has refused to obey reasonable orders in the face of a warning for prior disobedience, a tribunal is likely to find that a decision to dismiss is reasonable *unless* Alf has provided an explanation which justifies his disobedience.

If you are concerned that a tribunal might support Alf's explanation, and find that it was unreasonable of you to reject it (or to dismiss him having accepted it) then, clearly, you should not dismiss him.

6.19 If you decide to dismiss Alf, you must do so with notice – you will not be able to dismiss him summarily. You should write to him stating the following:

- That you refer to your meeting on January 28, 1999.

- You have carefully considered the matters that Alf put forward. State, briefly, what Alf's main points were.

- *Either* that you do not accept his explanation/excuse (and state the reason for disbelieving him).

- *Or* that you accept his explanation but, on weighing it up against the (repeated) failure to comply with instructions, do not think that you can continue utilising Alf's services.

- (If appropriate) that you have considered demotion or suspension, but you do not think that they would be appropriate. State that your business interests prevent Alf's continued employment and give a reason (such as you are spending an inappropriate amount of management time on him, or are losing business).

- That in the circumstances, you are dismissing him. State either that he is required to work out his notice period, and that his last day of employment will be January 28, 1999; alternatively, that you do not require him to work out his notice and will pay him ___ weeks salary in lieu of notice (see 4.46 for further details).

- That he has a right of appeal against your decision within, say, three working days. If he wishes to appeal, he should set out his reasons in writing in a letter to the appropriate person. See Chapter 11 for further information on appeals.

6.20   If Alf contacts you after receiving the letter, be firm but polite. Do not say anything that might prejudice your case at a tribunal hearing – he may be recording the conversation.

Likewise, be careful about offering references during the course of the next three months. See 3.24 for further discussion of this point.

7. DISMISSING FOR REDUNDANCY

Introduction

7.1 This is a highly complex area of law. You stand more risk of being found to have made an error on procedural matters when you dismiss for redundancy than when you dismiss for any other reason. There is also a close overlap with dismissals for business reorganisation (see Chapter 8). If you are able to dismiss Alf due to a business reorganisation, you are better off doing so since Alf will not be entitled to a redundancy payment.

This part is important: the word 'redundancy' has a specific legal meaning. Non-lawyers, employers and employees often use the word 'redundancy' to describe a dismissal where there is no blame to be placed at the employee's feet, i.e. when there is no misconduct or incapability involved. This is wrong, and you will fall foul of a tribunal if you make this mistake.

You can only dismiss for redundancy in specific circumstances. These are set out below. If there *is* a redundancy situation, a dismissal will still be unfair if you select Alf to be dismissed based on particular grounds (see 7.27), or if you fail to have a period of consultation with Alf and his colleagues before the dismissals. A dismissal may also be unfair if you select Alf for redundancy based on personal characteristics (such as he is too loud) rather than objective criteria (such as timekeeping and length of service). Finally, a dismissal for redundancy may become unfair if you fail to consider whether there is any alternative employment that can be offered to Alf.

If you are making large-scale redundancies, you would be wise to seek specific advice from a solicitor specialising in employment law. In particular, if you are proposing to make 20 or more employees at one establishment redundant within a period of 90 days or less then special rules will apply. These special rules are *not* addressed in this book and you must seek specialist legal advice.

7.2 This chapter is divided into two sections. The first section is an analysis of when you can declare redundancies. The second section sets out the procedure that you must follow when making Alf redundant.

When can you declare redundancies?

7.3   There is a very precise definition contained in section 139 of the *Employment Rights Act 1996*. This provides that an employee is taken to be dismissed by reason of redundancy if:

'the dismissal is wholly or mainly attributable to:

(a)   the fact that his employer has ceased or intends to cease:
    (i)   to carry on the business for the purposes of which the employee was employed by him, or
    (ii)   to carry on that business in the place where the employee was so employed, or

(b)   that the requirements of that business:
    (i)   for employees to carry out work of a particular kind, or
    (ii)   for employees to carry out work of a particular kind in the place where the employee was employed by the employer,

has ceased or diminished or are expected to cease or diminish.'

What does that mean? Essentially, you can declare redundancies in two types of situation, namely:

a   when you are planning to close down your business, or the part of your business for which Alf works, at the location where Alf is employed to work; or,

b   where your business no longer needs as many (or any) employees to carry on a particular kind of work.

Situation (a)

7.4   Although situation (a) sounds obvious, it is not always so. You may remember a brief discussion of mobility clauses at 6.5. Tribunals adopt a technical, and what is sometimes perceived as unrealistic, point of view about what is meant by the place at which Alf is employed to work. You may employ him to work in a car factory in Preston. However, if his contract of employment contains a mobility clause, stating that you can require him to move anywhere in the United Kingdom, then tribunals regard his place of work as being exactly that, i.e. anywhere in the United Kingdom.

This means that, even if you are closing down Alf's entire place of work, if your business operates out of other locations in the United Kingdom. you cannot dismiss Alf for redundancy unless situation (b) also applies (i.e. you now need fewer people to do the type of work that Alf was doing). If situation (b) does *not* apply, you must offer Alf alternative employment in one of your other locations, and a failure to do so will mean that the dismissal is not by way of redundancy (although it may be fair for 'some other substantial reason').

Note that in the above scenario, if Alf does *not* accept the alternative employment elsewhere in the United Kingdom, he is presumed *not* to be made redundant and you will not have to pay him any redundancy compensation.

Situation (b)

7.5   This can occur where you have a drop-off in business, and thus need fewer employees to cope with your business requirements. It might also occur where you are replacing employees with mechanical or computerised methods of working, and there is therefore a reduction in the need for human employees to carry on doing those particular tasks.

Be careful to distinguish this situation from a business reorganisation. If you decide to change your administrative staff to a night-shift, you have not reduced the need for employees to carry out work of a particular kind (i.e. administrative work) at that place of business, and accordingly any dismissals of employees who refuse to change hours will *not* be due to redundancy. It will, instead, be due to a business reorganisation (which, if handled properly, can avoid the need to pay a redundancy payment).

You can make Alf redundant even if *he* has not been doing the kind of work which you have less of a need for employees to do. The test to apply is two-fold, namely:

a   have the requirements of your business for employees to carry out work of a particular kind ceased or diminished (or are they expected to cease or diminish)?

b   if so, is the need for Alf's dismissal caused wholly or mainly by that state of affairs?

If the answer to both questions is 'yes', and if you have followed a proper procedure throughout, then you will be able to dismiss Alf for redundancy.

Example

A company which employs six production machines, each with its own operator, decides it only needs five machines and resolves to make one person redundant. A fork-lift truck driver who delivers materials to the machines is selected for redundancy, on a 'last in, first out' basis since he is the most junior employee, and one of the machine operators is transferred to be a fork-lift truck driver. The Employment Appeal Tribunal held this would be a redundancy since there was a reduction in the need for employees to do a particular kind of work (i.e. operate the production machines) and the fork-lift truck driver had been dismissed as a direct result of this, even though he was not one of the employees directly affected – *hypothetical scenario discussed in* **Safeway Stores v Burrell [1997] IRLR 201**

7.6   One important point is that a tribunal will *not* question your business decision to close down a particular location or dismiss employees due to a reduction in work. Provided your decision is not manifestly unreasonable, or a sham designed to dismiss employees by an illegitimate route, tribunals take the view that they should not interfere in business decisions. This is because it is not their function to substitute their view for yours of the way in which your business is run. Accordingly the commercial reasons for closure will not be investigated and you need have no concern about confidential information finding its way into a public hearing.

Example

An employer decided to close down its entire night-shift. An employee complained of unfair dismissal on the grounds that there was no need to do this. The tribunal decided that it was not entitled to consider the manner in which an employer decides to cut down the workforce, and refused to decide whether the redundancies were necessary – *Guy v Delanair (Car Heater) Ltd. [1975] IRLR 73*

It may, however, still be necessary for you to show that a redundancy situation existed. Thus you may be required to provide basic evidence to a tribunal to show that you *did* make a business decision to downsize, rather than you have simply decided to dismiss Alf (and, often, others as well) and wrongly attached the label 'redundancy'.

7.7   When dismissing for redundancy, the need to follow a proper procedure cannot be overemphasised. Going through the procedure is time consuming and thus costly. It is less costly, however, than paying an unfair dismissal award to somebody who no longer works for you. This is particularly the case when making multiple redundancies (when the cumulative cost of several awards can be substantial).

In essence, a tribunal will consider that even if a redundancy situation *did* exist, an employer would not be acting reasonably in making the decision to dismiss a particular employee unless he had considered all alternative options and consulted the employee first. The most frequent, and expensive, error that an employer can make is to assume that consultation would not make any difference. Other than in exceptional cases, which are addressed below at 7.18, the failure to warn and consult with employees will render a dismissal unfair. Ignore this requirement at your peril!

Procedures for instituting redundancies

7.8   In essence, the procedure falls into three stages:

* Stage 1: Consultation

- Stage 2: Selection

- Stage 3: Consideration of alternative employment

If mistakes occur during stages 1 or 3, a tribunal might find that any dismissal was technically unfair, but that a dismissal was inevitable anyway. It those circumstances, any award will be limited to the pay that Alf *would* have earned if he had remained employed a few weeks longer whilst you went through the proper procedures. Similarly, if stage 2 (i.e. your selection procedure) is unfair, the tribunal might find that under a proper selection procedure there was a 60% chance that Alf would have been chosen for redundancy – in which case any award will be reduced by 60%. This is discussed further in Chapter 13.

Redundancy procedure – stage 1 – consultation

7.9   Once there is a redundancy situation and you begin contemplating redundancies, it is necessary for you to consult or warn the workforce. This is to allow them the opportunity to put forward solutions to avoid job losses. Although some solutions that employees (or a trade union) suggest will be unworkable, a dismissal is likely to be unfair if you fail to warn and consult.

The first issue is whether you need to involve a trade union. This is straightforward – either your business recognises a trade union or it does not. You recognise a trade union if you negotiate with the union for collective bargaining purposes. If you do recognise a trade union, you should warn and consult the union *in addition* to individual employees (see 7.22 below). If you choose to consult with one and ignore the other, you face criticism from an employment tribunal.

Consultation with individual employees

7.10   As stated above, a tribunal will almost always find a redundancy to be unfair if you failed to warn and consult the employees in advance. Four questions arise out of this:

1   How long before dismissal should the consultations take place?

2   Which employees should you consult?

3   What should the consultations consist of?

4   Is there ever an exception to the need to consult?

(i) How long before dismissal should the consultations take place?

7.11   The short answer to this is: the longer, the better. The period over which consultation takes place will depend to a large extent on the size and administrative resources of your business, and on the urgency of the need to make redundancies. If a consultation period is very short (say, less than one week) then you risk a tribunal deciding that you were simply paying lip-service to the need for consultation.

If you are a small company and are not making multiple redundancies, you should have little problem if you allow a two-week consultation period for redundancies. Larger companies, or small companies making multiple redundancies, should try to allow at least one month. If you are able to give greater warning, you should do so.

You may be able to persuade a tribunal that it was reasonable to allow a shorter period if there is a good reason for not providing a lengthy consultation period. Examples might be where an announcement that your business was closing down, or having cash-flow problems, would harm your business. Do not deceive yourself into using this reason when any harm would be minimal – tribunals are quick to ferret out false labelling by employers or claims that the company's finances fall into categories which they do not.

(ii) Which employees should you consult?

7.12   You should consult all employees who fall into the pool from which you will be selecting those to be made redundant. In other words, you should consult everyone 'at risk' of redundancy.

Identifying a proper pool is important, as the following illustration shows. Assume that Alf works as a grade 1 mechanic. You obtain new equipment which results in you needing to employ fewer grade 2 mechanics. If your pool of potential redundancy candidates consists of grade 2 mechanics only, you will not have the option of dismissing Alf. If, however, your pool of redundancy candidates includes *all* grades of mechanics then, once you have established the *need* to make redundancies, you will be at liberty to dismiss Alf if he meets (or fails) the selection criteria.

Working out the pool of redundancy candidates can be fraught with risk. This is because, in practice, some tribunals view this particular step as an exception to the rule that tribunals should not interfere when an employer has acted reasonably (even though they should not do so).

You are unlikely to be criticised if you select any of the following as your pool of candidates:

- All those who work at a particular location, when you are closing down that place of business.

- All those in a particular division or sub-division, such as plastic manufacturing or telephone sales, when you are ceasing to carry on that part of the business.

- All those who carry out work of a particular kind, such as drivers, when your need for drivers has diminished.

Until recently there was considerable confusion over whether you had to examine each employee's contract of employment to see if they could be *required* to work elsewhere or do work of another description – if so, they did not necessarily fall into the pool.

This uncertainty has now been resolved. The current approach is the two-stage test set out at 7.5 above.

Employment tribunals should not interfere in your selection of the pool, providing that you have been sensible in selecting the pool. Although, often, the pool of candidates will be obvious, if you are unsure you should err on the side of caution and adopt a narrower pool.

7.13   There are two occasions where you might be looking to make *everyone* from the pool redundant. This will happen if:

a   you are closing down a place of work or a particular type of work; or,

b   if the type of work which you are dispensing with is done by a very small number of people, you may wish to make all of them redundant.

Even when this is the case, you should still go through the consultation procedure. This is because the employees might have sensible suggestions for re-employment. The failure to consult may render a dismissal unfair even when it is seems obvious that redundancy would take place (although any compensation would be low).

7.14   It used to be possible to 'bump' employees. This means that if you needed to make a salesman redundant, but wanted to dismiss Alf (a buyer) instead, you could move one of the existing salesmen to Alf's position as a buyer and dismiss Alf in his place. Until recently, Alf would have been regarded as dismissed because of redundancy – i.e. a diminution in the need for salesmen. Recently, however, the Employment Appeal Tribunal said that this would not be a redundancy, although you may be able to establish that Alf had been fairly dismissed due to a business reorganisation (see Chapter 8).

(iii) What should the consultations consist of?

7.15   The first step is to write to all the candidates for redundancy. The tone of the letter should be regretful yet formal. The letter should contain the following points:

- That you anticipate having to make redundancies in the near future. State the anticipated number of redundancies and, in brief, the reason for making redundancies.

- Unless the pool is obvious, such as when you are closing down an entire place of work, set out in one sentence how you identify the pool of candidates for redundancy. State that Alf is a member of the pool.

- Your timescale. State that you will be meeting with employees individually or as a group, and specify a time for such a meeting. State the anticipated date that the redundancies will take effect. If you are also consulting with the trade union, mention this.

- That the purpose of the meeting(s) is to discuss ways of avoiding redundancy and an examination of whether it may be possible to find alternative employment.

- Invite voluntary redundancies. Section 12.17 onwards deals with redundancy payments; it is common for voluntary redundancies to be rewarded with a slightly enhanced pay package. Make it clear, however, that if more people apply for voluntary redundancy than you actually intend to make redundant, that it will be *your* choice as to who is offered redundancy. State that anyone who wants to apply for voluntary redundancy should do so in writing by a certain date.

7.16 It is your choice whether to have individual meetings with each candidate, or whether to hold an initial meeting *en masse*. If you choose the latter, make sure that you give everyone the opportunity to speak. Public meetings are not necessary, but they have the advantage that there is an undeniable record of consultation. The disadvantage is that these meetings have the potential to become confrontational and emotive.

At the meeting(s), you must stay in control. Your employees will be concerned about their future. The more agitated they become, however, the more likely they are to develop a grudge and complain to an employment tribunal.

During the meeting(s), explain to your employees the reasons for deciding to make redundancies. Be candid with them – they are less likely to complain to an employment tribunal if they recognise you are telling the truth. If you have been able to find alternative employment (see 7.30) then you must offer it (this should be confirmed in writing). If not, ask them if they have any suggestions.

You should tell your employees of the selection criteria you are intending to adopt and, if applicable, discuss their ratings with them – see 7.25 which discusses selection criteria and scores. Although in the past some tribunals have viewed this latter step as unnecessary, there is now a movement towards fuller consultation to the extent of giving employees the opportunity to comment on individual ratings. Further, some employees lodge complaints to the tribunal for no other reason than they want to know why *they* were selected for redundancy. If you tell them voluntarily, you may avert their claims. Do not, however, disclose or discuss anybody else's 'scores'.

7.17   Once you have held the consultation meetings, you will be able to take a decision on whom to select for redundancy. If your employees have made any sensible suggestions as to possible reorganisation of the business or re-employment for themselves, take these suggestions seriously. If you do not adopt them, ensure that you will be able to justify to a tribunal why you, as a reasonable employer, have not adopted the suggestions which would enable you to avoid dismissals.

(iv) Is there ever an exception to the need to consult?

There are, in fact, two exceptions to the need to consult.

7.18   The first is where you are able to form the view, at the time of the redundancies, that consultation would be futile. The courts have recently clarified that this exception extends to an employer who did not consider consultation at the time, in circumstances where a 'reasonable' employer *would* have decided at the time that consultation was futile. Since it is expected that you are reading this book before implementing the redundancies, the nuances of this distinction should not apply.

In reality, tribunals almost never accept this as a reason for failure to consult. This is not because they disbelieve that you *thought* consultation would be futile (although this is one of the commonest defences raised, and tribunals do view it with a certain scepticism), but because tribunals rarely accept that consultation *would* have been futile. You, as an employer, never know what suggestions employees may come up with. Solicitors will rarely advise employers to assume that consultation will be futile because of the substantial risk that a tribunal will disagree. If the tribunal disagrees, the dismissal will be unfair (although the compensation may be low – see Chapter 13).

7.19   The second occasion on which consultation can be dispensed with is where the effect of the delay caused by consultation will be fatal to the business. Thus, for example, if there was a truly dire cash-flow emergency so that the business would collapse unless there was an immediate reduction in the wages bill, then an employer might not be considered unreasonable if he fails to take the time to consult. Again, it will be rare for an employer to invoke this exception successfully.

7.20 If in doubt, consult. The risk entailed in a failure to consult is considerable. Most employers who fail to consult do so for one of four reasons:

    a   They are unaware of the need to consult and do not seek legal advice.

    b   They find the entire process of consultation embarrassing, in that they do not want to have awkward conversations with long-standing employees (who may also be friends). Imagine, though, the position if your roles were reversed. Would you prefer to have several weeks' warning of impending dismissal, and the opportunity to seek employment elsewhere? Or would you prefer to receive a letter one morning telling you that you need not report to work next Monday? Provided it is handled with tact, a sensible employee will be grateful for the consultation rather than resent you for it.

    c   They hope it will not come to redundancies. This is hiding your head in the sand. Either redundancies will occur or they will not. If they do occur, you will have established your position up front and enabled yourself to dismiss your employees fairly. If they do not occur, the one thing which is certain is that your employees will have been given a very legal scare. Consider the effect on productivity!

    d   They think that none of their employees will claim against them. This is a dangerous assumption. The absence of warning and consultation will make an employee more, not less, likely to seek advice on their rights. A chat in a pub, followed by a visit to the local Citizens' Advice Bureau or a solicitor, will very rapidly start the ball rolling.

7.21 There are two very distinct advantages in warning your workforce of impending redundancies. Firstly, every person who volunteers for redundancy is one less employee who may claim for unfair dismissal. Secondly, some employees might use the consultation period to search for employment elsewhere. If they find employment elsewhere, and resign to take it up before you have formally notified them that they have been selected for redundancy, they will be unable to claim unfair dismissal (since they will not have been dismissed, and thus cannot have been *unfairly* dismissed).

Consultation with a trade union

7.22   This section assumes that you recognise a trade union for the purpose of collective bargaining. If you do not, this section can be ignored.

If you are dismissing less than 20 employees within a period of 90 days then, provided you have fully consulted your employees, you can probably get by without consulting a trade union. If you *are* dismissing 20 or more employees within a period of 90 days, then special rules apply which fall outside the scope of this book. Consult a solicitor.

Nevertheless, if you do recognise a trade union, it will impress a tribunal if you have taken these additional steps since it will enforce your image as a reasonable employer.

There is another practical reason for consulting with a trade union. If the employees who belong to the union believe that they have been unfairly dismissed, they will seek help from the union. If the union perceives itself as having been snubbed or ignored by you, it is more likely to provide financial or legal assistance for claims against you.

The corollary of this is that if the trade union has been involved throughout, has been fairly consulted and any agreements have been honoured by you, it is far less likely to advise employees that they have a claim against you (or, indeed, to fund any such claims).

7.23   Write to the trade union at the same time as warning/consulting the employees. Explain the need for redundancies and invite a representative to a meeting to discuss whether there are any alternatives to redundancy, and how the selections for redundancy should take place (see 7.25). Take their views into account, but do not forget that employment law requires consultation, not obedience. If you are able to agree selection criteria with the union, it is almost inconceivable that a tribunal will decide that the procedure is unfair.

Once you have agreed the selection criteria, the trade union should not be involved in applying the criteria. It is for you to assess employees and determine which ones are to be selected for redundancy. It is important to retain firm control over this – you must avoid any accusations of delegating the decision on who should be dismissed to somebody outside your organisation. In reality, few trade unions will want to be involved in the actual selection since it entails favouring some members over others.

Further, once you have applied the selection criteria and identified those to be made redundant, you should not reveal the employees' scores to the union. There can only be one reason for such a request – the union is fishing for evidence that you have, or have not, applied the criteria in a way which *they* would consider fair. There is no obligation on you to disclose this information. Do not fall into the trap of doing so.

Redundancy procedure – stage 2 – selection

7.24   You have identified the pool of potentially redundant employees. You have invited volunteers for redundancy, and may have had some responses. You are now in the position where you have to select a pre-determined number of people from a pre-determined pool. These people will be dismissed by you. Whom do you choose?

There is no golden rule, other than the fact that in selecting people for redundancy you must use objective, rather than subjective, criteria. In other words, you must use criteria that can be judged objectively, such as length of service or frequency of absence, rather than criteria that depend largely on the views of person doing the judging (such as friendliness to customers).

During the 1970s and 1980s, trade unions and industrial tribunals regarded the vital (and, often, only) factor in redundancy selection as length of service. Redundancies would be fair only if the most junior people were dismissed before people with longer service records, irrespective of how good they were or the disadvantage of leaving a company with an older workforce and bereft of young talent. This principle is commonly known as 'LIFO' (which is an acronym for 'last in, first out'). An occasionally acceptable alternative was 'FIFO' ('first in, first out') which had precisely the opposite effect.

In the last decade, trade unions and tribunals have begun to appreciate that length of service should not be the conclusive factor in determining who is to be selected for redundancy. It can, however, remain an *important* factor. The reason for requiring an objective system of selection is to ensure that an employer does not use the excuse of redundancy to dismiss employees whom he would be unable to dismiss legally in more salubrious times.

Choosing the criteria for selection

7.25   If you have agreed selection criteria with a trade union, you should apply them to the pool of employees in the same way as if you had chosen the criteria yourself.

As stated above, the criteria must be objective. Provided that the criteria are objective, are reasonable (e.g. hair colour of employees, although objective, is not a reasonable factor to take into account in selecting for redundancy) and are applied in good faith a tribunal will uphold your selection.

It is common nowadays to use a combination of several criteria. A table can then be built up of employees' scores under the various criteria, and those with the lowest totals are the ones selected for redundancy. This is shown in the example below.

	Length of service (years)	Attendance record	Technical expertise	Disciplinary record	Productivity	Total
Alf	6	4	5	4	3	22
Jeremy	12	2	3	4	4	25
Catherine	6	5	5	5	2	23
Jennifer	2	4	1	4	4	15

Key: 5 Excellent
     4 Good
     3 Above average
     2 Satisfactory/requires training
     1 Unsatisfactory/requires training

In this example, if it were necessary to select two of the pool of four for redundancy, Alf and Jennifer would be the two selected since they have the lowest total scores.

7.26   Theoretically, you can use as many criteria as you like and perform 'weighting' exercises (i.e. give more importance to some factors than others). This will not, however, impress a tribunal. A tribunal wants to see a simple, easily implemented and objectively fair method of selecting people for redundancy. A technical and convoluted scheme indicates too much forethought and may be interpreted as an attempt to fix the criteria so as to arrive at a pre-determined result.

7.27 There are a number of factors that must not be used in selecting your employees for redundancy. If your decision to dismiss is caused by, or is based upon, any of certain prescribed reasons then it will be automatically unfair. The reasons are set out, at length, in the employment legislation but broadly fall into the following categories:

- involvement with health and safety matters;

- pregnancy, birth of a child or exercising rights to maternity leave;

- being unable to work due to incapacity arising out of the birth of a child;

- any allegation (including bringing proceedings) that you have infringed any of his/her rights conferred by the employment legislation (note: not all the employment legislation falls within this category – but even if you select somebody because they have asserted you infringed one of their non-protected rights, a tribunal is unlikely to consider this reasonable behaviour);

- any involvement in, or membership of, a trade union (or, likewise, non-membership of a trade union).

These reasons are set out in more detail at 18.2.

7.28 The degree of consultation over selection will vary depending on the size of your business and the inevitability of dismissal. If you are going to be making all the pool candidates redundant, any consultation over the method of selection will not need to be as thorough as if you are making a small number of people from within the pool redundant (where the selection criteria, and the scores under those criteria, will be vital).

During the consultations with individual employees, you should tell them what their provisional scores are under the various headings. Invite their comments. If they have a good explanation for a low score, for example if their 'attendance' score is low due to a recent illness which is unlikely to recur, you should

reconsider the provisional score in the light of their explanation. Keep careful notes of any comments made by the employees
during these meetings. This will be evidence that you *did* consult
properly and, just as importantly, will be evidence of what was
(and thus what was not) raised by the employees during the
consultation.

7.29   After the selection stage you should have established the identity
of those to be made redundant, whether by reason of selecting
the whole pool (as when you are closing down a location) or
because you have drawn up a table and chosen those with the
lowest scores. The final stage is to consider alternative employment for each of those employees.

Redundancy procedure – stage 3 – alternative employment

7.30   No matter how fair your selection and consultation procedures
may be, an employment tribunal is likely to find a dismissal to
be unfair if you have not considered whether you can redeploy
any of your redundant employees. This requirement is justified
on the basis that a reasonable employer would not dismiss an
employee due to redundancy if he can redeploy him elsewhere.
The need to consider alternative employment is mandatory even
for small business (although, in such cases, there will usually be
no possible alternative employment available).

What alternative employment must you consider?

7.31   Do not fall into the trap of thinking that employment is not
suitable because it entails a demotion or a reduction in wages.
If there is any position, unless manifestly unsuitable, which Alf
would be reasonably capable of doing, you should offer it to
him. He may reject it – but it should be his decision and not
yours. If you decide that a job *is* available, but you do not think
Alf has the necessary attributes to fulfil it, make a note as to
why he is not suitable and keep the note on his personnel file.

   In addition to determining whether there are any alternative
positions at your company, you must also take steps to ascertain
whether there is any available employment at any associated
companies. This means you should contact any subsidiaries or

parent companies, as well as any *other* subsidiary of your parent companies and ask them to investigate whether they have any suitable positions available. If they do not respond to you, ensure that you chase them up (and keep a record of doing so) so that you can establish that your original request was not simply a sham.

If a job *is* available which Alf is capable of doing, you must offer it to him. This is for four reasons:

a   if suitable employment *is* available and you do not offer it to him, the dismissal will be unfair;

b   if he accepts the job, you will not have to pay him a redundancy payment;

c   if he unreasonably refuses a suitable job, you are not obliged to pay him a redundancy payment (see 7.39);

d   if he does not accept the job and claims unfair dismissal, the fact you have offered him alternative employment will assist your case and, in any event, may reduce any award he receives if the dismissal is found to be unfair (see 13.15).

If no alternative employment can be found

7.32   Do not merely consider alternative positions for Alf. Also ensure that you have a contemporaneous record of doing so. The best way to do this is to combine it with consultation (which is also an ingredient in making the redundancy dismissal fair). Write to Alf in the following terms:

• That, further to (your meeting on. . .) *or* (your letter dated. . .), you regret to inform him that he has been selected for redundancy.

• You have reviewed the position within the company and, after full consideration, are sorry to say that there are no suitable alternative vacancies available for him. If you have contacted associated employers, state this, identify the companies you have contacted and state that your efforts have not been successful.

• That if he has any suggestions as to possible redeployment, or if he is aware of any vacancies elsewhere that you could recommend him for, that he should contact you as soon as possible.

- Alternatively, if he would like to meet to discuss the situation further, he should contact you to arrange a convenient time.

- That you will continue reviewing the possibility of alternative employment; however, if nothing comes available, that his last day of work will be January 28, 1999. This will normally be *at least* his notice period away (see 12.11) – otherwise you will have to pay him in lieu of notice.

You should also give details in this letter as to how his redundancy pay will be calculated. This is discussed further at 12.17.

7.33   If Alf does make any suggestions, you must consider them carefully. If his suggestion is impracticable, write to him and explain your reasons for rejecting it. If he has suggested another position within your company and you are unsure as to his suitability, you may wish to consider employing him on a trial basis. The failure to try Alf in a position which he may be suitable for might make an otherwise fair dismissal unfair.

Once Alf's employment has terminated, assuming you have been unable to find any alternative employment, you should pay him his full redundancy entitlement together with any contractual redundancy entitlement or pay in lieu of notice (if appropriate). Err on the side of caution and overpay, rather than underpay in borderline cases, to avoid unnecessary grievances.

If alternative employment is found

7.34   If you have managed to find alternative employment for Alf then, unless the job is essentially the same as he was already doing (which might be the case if you have closed down one place of work and moved Alf to a nearby location to do the same job), he is legally entitled to a four-week trial period during which his right to a redundancy payment is unaffected.

You should write to Alf in the following terms:

- That, further to (your meeting dated. . .) *or* (your letter dated. . .), you regret to inform him that he has been selected for redundancy.

- You are able to offer him alternative employment within the company (or with an associated company – state its name). State the job title and description, the salary and any other relevant details. If you have a written job description or contract of employment, enclose it with your letter.

- Inform him of the date that his existing job will disappear. Again, this will normally be *at least* his notice period away (see 12.11), otherwise you may have to pay him in lieu of notice if he does not take up the new job.

- Tell him of the start date for his new job. This *must* be within four weeks of the old job finishing, although if the old job finishes on a Friday, Saturday or Sunday then you are entitled to an extension until four weeks on the following Monday. Note that you need not pay him during these four weeks.

- That he is entitled to a four-week trial period in order to decide whether the new job is suitable.

- Ask him to confirm in writing, within seven days, that he will accept the new job. If he does not do so, you should speak to him and get him to write out, in your presence, an acceptance or a rejection of the new job (subject to the trial period).

Do not try to make the job offer conditional on *not* having a four-week trial period. This will render the alternative employment unsuitable (since it deprives Alf of a right to which he is legally entitled) and will make the dismissal unfair.

7.35　If Alf does not accept the job, you should continue searching for alternative employment for him until he is dismissed. You may not, however, be obliged to pay him a redundancy payment if he has unreasonably refused suitable employment. This is discussed further at 7.39.

Make sure that you do actually offer Alf any alternative position, even if he has told you in advance that he will not accept any further employment with you. If you fail to make a specific job offer, there will be no offer of employment that Alf has unreasonably refused. Accordingly you will not be able to rely on this escape clause to avoid paying a redundancy payment.

The trial period

7.36   Alf is entitled to a four-week trial period in which to assess his new job, unless the new job is identical, for all practical purposes, to the old one. If, during this four-week period, he decides that he does not want to continue with the new job, he is entitled to resign and will be deemed, legally, to be in exactly the same position as if you had offered him the new job after he was selected for redundancy and he had *not* accepted it.

If Alf resigns *after* the four-week trial period, then the resignation will be deemed to be an ordinary resignation and he will *not* be entitled to a redundancy payment. Further, unless he can bring himself within the rules for constructive dismissal (see 17.2), he will have resigned in the ordinary way, thus not have been dismissed and will be unable to claim unfair dismissal.

The four-week trial period means four *calendar* weeks, rather than four working weeks. Accordingly if your place of work closes for a week, this will not suspend the running of time for the purpose of calculating the four week trial period.

Example

An employee was made redundant. His trial period for his alternative employment started on 21st December 1986. His workplace closed for seven days over Christmas. He resigned on 19th January 1987. The tribunal held that the four-week period continued to run over Christmas, even though the workplace was closed, and thus it had expired on 18th January 1987. The employee's resignation was therefore one day outside his four-week trial period and he was not entitled to a redundancy payment – **Benton v Sanderson Kayser Ltd [1989] ICR 136**

7.37   It is possible to extend the four-week trial period. This can only be done by agreement in writing before Alf starts work in the new position, and it can only be done if the purpose of the extension is to allow time for retraining Alf. The agreement must also specify the terms and conditions of employment that will apply if Alf stays on after the trial period. Unless these conditions are complied with, the extension of time will not be valid and Alf will lose his right to a redundancy payment. It is apparent that there is little incentive for an employer to suggest, or agree to, such an extension.

7.38 If Alf remains in employment after the trial period, he is deemed for all practical purposes never to have been dismissed (even if there was a break in his employment of up to the permitted four weeks between the old job and the new job). In particular, his length of employment will not be re-set to zero by the new job, but will continue as if uninterrupted, for the purpose of establishing whether Alf has been working for two years (so as to gain employment rights) if you try to dismiss him in the future.

Unreasonable refusal of suitable alternative employment

7.39 If Alf declines the new position, whether during his trial period or when the job is first offered to him, then the termination of his employment is still regarded as being caused by the redundancy (rather than by his refusal to take up the new job).

However, Alf may disentitle himself to a redundancy payment if two criteria apply. These criteria are:

a   that the alternative employment offered was suitable for him; and,

b   that his failure to accept it was unreasonable.

If this exception applies, Alf will not be entitled to any redundancy payment (although he may still be entitled to pay in lieu of notice if you did not give him sufficient notice when telling him of his final day of work – see 12.11).

This part is important: if your redundancy selection was fair, then the fact that you rely on this exception to avoid making a redundancy payment will *not* make an otherwise fair dismissal unfair. If you withhold a redundancy payment on the basis that Alf has unreasonably refused a suitable job offer, this is not something which goes towards the fairness or unfairness of the dismissal. The worst that can happen if, in reality, you are not entitled to withhold payment is that Alf will successfully claim against you in the employment tribunal for the redundancy payment that you would have paid him anyway. In such circumstances, you will be no worse off.

There is a certain amount of overlap between the above two criteria – some factors will be relevant both to the suitability of the new job and whether Alf is acting unreasonably in declining it. However, tribunals will address the two criteria separately, and so it is sensible to deal with them in a similar way.

Suitability

7.40   Employment will be 'suitable' for Alf if, objectively, it is similar in terms of pay, duties, hours, responsibility and status. Note that the new job does not have to be 'equal' to the old one in order for it to be suitable. The pay can be slightly lower, the responsibility slightly less. The basic test is that the overall package must be appropriate for somebody of Alf's skills, abilities and working history.

Example

Headmaster, with many years of experience, offered a job in a mobile pool of teachers with his pay frozen at his current level. The drop in status made the new job 'quite unsuitable' – *Taylor v Kent County Council [1969] 2 QB 560*

Example

Nightworkers offered double-day shiftwork held to be unsuitable – *Morrison & Poole v Ceramic Engineering Co Ltd [1966] 1 ITR 404*

Example

Old job had compulsory overtime; the new job had no overtime. This was held to be unsuitable – *O'Connor v Montrose Canned Foods Ltd [1966] 1 ITR 171*

Example

Employee required to move from Bournemouth to Bristol, but was given an increased salary to compensate. This was held to be suitable – *Gotch v Guest [1966] 1 ITR 65*

Example

Additional daily journey time of between one and four hours depending on traffic held to be unsuitable – *Bass Leisure Ltd. v Thomas [1994] IRLR 104*

Note that the *number* of jobs you offer to Alf is immaterial – suitability is concerned with quality of alternative employment, and not with the quantity of jobs offered.

Unreasonable refusal

7.41   If you consider that the employment was suitable for Alf, the next step is to decide whether he acted reasonably or unreasonably in refusing it. This is a subjective test – i.e. the question is whether *Alf* himself is acting reasonably, not a hypothetical employee. The factors here will often be more personal and, indeed, you may sometimes be unaware of the factors which cause Alf to decline a new job. However, as mentioned above, if you do withhold his redundancy payment, the worst that can happen is that a tribunal orders you to pay it. It will not result in a finding of unfair dismissal against you.

The main factors which will be taken into account are the following:

- other employment: if Alf has already obtained another job, particularly if there has been delay before your offer of alternative employment was made, he will usually not be acting unreasonably in declining your alternative job offer;

- hours: if the new job entails a fundamental change of hours, such as moving to a night-shift, it is likely to be reasonable to refuse it;

- location: if the new job entails moving to a new part of the country, it will probably be reasonable to refuse;

- track record: if Alf has genuine grounds for believing that your offer is a sham, designed to prevent him claiming a redundancy payment, or if he reasonably believes that your company is in dire financial straits and may be unable to pay him, he may be reasonable in declining the new job.

Example

Employee had been employed for five years in Newcastle. He had two children at the local schools, one of whom was about to sit GCE exams and the other the 11-plus. He was offered a three-year contract in Glasgow, to be followed by a job in Leeds. It was held that his refusal to move was reasonable – *Bainbridge v Westinghouse Brake and Signal Co. Ltd [1966] 1 ITR 89*

Example

Offer of new position made at 3.30pm on Friday, but not confirmed in writing until 9.00am Monday. An answer was required by 10.30am on Monday and, at 11.30am, the position was given to somebody else. It was held that the refusal was reasonable – *Barratt v Thomas Glover & Co. Ltd [1970] 5 ITR 95*

Example

Firm moved from Essex to Devon. The employment offered might not have been suitable, but the employee refused even to go and inspect the new location (without giving any proper explanation). It was held that the refusal was unreasonable – *Douce v F Bond & Sons Ltd [1966] 1 ITR 365*

Starting to recruit again

7.42   Redundancy dismissals only occur, in general, when you need to reduce the size of the workforce. This is inconsistent with recruiting from outside to fill positions (unless the new jobs are of a wholly different nature from those from which you are dismissing people, and could not reasonably be considered suitable alternative employment).

If you are justifying a redundancy dismissal to an employment tribunal, a question you are almost guaranteed to be asked is whether you replaced Alf or whether you recruited anybody else to fill any new positions. If you have replaced Alf, you will have great difficulty persuading the tribunal that the strict definition of redundancy applies (see 7.3) and you are highly likely to be found to have unfairly dismissed Alf.

As a rule of thumb, you should not replace Alf for at least three months – preferably six. If you *do* decide to re-open his job, you should offer the job first of all to Alf. If you do not do so, a tribunal is likely to draw the inference that the entire redundancy procedure has been a sham, and that you had a concealed reason for dismissing Alf which you dressed up as a redundancy situation. Although Alf normally has to bring an unfair dismissal claim within three months of being dismissed, if you replace him just outside this period then this might entitle him to an extension of time on the grounds that it was not reasonably practicable to bring a claim before he became aware of the replacement. Extensions of time for bringing unfair dismissal claims are discussed in more detail at 18.9.

8. BUSINESS REORGANISATION/ CHANGING AN EMPLOYEE'S CONDITIONS OF EMPLOYMENT

8.1   When reorganising your business, you may wish to make changes to Alf's duties or terms and conditions of employment. The most common changes will include reducing his pay, changing his working hours, introducing confidentiality or non-competition agreements or changes to job title.

Bear in mind that there is a close overlap between business reorganisations and redundancies. You are advised to consider Chapter 7 to ensure that what you propose to do does not fall within the definition of redundancy.

Legally, you are not entitled to make any changes to Alf's terms and conditions of employment unless he agrees. A contract of employment cannot be changed by you alone, just as Alf cannot change it alone (by, for example, awarding himself a pay rise). If you therefore make changes, or threaten to make changes, to Alf's contract of employment, he is entitled to resign and claim constructive dismissal.

Having a claim of constructive dismissal brought against you is not fatal – if you have acted fairly and it is necessary in your business's interests to make the changes to Alf's terms and conditions of employment, then the constructive dismissal should be found to be fair. Constructive dismissal, as a general concept, is considered at 17.2.

8.2   In order for a dismissal (whether actual or constructive) to be fair, you must establish that the reason for the dismissal is either capability (Chapter 2), conduct (Chapters 3 to 6), redundancy (Chapter 7), contravention of a statutory provision (10.3) or 'some other substantial reason'(*Employment Rights Act 1996, s98*). Changes to Alf's terms and conditions of employment because of business reorganisations, are capable of amounting to 'some other substantial reason'.

8.3   Ideally, you should make the change to Alf's terms and conditions by obtaining his consent. Provided that there is a formal agreement between you, it will be binding on him and he will not be entitled to resign and complain about it later. The agreement need not be in writing (although it is prudent to record it in writing).

Alternatively, if Alf declines to consent, you may have to implement the change by delivering an ultimatum. If Alf then refuses to comply, you can dismiss him (provided you go through the correct procedure). If he resigns and claims constructive dismissal, you will have a defence to the claim.

Obtaining Alf's consent to the change

8.4   Ideally, you should try to obtain Alf's consent to the change. A mere acquiescence is insufficient: you need to show that you have provided 'consideration' for Alf's agreement to the change. The 'consideration' can take the form of a nominal pay rise, a slight reduction in working hours or an increase in holiday entitlement – however, it has to be something to Alf's benefit (or your detriment).

Because of the need to provide consideration when obtaining Alf's consent to a change in his terms and conditions, it is common practice to combine the changes with an annual or half-annual salary review. Alf does not have an entitlement to a salary increase each year (although if you give everyone else a salary increase but not Alf, he may claim constructive dismissal on the grounds that you are treating him arbitrarily and unfairly).

If you are able to combine the change to his terms and conditions with a salary increase, you should write to him in the following terms:

- That you are making a number of changes to the organisation of your business, and that you wish to make the following changes to his terms and conditions of employment. Set out the change carefully – if you are introducing a non-competition or confidentiality clause, ensure the text of the clause is set out.

- That you seek his consent to the change. If he accepts the change, you propose to increase his salary to £x or increase his holiday entitlement to y days per year. It is not anticipated that there will be any other salary increases in the next year.

- If he accepts the change, sign and return a copy of the letter. The salary increase will take effect from date.

If Alf does sign the letter, you will have covered yourself and he will be unable to complain of the changes at a later date.

8.5   What if Alf does not consent to the changes? If the job involves a pay cut or a loss of prestige, Alf may be unwilling to consent to the changes. In that case, you have to impose the changes upon him. Provided this is done in a fair manner, and provided you can establish a sound, good business reason for imposing the change, you will be able to satisfy the tribunal that the dismissal was fair if Alf resigns and claims constructive dismissal.

Imposing the changes upon Alf

8.6   If Alf will not consent to the changes, or your business is in financial difficulties and you cannot afford to offer Alf a pay-rise or increased holidays, you may need to impose the changes to his terms and conditions of employment upon him.

When can you impose changes on Alf?

8.7   You cannot impose changes on Alf just because you feel like it. You need to be able to establish that there is a 'sound, good business reason' for the change (***Hollister v National Farmers' Union [1979] IRLR 238***). This does not mean that you need to establish that your business is on the edge of insolvency and that it will collapse if the changes are not made. You do, however, need to show that there is a good reason for adversely affecting Alf's rights – merely increasing business profitability on an already profitable business is unlikely to be enough, particularly if the changes to Alf's contract involve a financial detriment to him.

In essence, the more detrimental the changes are to Alf, the more fundamental the business justification must be. By contrast, when the proposed changes do not act to Alf's financial detriment (such as changing, without increasing, the hours worked), it will be easier to justify them. It will also be easier to justify changes if other employees have agreed to them (which is why it is important to seek consent before trying to impose the changes).

If the changes involve increased working hours for Alf, you may have difficulty persuading a tribunal that you are acting fairly unless you offer Alf a *pro rata* wage increase (unless you can establish that your business genuinely cannot afford pay increases).

Bear in mind that a mere assertion by you that you have a sound, good business reason for the changes to Alf's contract will not be enough. You will need to provide evidence to satisfy the tribunal – this might take the form of accounts, business plans, profitability projections or management consultant appraisals.

Example

An employee's contract stated he had to work during daytime hours. He was asked to work a night-shift one week in six and refused. The tribunal thought that there was a proper reason for the change and held the dismissal to be fair – *Knighton v Henry Rhodes Ltd [1974] IRLR 71*

Example

Ms Moreton worked during school term-time only. She was asked, and given 12 months' notice, to work during school holidays as well as during term-time since it was necessary for her employer's business. She refused. The tribunal held that there was a fair business reorganisation, thus Ms Moreton's claim for unfair dismissal failed – *Moreton v Selby Protective Clothing [1974] IRLR 269*

Imposing the changes

8.8   Provided you can justify the changes, there is no real procedure that you need to go through when imposing the changes on Alf. You should write to him in the following terms:

- That further to your last letter, you note that he has not responded. If you have sought to introduce changes for other employees, and they agreed, state this (although do not mention any other employees by name).

- Despite the fact that he has not replied, you consider it necessary for business reasons to introduce the changes to his terms and conditions. Set out the precise changes you are proposing again.

- If you offered a pay-rise, or other benefits, state that you intend to stand by the additional benefits you were previously offering to him.

- The proposed changes will apply from date.

- If Alf wishes to discuss the reasons for, or the effect of, the changes with you, he should feel free to come and ask/arrange a meeting.

8.9   What happens next is up to Alf. He can do one of three things, namely comply with the changes, resign or continue working but refuse to comply with the changes.

If he refuses to comply with the changes, you will be entitled to dismiss him. The reason for the dismissal will be both 'conduct' and 'some other substantial reason'. You should adopt a formal dismissal procedure, namely that set out in Chapter 6 (dismissing for refusing to obey instructions).

9. DISMISSING WHEN TAKING OVER A BUSINESS OR CONTRACT

Introduction

9.1   Like redundancies, this is an area of law that is fraught with hazards. The rules relating to dismissing employees when you take over a business are governed by a European Directive which was incorporated into English Law by *The Transfer of Undertaking (Protection of Employment) Regulations 1981* – commonly known by its acronym as '*TUPE*'. These Regulations have generated more appeals and more complexity than any other area of employment law.

If you are taking over a business which employs more than a small number of people (say, over 10 employees), and you are considering dismissing them or changing their terms and conditions of employment, it is highly recommended that you seek advice from a specialist employment solicitor.

This chapter can do no more than set out when complex issues of employment law are likely to arise. It deals with two separate situations, namely:

a   dismissing employees when buying a business; and,

b   dismissing employees when taking over a contract.

Both of these scenarios may be governed by the rules contained in *TUPE*. Before turning to the practical steps to take in these situations to minimise liabilities or dismiss employees, it is sensible to consider an overview of the law relating to transfers of businesses or contracts.

Overview of *TUPE*

9.2   In essence, *TUPE* provides that where an 'undertaking' is transferred from one business to another, all of the employees formerly employed by the first company are automatically transferred along with the business, so that they become employed by the second company. If either the first or the second company tries to dismiss them because of the transfer, the dismissal will automatically be unfair (except in particular circumstances, namely where there is an economic, technical or organisational reason for the dismissal).

In addition, after the transfer the employees remain employed on the same terms and conditions as before the transfer. Accordingly, the new company cannot change the employees' contract of employment (including their hours or pay) – if they do, the employees are entitled to resign and claim constructive dismissal.

The effect of *TUPE* is that when you buy a business, or take over a contract, you may often find yourself legally responsible for all the employees who worked for that old business or on that contract.

What is an 'undertaking'?

9.3   The *TUPE* Regulations only apply to transfers of 'undertakings'. The courts are constantly changing their minds on what is meant by an 'undertaking'. There are no hard and fast rules – simply a number of indicators – and it quite conceivable that one employment tribunal would consider a certain takeover to include an 'undertaking', whereas on the same facts another tribunal would not consider there to have been a transfer of an 'undertaking'.

Essentially, for there to be an 'undertaking' there has to be a recognisable economic entity transferred. If you buy a high-street printing shop – purchasing the premises, the machinery, the stock, the name and the goodwill – you would have purchased an entire economic entity. Accordingly *TUPE* will apply and all of the printing shop's employees will automatically transfer to your employment. If you dismiss any of them (which, since they have been automatically transferred to you, includes not providing them with work and a salary), you are deemed to have automatically unfairly dismissed them (unless you can bring yourself within the defence at paragraph 9.6).

Very frequently, however, it is not clearcut as to whether there has been a purchase (or transfer) of an economic entity. The core question is whether the business remains the same business, but in different hands. The following factors are often considered by tribunals in deciding whether an undertaking has been transferred:

- whether you carry on business in the same manner as before;

- whether there has been an assignment of goodwill or book debts;

- whether there has been an assignment of stock;

- whether you have taken over the old business's premises or trading name;

- whether you have taken over outstanding contracts/work in progress;

- whether you are taking on a significant number of staff from the old employer.

If the answer to any one of these questions is 'yes', there is a risk that a tribunal will find that a transfer of undertakings has occurred. If the answer to more than two or three of the questions is 'yes', it is likely that a tribunal will find that a transfer of undertakings has occurred.

9.4   It is not necessary for you to take over an entire business for *TUPE* to apply. If you take over a contract, and the contract forms an economic entity in its own right (by being a separately identifiable part of the seller's business), then *TUPE* may apply and you may find yourself liable for all the employees that the seller employed to deal with the contract.

Example

A health authority contracted out cleaning services to company A. When the contract was re-tendered, company A lost the cleaning contract and company B won it. Many of the employees of company A were taken on by company B, which had provided its own cleaning equipment, management and materials. The Court of Appeal held that there was a transfer of undertakings, since the provision of cleaning services amounted to a separate undertaking in its own right. Since company B had reduced the wages of the cleaners it took on, they claimed constructive dismissal and were held to have been unfairly dismissed – *Dines v Initial Healthcare Services [1995] ICR 11.*

Note that for *TUPE* to apply, there must be a specific undertaking which transfers. It is unlikely that the transfer of a short-term, one-off contract, as contrasted with a longer-term contract involving a series of activities (such as an annual cleaning contract), would be sufficient to amount to a *TUPE* transfer. Thus if you run a printing shop and take over one of a competitor's contracts, or even one of a competitor's main clients, but the contract/client does not form an separate economic entity for your competitor in its own right, the *TUPE* rules are unlikely to apply and you will not be obliged to take on any of his employees.

What happens when TUPE applies?

9.5   When *TUPE* applies, all the employees who had been employed by the seller/previous contractor are automatically transferred into your employment. If you fail to provide work, you are deemed to have dismissed them (i.e. constructive dismissal). If you change any of their terms and conditions of employment, including pay, they are entitled to resign and claim constructive dismissal. If you dismiss any of them, whether directly or constructively, any such dismissal is automatically unfair if the transfer is the reason (or principal reason) for the dismissal. Justifications such as redundancy, capability or conduct do not apply if the true reason for the dismissal is the transfer.

9.6   There is one defence to the dismissal being *automatically* unfair. If you can establish that the dismissal was for an 'economic, technical or organisational reason entailing changes in the workforce' (***TUPE**, regulation 8(2)*), then the dismissal will be *potentially* fair provided you can show that you have gone through a proper procedure of consultation and consideration as to *who* should be dismissed. This is a very useful exception to the *TUPE* rules and should be carefully investigated to see if an economic, technical or organisational reason can apply.

9.7   What is an economic, technical or organisational reason? There are no real guidelines as to what amounts to an economic, technical or organisational reason: however, the words are ordinary words and are treated as bearing an ordinary meaning. It is unlikely to be enough to dismiss somebody for 'economic' reasons because it would increase the profitability of your business – this would apply to most transferred employees and would destroy the purpose of *TUPE*. Instead, you would probably need to establish some fundamental business need, perhaps falling short of a risk of insolvency but going beyond mere convenience.

It is important to note that the 'economic, technical or organisational reason' must be one which entails a change in the workforce. The reason must be one which requires change in the numbers of, or nature of, the workforce. If there are technical reasons for no longer employing Alf, but the reasons do not entail a change in the workforce, then this defence will not apply.

9.8   A final point to note is that you cannot avoid the effect of *TUPE* by requiring the seller of the business to make redundant or dismiss employees for other reasons prior to the transfer. The courts have said that any dismissal in anticipation of such a transfer is void, and the employees will still transfer over to your employment. As a result, you will be liable for their automatic unfair dismissal.

Dismissing employees when buying a business

9.9   There are two methods of buying a business:

a   Purchasing the shares of the company, so that the company remains the same but you become the new owner. This can only be done with limited companies: if you are buying a firm or a sole trader's business, you can only use method (b) below.

b   Purchasing the assets and liabilities of the business but, if it is a company, not the company itself.

Method (a): Buying a company by purchasing its shares

9.10   When you buy the shares of a company, there is no transfer of undertaking. Legally, there has not been any transfer of an economic entity – the business was there in its existing form before you purchased the shares, and it remains in the same form after you have purchased the shares.

Accordingly, *TUPE* does not apply. You do not need to worry about dismissals being automatically unfair, or about establishing an economic, technical or organisational reason for the dismissal.

However, the fact that you have purchased the shares of a company does not give you an immunity from general unfair dismissal law. The normal rules apply, namely that you have to have a valid reason for dismissal and have to act reasonably. You will therefore need to come within one of the other reasons for dismissal such as capability, conduct, business reorganisation or redundancy, and follow the dismissal procedures set out in those chapters.

Method (b): Purchasing the assets and liabilities of a business

9.11   When you purchase the assets and liabilities of a business, and take over its goodwill, there will almost always be a transfer of an undertaking. In this situation, any dismissals caused because of the takeover will be automatically unfair *unless* you can establish an economic, technical or organisational reason for the dismissal entailing a change in the workforce.

Hint

When negotiating the purchase, if you do not want to take on certain employees, see if you can negotiate an indemnity or contribution from the seller in case you are found to have unfairly dismissed them. Any such indemnity should be backed up by personal guarantee otherwise, since you are taking all the assets of the business, the seller may have no assets against which to enforce an indemnity.

9.12   Presumably, prior to purchasing the assets and liabilities of the company, you will have formed an idea as to which members of staff you wish to retain and which you wish to dismiss. Note that this chapter gives guidance as to an appropriate procedure to adopt for dismissing employees fairly *provided* you can establish an economic, technical or organisational reason for doing so. There is no method of avoiding the protection that employees receive as the result of *TUPE*: i.e. you must still persuade a tribunal that there was a genuine economic, technical or organisational reason warranting the dismissals. If you cannot satisfy this requirement, you will be found to have unfairly dismissed those employees you have not kept on.

Step 1: Identify the changes you need to make in the workforce

9.13   A tribunal will not be impressed if you try to trick employees into believing that their employment has not transferred to you. If you try to deny that Alf has become your employee when you take over the business he used to work for, it will be extremely difficult to persuade a tribunal later that you have acted fairly even if you can establish an appropriate economic, technical or organisational reason.

This is not to say that you should admit that Alf's employment has transferred to you if you are unsure that it has, since in such circumstances you may well be found to have voluntarily employed Alf. If the position is not clear, you should consult a solicitor specialising in employment law.

9.14   The first thing to do, therefore, is write to all employees who were employed by the old business. This can be done after contracts are signed but before the date of the takeover. Your letter should state the following:

- Their old employer has sold the business to you. State your full name (or the name of your firm/company) and, if a company, your registered address.

- The date on which the transfer will happen and that, from that date, they will all be employed by you.

- Their terms and conditions of employment will remain the same after the transfer of employment.

- Any employee is entitled to object to their employment being transferred. If they do object, they should contact you in writing. Note that there is no obligation to tell an employee of his right to object; however, if any employee *does* object, his employment will not be transferred and thus you cannot be found to have unfairly dismissed him. It is not necessary that his objection be in writing: however, if the objection is verbal only it may cause difficulties if he subsequently denies having objected to the transfer.

- As a result of the transfer, some organisational changes are going to be made to the company. Set out in one or two sentences the reasons for the changes (fuller reasons will come later). State that it is possible/probable that some jobs are going to be lost.

- If you wish to do so, invite volunteers to object to being transferred and offer a compensation package for such volunteers. When you dismiss people properly following a business takeover, you do not need to pay them any redundancy payments – you only need to pay their notice. If you wish, you may point this out in the letter and demonstrate how volunteers will receive a better financial package than those selected for dismissal later.

- You are available to discuss the above (giving contact details) and, in any event, you would welcome any written comments or suggestions on how to avoid job losses.

9.15   If the company you are buying, or your company, recognises a trade union, you should contact the trade union and discuss with it methods of avoiding job losses and selecting employees for dismissal. The advantages of doing this are set out at 7.22. This consultation should be ongoing throughout the entire dismissal process.

9.16   Once you take over the business, you should decide exactly what changes need to be made. Remember you will have to justify any dismissals as falling into a economic, technical or organisational category entailing a change in the workforce. Take these words seriously – an employment tribunal will. If you have board or management meetings, discuss the changes that need to be made at a meeting and ensure that full minutes are taken. If you own your own business and do not have board meetings, draw up a business plan detailing the precise changes that you wish to make to the structure or organisation of the business. Do not identify people who are to be dismissed at this stage. Ensure that the business plan is dated.

Note that you will not be able to dismiss all (or some) of the old employees and replace them with new employees selected by yourself: this is because such dismissals are unlikely to be capable of being categorised as economic, technical or organisational reasons and, in any event, are not reasons entailing a change in the workforce.

Step 2: Select the employees to dismiss

9.17   Once you have decided what changes are to be made, and the number of people who are to be dismissed (and, if appropriate, from what department), you should write again to all employees in the following terms:

- Now that the transfer has taken place, it is necessary to make a number of changes within the workforce. Set out your reasons in one or two paragraphs and explain why jobs are going to have to go.

- If you are consulting with a trade union, refer to this in your letter and state the name of the trade union representative with whom you are consulting.

- Your provisional position is to dismiss *x* number of people from each department in which you intend to make dismissals.

- Again, if you wish to do so, invite volunteers and offer a compensation package.

- State that if there are an insufficient number of volunteers, you will have to select candidates for dismissal. State your selection criteria (see below).

9.18   If you need to select people for dismissal, what selection criteria should you use? If you have been consulting with a trade union, you should agree selection criteria with the union. Provided these criteria are properly implemented, a tribunal will accept them as being fair and reasonable. See 7.24 for further details.

If you have not been consulting with a trade union, or cannot agree selection criteria, you must choose your own. It is crucial that the criteria be objective – see 7.25 for more details on choosing selection criteria.

There is one difference between selecting employees for dismissal when taking over a business, and when making redundancies in your own business. In the latter case, you will know the employees and be able to judge them within the framework of the selection criteria. With new employees, particularly if the old company did not keep detailed personnel records, it will be much harder to make assessments. In such circumstances, you may have to fall back on basic criteria such as 'LIFO' (last in, first out), 'FIFO' (first in, first out), qualifications, or an impression as to dedication and ability from interview (which is inevitably subjective, but which may be the best you can do in such circumstances).

When taking over some businesses, you may inherit a preexisting management structure and you may be able to rely on these members of management to undertake a more detailed assessment based on their knowledge of individual employees.

Step 3: Consider alternative employment

9.19   By now you will have realised that the procedure for dismissing after a takeover is broadly similar to that for redundancy, except that you have to establish an economic, technical or organisational reason *rather* than a diminution in the need for employees to do work of a particular kind. The third stage, after you have provisionally selected which employees to dismiss, is to consider alternative employment.

Unlike a redundancy situation, there is no formal legal obligation to consider alternative employment. Also unlike redundancy, employees are not entitled to a four-week trial period in which to consider their position. However, many tribunals will not consider you to have acted reasonably unless you consider whether you can save jobs by offering alternative employment.

The procedure to go through when considering alternative employment is set out at 7.30.

Step 4: Consultation

9.20   After selecting the employees to dismiss, you should write to them in the following terms:

- following extensive review and consideration, you have provisionally selected Alf as one of the people to be dismissed because of the technical/economic/organisational reasons set out in your last letter.

- You have considered alternative employment (if you have any associated companies, name the companies at which you have considered alternative employment) but there are no suitable jobs available.

- Invite each employee to a meeting with you to discuss the process of selection and discuss any suggestions they may have for alternative employment. State a date and time for the meeting – there is no reason why it should not be arranged quickly – but if it is inconvenient for the employees you should re-arrange the meetings.

- State the period of notice to which they are entitled (see 12.11) and state whether you will want them to work out their notice periods or whether you will pay in lieu of notice.

- If you are offering a termination payment, state what it is. Remember that when dismissing because of a takeover, you are not legally obliged to pay a redundancy payment.

- Emphasise that your letter is not a letter of dismissal, and that they remain employed by your company until further notice.

9.21   At the meeting with each employee, you should try to have someone available to take notes. Go through your selection criteria and explain to the employees the reasons for selecting them. If they disagree with your use of the criteria (for example, they say that they have been employed for eight years and not two), you will need to take this into account and may need to reconsider your selection. If they disagree with your choice of selection criteria (for example, say that you should have worked on a 'LIFO' not 'FIFO' basis), explain to them that the choice of selection criteria was a business decision and it is too late to change them.

You should also ask each employee whether they have any suggestions as to alternative employment, and whether there are any people whom you could contact on their behalf to try to help with finding a new job. Make a note of every suggestion made.

The letter of dismissal

9.22   You should allow a day or two to elapse after your meetings with the employees. If any suggestions were made for alternative employment, you should consider these (and ensure, if possible, that there is some record – such as a memo to a colleague in another department asking if a particular vacancy is still available). You can then write to the employees in the following terms:

- Thank them for attending the meeting with you (or, if they failed to attend, make reference to this).

- If they agreed with your application of the selection criteria, mention this. If they disagreed, briefly set out the reasons for their challenge and state why these reasons are not valid.

- Refer to any suggestions they made for alternative employment. Mention what steps you have taken to look into these suggestions, and explain why it is not possible to offer the alternative employment. If alternative employment *is* available, set out the terms of the job offer and ask them to confirm their acceptance within, say, seven days. If they did not make any suggestions as to alternative employment during your meeting, mention this. State that you will continue considering them should any suitable job vacancies arise over the next few months.

- State what their last day of work will be. If you are paying monies in lieu of notice, set out your calculation of the notice pay in your letter. Set out any termination payment that you are making voluntarily, making sure you state that it is an '*ex gratia*' payment. Enclose a cheque or state when a cheque can be expected.

- Enclose a copy of the employee's P45 or state when it can be expected.

- If possible, add a personal paragraph so that the letter does not appear mass produced. State that you will happily provide references. Note that, unlike with dismissals for misconduct (see 3.24), there is no reason why you should not give good references for employees.

Dismissing employees when taking over a contract

9.23   It can be particularly difficult to tell, when taking over a contract, whether the contract amounts to an 'economic entity' or 'undertaking' so as to make *TUPE* apply. If *TUPE* does apply, you are deemed to have taken over the employment of all the employees who worked exclusively on that contract. It is also likely (although the law is not so clear on this) that any employees who spent the vast majority, but not all, of their time working on the contract would likewise transfer into your employ.

Theoretically, you should be able to negotiate an indemnity or contribution from the person providing you with the contract in case there is a transfer of employees and you are found to be liable for unfair dismissal. In practice, however, if you have obtained the contract in a competitive tender situation, you will be unlikely to be able to negotiate such an indemnity.

When will a transfer take place?

9.24   A one-off contract, on its own, is unlikely to amount to an economic undertaking. If you take over such a contract, and nothing else, you are probably safe and will not find that you are responsible for taking over the old contractor's employees.

If, however, you take over other aspects associated with the contract, for example equipment, materials or even some members of staff, you are at risk of an employment tribunal finding that *TUPE* applies.

If there are a number of employees who worked for the old contractor, and you consider yourself to be at risk of a tribunal finding that *TUPE* applies, you are well advised to seek specific advice from an employment law solicitor.

What if TUPE applies when taking over a contract?

9.25   If *TUPE* does apply when taking over a contract, you will need to go through exactly the same procedure as when taking over a business, as set out above.

10. DISMISSALS FOR OTHER REASONS

10.1   In order for a dismissal (whether actual or constructive) to be fair, you must establish that the reason for the dismissal is either capability, conduct, redundancy, contravention of a statutory provision or 'some other substantial reason' (*Employment Rights Act 1996, s98*).

The most common 'other substantial reason' will be a business reorganisation or taking over somebody else's business and dismissing employees (see Chapters 8 and 9 respectively). This chapter deals with dismissals for other common reasons. Theoretically, anything may be capable of amounting to a fair reason for dismissal: however, in practice a number of identifiable categories have arisen over time. These are:

(a)   where continued employment would contravene a statutory requirement – this is not strictly an example of 'some other substantial reason', but is a express reason for dismissal in its own right;

(b)   where there are personality clashes between Alf and other employees;

(c)   where you are put under pressure to dismiss Alf by a customer or supplier;

(d)   where Alf reaches retirement age;

(e)   where Alf was engaged for a fixed period or for a fixed task;

(f)   other, miscellaneous reasons.

When dismissing for any of these reasons, except reason (d), you will have to give Alf his full notice. See Chapter 12 for what you must pay on a fair dismissal.

10.2   Note that in the above cases, you will often have to go through a consultation procedure with the employees or consider alternative employment. It is not proposed to set out the detailed requirements for these in this chapter – such procedures are set out in full in preceding chapters.

(a) Where continued employment would contravene a statutory requirement

10.3 If continuing to employ Alf would place either him or you in breach of a duty or restriction imposed under an enactment, you will be entitled to dismiss Alf (provided you first consider alternative employment, or making adjustments to his duties so that he can continue in employment).

The most common example of this occurs if Alf needs to drive as part of his duties, and he is banned from driving (thus rendering it illegal for him to continue driving for you). Note that if driving is only a small part of Alf's duties, and you could allocate the driving to somebody else and find alternative work for Alf, then a dismissal is likely to be unfair. Likewise if Alf was able to use public transport rather than driving himself, and doing so would not significantly affect his work, you would also be acting unreasonably in dismissing him.

If you wrongly believe that the ongoing employment of Alf would be in breach of an enactment, this will not suffice under this heading. It may, however, be sufficient to justify 'some other substantial reason'.

Example

Trust House Forte dismissed an employee after being wrongly told by the Department of Employment that he would not qualify for a work permit. In fact, he did qualify and the Department had misinformed the employers. The Employment Appeal Tribunal held that the employers were not entitled to claim that continued employment would be a breach of an enactment, but that their reasonable and genuine belief that they would be in breach amounted to some other substantial reason justifying the dismissal – **Bouchaala v Trust House Forte Hotels [1980] IRLR 382**

(b) Personality clashes between Alf and other employees

10.4 If other employees do not get on with Alf, and the personality clashes cause significant disharmony in the workplace, this may amount to some other substantial reason enabling dismissal of Alf.

***

Example

Ms Treganowan worked in an office with other women who disapproved of her loose morals. She had an illegitimate child, of which the other workers disapproved, and would boast of a relationship with a boy almost half her age. The atmosphere in the office had become extremely tense and hostile and was seriously affecting the company's business. It was held that the dismissal of the employee was fair for 'some other substantial reason' – *Treganowan v Robert Knee & Co. Ltd [1975] IRLR 247*

***

If the personality clash is between two people only, you may have some difficulty justifying dismissal of one as contrasted with the other, since it may not be easy to establish who is at fault. In such a case, if the personality clashes make it impossible for you to carry on employing them, you may be able to dismiss both. Ensure that you have given both of them formal warnings. Also consider whether either or both staff members can be moved to a different department or given some other form of alternative employment.

10.5   If the personality clash is more general, and the majority of your workforce cannot work with Alf, you will need to go through the following steps:

- Ask the other employees to put their grievances relating to Alf in writing (this will be extremely helpful evidence at a tribunal hearing).

- Give Alf at least one, and preferably two, formal warnings in writing. Ensure you meet him to discuss ways in which he can attempt to improve his relationship with other members of staff.

- Discuss the situation with other employees. Satisfy yourself that there is no likelihood of matters improving. Keep notes of these conversations.

- Consider whether Alf can be relocated or offered some other alternative employment.

- If there is no alternative, dismiss him.

10.6   Personality clashes arising from Alf's sexual orientation: As the law presently stands, sexual orientation does not come within the definition of sex discrimination.

Although it would be unlawful to dismiss Alf because of his sexual orientation alone (since you would be unable to establish a fair reason for dismissal), if his sexual orientation causes difficulties with other employees, then this may be a sufficient reason to dismiss him.

Example

An audit clerk insisted on wearing various badges proclaiming that she was a lesbian, including badges saying 'Dyke', and 'Lesbians Ignite'. She ignored instructions from her employers to remove the badges and was eventually dismissed. The Employment Appeal Tribunal held that a balance must be struck between the freedom of the employee and the needs of the business (which included avoiding badges which were potentially offensive to customers and other employees). Accordingly the dismissal was fair – *Boychuck v HJ Symons Holdings [1977] IRLR 395*

10.7   Industrial action by other employees: Although it may be legitimate to dismiss Alf if other employees complain about him and cannot get on with him, if matters go further and the other employees begin or threaten industrial action (such as a strike) in order to put pressure on you to dismiss Alf, this industrial pressure must be disregarded in assessing whether or not Alf's dismissal is fair. This is discussed further at 18.14.

(c) Pressure by customers or suppliers to dismiss Alf

10.8   Sometimes a major customer or supplier may be unwilling to work with Alf. Alf may have upset them in some way and they choose to exercise their commercial muscle in order to secure his dismissal.

Example

An employee of a company, whose biggest client was the US navy, stole a lighter belonging to a naval officer. The navy insisted that the employee be dismissed, and it was held that the employer had not acted unreasonably in bowing to the demands of their best customer in a situation such as this – *Scott Packing v Paterson [1978] IRLR 166*

In order to establish that the dismissal of Alf in these circumstances is fair, you will need to prove that you have balanced the potential injustice to your business if the customer goes elsewhere against the injustice to Alf if you dismiss when there is no fault on his part. Bear in mind that it may be easier to justify dismissing Alf when the pressure comes from a major customer rather than a major supplier. If the customer is only a minor one, you may also have difficulty justifying Alf's dismissal.

Before dismissing Alf you should take the following steps:

- If you feel able to do it, ask the customer/supplier for a letter confirming that they insist Alf be dismissed and setting out their reasons. Unless you feel it wholly inappropriate, write to the customer/supplier and ask them if they would be satisfied if you issue Alf with a final written warning instead of dismissing him. If you prefer to do this orally, keep notes of the relevant conversations.

- Consider if there is any alternative employment you can offer Alf, possibly with an associated employer, which would not involve Alf coming into contact with the customer.

- Consult Alf while this is going on (and, if appropriate, forbid him from contacting the customer/supplier). Make sure Alf is kept fully informed (and keep notes of your discussions with him).

- If the person putting pressure on you is a supplier rather than a customer, consider whether you can go elsewhere to purchase the items you buy from the supplier. This will not be possible if the supplier is a monopoly supplier or considerably cheaper than his competitors; however, it will impress a tribunal if you can show you have considered finding alternative sources for your materials.

● If all else fails, you can go ahead and dismiss Alf.

(d) Dismissing Alf when he reaches retirement age

10.9   At present, the law provides that employees cannot claim unfair dismissal or redundancy once they reach or exceed retirement age. If there is no contractual or 'normal' retirement age, the retirement age is deemed to be 65 for both men and women.

This rule, known as the 'upper qualifying age', is presently under challenge before the courts as being in contravention of European law. It is likely to be several years before the matter is finally resolved: however, if the courts decide that the upper qualifying age is unlawful and that people over 65 are entitled to claim unfair dismissal, it is almost certain to be held to be fair to dismiss somebody who has reached or exceeded a contractual retirement age. If there is no normal retirement age, it is unknown whether the courts will say exceeding 65 is a fair reason for dismissal (being 'some other substantial reason') or whether they will insist that Alf has a right to continue working until he is no longer capable of doing the job.

(e) Where Alf was engaged for a fixed period or task

10.10   If Alf is engaged for a fixed period or task, and the period expires or the task is completed, you may no longer wish to employ Alf. Ordinarily the completion of the task will be a 'substantial reason' for dismissing him.

If Alf has been employed on a fixed-term contract which expires, the failure to renew the contract is regarded by tribunals as a dismissal *unless* the fixed term is at least one year and Alf has agreed in writing to waive unfair dismissal rights – see 17.16.

You will need to establish that the fixed period or task was well known to Alf and made clear to him at the time he was engaged. This may be difficult to establish in the absence of a letter to Alf when he was first employed setting out the fixed period or nature of the task he was employed to do. Tribunals are keen to avoid situations where you provide Alf with a series of short fixed-term contracts or many single tasks in an attempt to bypass unfair dismissal protection. Assuming that you can persuade the tribunal that the one-off nature of your employment relationship is not a sham, a dismissal of Alf in these circumstances will be fair.

(f) Other, miscellaneous reasons

10.11 The following is a list of some other cases in which tribunals have decided that the employer has established 'some other substantial reason' for the dismissal. Remember that the fact that other employers have persuaded a tribunal that their dismissal was fair does not mean that you will be able to persuade a tribunal that *your* dismissal of Alf was fair in similar circumstances – the overriding test is that you have to have acted reasonably in accordance with the merits of the case.

- where Alf is about to go and join a competitor – ***Davidson v Comparisons [1980] IRLR 360***;

- dismissal of a spouse where the husband and wife lived together for work and the other spouse had been dismissed – ***Kelman v Orman [1983] IRLR 432***;

- where Alf was in prison and thus unable to carry out his duties – ***Kingston v British Railways Board [1984] IRLR 146***;

- where an employee said he intended to resign to go and live in Australia. The employers treated him as having ceased working even though he never formally resigned. After he changed his mind he claimed unfair dismissal. The belief that the employee had resigned was some other substantive reason justifying the dismissal – ***Ely v YKK Fasteners [1993] IRLR 500***.

10.12 By contrast, the following situations have been held *not* to give rise to 'some other substantial reason' justifying the dismissal:

- a rumour that Alf is about to leave and set up a rival company – ***Betts v Beresford [1974] IRLR 271***;

- dismissal of a spouse where his wife, also previously employed by the same employer, is dismissed after stealing from the employer – **Wadley v Eager Electrical [1986] IRLR 93.**

It can be seen that these cases are similar to the respective examples of *Davidson* and *Kelman*, set out in 10.11 above, and thus demonstrate that tribunals vary enormously in their approach (as can circumstances in individual situations).

11. INTERNAL APPEALS

Introduction

11.1   Tribunals regard providing a right to appeal as an integral part of the law of dismissal. Unless you are a very small company, and the decision to dismiss was taken by the senior manager (and thus there is nobody to appeal to), the failure to provide an appeal may often make a dismissal unfair.

An appeal can often be of great advantage to an employer. Although it means that a certain amount of management time will have to be written off, the following two benefits come about:

a   if there were procedural defects in your original decision to dismiss, a properly held appeal can cure those defects and prevent the dismissal from being held to be unfair;

b   Alf may be more inclined to regard himself as having been treated fairly and reasonably. This may, in some cases, actually ward off an application to an employment tribunal.

For these reasons, the opportunity to appeal should always be offered (whether or not the right to appeal appears in Alf's contract of employment).

The appeal hearing

11.2   Unless totally impracticable to do otherwise, someone other than the person who took the decision to dismiss should conduct the appeal. However, for the sake of consistency, the word 'you' will continue being used in this chapter to describe the person chosen to handle the appeal procedure.

An appeal hearing can take two forms. In the absence of Alf's contract of employment dictating the form it should take, you can choose whichever form suits you best. The two types of appeal hearings are these:

a   Rehearing: this involves you having another hearing at which all the evidence is presented from scratch and Alf presents his arguments all over again. It is essentially a second bite at the cherry, but will allow you to remedy any procedural defects that happened first time around.

b   Review: this is simply giving Alf the opportunity to question the decision-making process by suggesting, for example, that you did not have all relevant information last time, or you took irrelevant information into account, or that you were biased.

Decide whether you prefer a rehearing or a review. A review will normally be more appropriate when the issue that Alf is appealing about is one of selection for redundancy. Further, if there are a substantial number of witnesses, a review will often be easier. However, reviews lack the main advantage of rehearings in that rehearings are usually more effective at curing any defects in the original procedure.

11.3   You will have invited Alf to request an appeal in writing in the dismissal letter. Insist on it being done in writing – do not allow an oral request for an appeal (unless Alf cannot write!). If you have given him a reasonable time limit during which he has to present his appeal, you are justified in refusing to hold an appeal if he fails to appeal within that time. However, you run the risk of a tribunal saying that the period you allowed was too short. A week should almost always be sufficient.

Even if Alf were to present his request for an appeal a few days late, you may often be better off by conducting the appeal in any event. The reason for this is simple. If you refuse to allow Alf to appeal, he will feel hard done by and will consider that you are acting unfairly (in a moral, rather than legal, sense). This may encourage him to complain to an employment tribunal in circumstances where he might not otherwise do so.

Who should conduct the appeal?

11.4   If you are a medium or large company, the appeal should *always* be conducted by somebody other than the person who conducted the original disciplinary proceedings. Historically, tribunals used to regard it as unfair if there was any discussion about the case between these two people; however, nowadays tribunals realise that discussion is inevitable.

Bear in mind that if the case proceeds to a tribunal, you will probably be cross-examined on the degree of interaction that the original decision-maker had with the appeal decision-maker. An employee's lawyer will be keen to establish that there had been considerable discussion and that the appeal decision-maker, therefore, had not come to the appeal with an open mind. Avoid this by minimising your discussions about the merits of the appeal.

If you are from a small company, and there is nobody else of suitable managerial status who can conduct the appeal, you are encouraged to hold it yourself (rather than not allow an appeal at all). If you are doing the appeal yourself, a rehearing will usually be inappropriate and a review is the better, and easier, approach to adopt.

Conducting a rehearing

11.5   After you receive Alf's letter indicating a desire to appeal, you should write to him stating as follows:

- You will arrange an appeal hearing. State a date, time and place. Indicate that the date can be rearranged if inconvenient for him. If known, state the name of the person who will be conducting the appeal hearing.

- The appeal will take the form of a rehearing. This means that he will be allowed to make any submissions he wishes on whether or not he committed the act(s) you dismissed him for, or whether he was not performing his duties properly, and whether dismissal was an appropriate sanction. He will also be allowed to call witnesses or put forward any other documents that are relevant, whether or not he relied on them at the original hearing(s).

- He can have a representative present if he wishes.

- (If appropriate) the person conducting the appeal will not discuss the matter with the person who took the original dismissal decision except insofar as is necessary for a basic understanding of the case.

- That, if he prefers, he can simply put submissions in writing (rather than having an oral hearing).

If Alf elects to put his submissions in writing, you should treat it as a review rather than a rehearing. Consider the submissions and decide whether you think the original decision was reasonable or unreasonable. If you are satisfied that the original decision to dismiss was reasonable, you should write a full letter to

Alf setting out your reasons and confirming that the dismissal will stand – see 11.13. It is important to take care over this letter since it will be the only evidence a tribunal will see as to whether or not you conducted the appeal properly or merely treated it as a rubber-stamping exercise.

If, by contrast, you decide that the original decision to dismiss was not reasonable, see 11.14.

11.6   If Alf does not attend the appeal, and does not contact you in advance, you will be justified in dismissing his appeal and not offering him another opportunity unless he has an extremely good reason for missing the original meeting.

11.7   As ever, it is important that someone take a note of what is said at the appeal meeting. You should open the meeting by introducing everyone (unless to do so would be ridiculous) and confirming to Alf that you have not discussed the facts surrounding his dismissal with the person who took the original decision. Explain to him that you are going to re-examine the evidence, listen to everything he has to say and then make a completely fresh decision.

If there were witness statements from the original hearing, it is up to you whether you rely on these alone or invite the witnesses to the appeal hearing. If Alf is alleging that they have fabricated their statements, it may be desirable to actually see them so that Alf can put his allegations to them. However, on an appeal hearing you have more latitude than at the original hearing and you should not be criticised for relying on witness statements alone or for refusing to allow Alf to cross-examine the witnesses.

Alf must be allowed to make any other representations that he sees fit. You should examine any documents he puts forward. Do not be afraid to ask him questions or test his evidence – as with the original hearing, you should allow him the opportunity to explain any inconsistencies in his evidence (and his failure to do so will strengthen the case for upholding the dismissal).

Ensure that Alf understands that he is entitled to appeal against *both* the finding of culpability (or incompetence) *and* the decision to dismiss (rather than impose a warning or suspend). If he chooses to make representations on the latter, take a careful note of what he has to say.

Conclude the meeting by saying that you will write to Alf over the next few days with your decision. Do not be pressed into giving a preliminary answer.

11.8   Once the meeting is over, consider the evidence afresh. You should take into account the matters mentioned in paragraphs 4.20 and 4.44. If you are of the view that Alf probably did commit the acts complained of (or was incompetent), and that dismissal is a reasonable sanction, you should uphold the decision to dismiss. See 11.13 for information as to what your letter to Alf should contain.

On the other hand, you may think that dismissal is not appropriate. If so, you should write to Alf and formally reinstate him. This will involve making up all back pay that he lost between the time of his dismissal and the date of reinstatement (or, if you gave Alf pay in lieu of notice, it may entitle you to demand some of that money back again). See 11.14 for information as to an appropriate letter.

Conducting a review

11.9   If you prefer to conduct a review, rather than a full rehearing, you will be examining the decision-making process and deciding whether the decision to dismiss was a reasonable one. This may involve reconsidering Alf's scores under the selection criteria when he was dismissed due to redundancy. When doing this, you will still need to consider the original evidence, but will be more concerned with whether the original decision-maker took into account irrelevant facts (or failed to take into account relevant ones) or was biased when deciding what to do.

The main danger with this approach is that it can be seen as a simple rubber-stamping procedure. Little can be done about this, so you need to be as open and candid about reviewing the original evidence as you can be.

11.10   Write a letter to Alf, as in 11.5 above, inviting him to an appeal hearing. This letter should refer to an appeal by way of review, and state that Alf will be allowed to challenge the original decision on the grounds that irrelevant matters were wrongly taken into account, or relevant matters omitted. Say in the letter that it is *not* a rehearing, and that although Alf will be allowed a representative, he should not bring any witnesses unless there is new evidence which was not presented at the original hearing.

Again, if Alf is content for the appeal to take place on paper, you should review the evidence before the original decision-maker and consider whether the decision to dismiss was reasonable or unreasonable.

11.11 At the review hearing, you must be careful not to give Alf the impression that you are deciding the matter from scratch. Ensure that a careful note is taken so that you will be able to prove the content of the meeting to a tribunal should matters progress that far.

Explain to Alf that you are concerned solely to review the original decision to dismiss and not to re-determine his guilt or innocence. Do your best to ensure that he understands the distinction – if he feels that you are trying to confuse him with terminology then he is more likely to lodge a claim against you.

Ask Alf to take you through his grounds of complaint. Try to help him focus on discussing the evidence that came out during the original investigative hearing and not, instead, developing new lines of argument. If, however, he does have new evidence which was not considered first time round (for example, a witness has come forward and said that he saw somebody else stealing the money from the till) then you will need to consider this evidence to see if it puts a wholly different complexion on the matter.

Once Alf has made all of the points that he wishes to, you should tell him that you wish to consider your decision. Do not give any indication, at that stage, what your decision is likely to be.

11.12 When considering your decision, you are not concerned with whether the original decision to dismiss was the right one in the circumstances, but whether it was a *reasonable* one in the circumstances. Consider each of the points raised by Alf and decide whether it indicates bias or inappropriate considerations by the original decision maker. Once you have been through Alf's arguments, and considered each one in turn, decide whether the original decision was a reasonable one.

If you consider it to be reasonable, you will uphold the decision to dismiss. If you consider it to be unreasonable, you will need to reinstate Alf. As discussed above, this will entail making up all back pay that Alf lost between the time of his dismissal and the date of reinstatement. Alternatively, if you gave him pay in lieu of notice, you may be entitled to demand some of that money back again.

You will need to write to Alf in appropriate terms, informing him whether you have upheld or reversed the decision to dismiss.

Upholding the decision to dismiss

11.13   Your letter should state the following:

- That you write further to your meeting on January 28, 1999. State who was present at the meeting, and whether it was a rehearing or a review.

- If it was a rehearing, summarise the gist of the evidence and state your conclusions of fact. It is unwise to take more than two or three paragraphs for this – the more detail you go into, the more you are opening yourself up to cross-examination at an employment tribunal hearing. State that you have reconsidered the sanction and that you think dismissal is appropriate.

- If it was a review, list Alf's main points of criticism. Answer each one with one sentence; this may be no more than 'we feel that the original decision was reasonable and can be justified on the evidence'. If possible, however, go into a little more detail so that a tribunal can see you have given full consideration to Alf's points.

- State that, in the circumstances, you are upholding the decision to dismiss. It is not necessary to state that there is no further appeal as it makes the tone of the letter appear harsh.

The letter should be posted to Alf's home address (since, by this stage, he will already have been dismissed). This will conclude the dismissal process.

Reversing the decision to dismiss

11.14   There are two possibilities. You may have decided that you cannot justify the original decision that Alf was guilty of misconduct or incompetence; alternatively you may be satisfied of his culpability but think that dismissal is too excessive a punishment. If the latter is the situation, you may wish to issue a formal written warning.

Your letter should contain the following points:

- You refer to your meeting on date.

- After carefully considering what Alf had to say, you are pleased to inform him that you are reversing the original decision to dismiss. As a result he will be reinstated in his old position and should come back into work on date.

- If you are going to issue a warning, state that you are instead issuing a formal warning in respect of his conduct/capability. Inform him that if he commits the same breach or offence, or any other offence, or fails to improve his work standards (as appropriate) he may face dismissal in the future. State that you take his actions extremely seriously and have only reinstated him because of the matters he raised on this occasion (you may need to change this around to find the right form of words).

- Set out the position on pay (subject to the point at 11.15 below). Whether or not you have issued a formal warning, you will need to put Alf back in the financial position that he would have been in if you had not purported to dismiss him.

- If you are reversing your decision on your findings of fact (i.e. you are no longer satisfied that Alf is not up to the job or that his conduct was improper) you may wish to apologise for any inconvenience caused. It is worthwhile being gracious since, if you should have reason to dismiss Alf on a later occasion, you do not wish to be accused of harbouring a grudge against him.

Send the letter to Alf by post. If you do not hear from him, contact him by telephone and ask him whether or not he is returning to work. You should be aware that you can still be found liable for unfair dismissal even when you have offered the job back – your offer of reinstatement may have an effect on the award which Alf receives, but will not prevent a tribunal from regarding him as 'dismissed'.

11.15   On reinstatement, you will need to pay a sum to Alf which puts him back in the position he would have been in if he had not been dismissed. It may be that you will wish to wait and see if Alf chases you up for this sum; he may be so relieved at being reinstated that he will not think to claim the days'/weeks' missed pay.

If you are going to compensate him for the difference, you should calculate the number of days' earnings that he has lost and add it to his next paycheque. Alternatively, you may prefer to enter into an agreement with him expressing the payment to be damages for lost earnings during a period of unemployment. If you adopt this approach, you need only pay him his *net* loss – i.e. his loss of earnings after deductions both of income tax and any sums he received by way of income support or unemployment benefit (NB he is unlikely to have received the latter if he was dismissed because of his conduct). This may be financially advantageous to you; however, there is a danger in doing this because, if Alf does not accept reinstatement, the letter can be used against you as an admission of liability. If you wish to adopt this approach, it is best to wait until Alf has agreed to reinstatement.

If you paid Alf pay in lieu of notice, it may be the case that his lieu of notice period takes him beyond the reinstatement date. In that case, there will be monies owing from him to you! It is a commercial decision for you to make as to whether you wish to pursue this sum. You are not entitled to set-off these excesses against Alf's next paycheques (unless he has agreed that you may do this in writing in advance) – this would amount to an unlawful deduction of wages. Instead, you should bring proceedings to reclaim the balance in the County Court (almost certainly by way of small claims arbitration, which currently deals with all claims worth under £3,000 – to be increased in April 1999 to £5,000).

12. WHAT YOU MUST PAY WHEN DISMISSING SOMEONE

12.1 When you dismiss Alf properly, you will often have to make some sort of payment to him. This will usually fall into one or more of the following categories:

    a   Pay in lieu of notice, if you have not required Alf to work out his notice period.

    b   Associated entitlements, such as outstanding holiday pay and accrued bonuses or commissions. This also includes any contractual payments that you must pay if you are dismissing him for particular reasons.

    c   A redundancy payment, if you have dismissed Alf due to redundancy.

You may also wish to give Alf an *ex gratia* payment – i.e. one which you strictly do not have to pay but you wish to pay voluntarily as additional compensation. Each of these is discussed below.

12.2 The obligation to pay monies on dismissal is entirely separate from the issue of whether the dismissal is fair or unfair. If you fail to pay monies that are properly owing to Alf, such as pay in lieu of notice, it will *not* make his dismissal unfair. It is risky to not make these payments, however, for the following reasons:

    a   Whereas Alf might not have considered an unfair dismissal claim, he will justifiably resent your failure to pay him his entitlements. If he puts in a claim for monies owing in such circumstances, he is far more likely to add a claim for unfair dismissal. He is certainly likely to seek legal advice which, in turn, may increase the chance of an unfair dismissal claim being brought against you.

    b   If and when he does claim these sums from you, he will succeed. If the claim is brought in the small claims court (which deals with all claims under £3,000 – to be increased to £5,000 in April 1999), you will have to pay the costs of issuing the summons, interest, together with Alf's loss of earnings in going to court and travel expenses. There is also a small risk of you having to pay full legal costs if the court decides you have acted unreasonably.

c   If a claim for unfair dismissal is brought against you, although your failure to pay these sums will not make the dismissal unfair, a tribunal might consider your conduct unreasonable. This may, in turn, have some bearing on their perception of you in determining whether you have acted reasonably in connection with other matters relating to the dismissal.

Clearly if there is a genuine dispute over whether Alf is entitled to monies, such as commission payments, you would be justified in withholding the monies and either seeking resolution through the courts or settling the matter amicably with him. Nevertheless, where Alf's entitlement is clear you should pay the monies at the time of his dismissal.

12.3   It is also important that you make it very clear how you have calculated any payments made to Alf. This is for two reasons. Firstly it is a criminal offence *not* to specify exactly how certain payments, such as a redundancy payment, are calculated. Secondly, if Alf later challenges your calculation of his payments, there will be a clear record of how those calculations were performed.

(a) Pay in lieu of notice

12.4   This is often considered a simple matter to calculate but can, in fact, be quite complex. There are two questions. Firstly, when is Alf entitled to pay in lieu of notice? Secondly, how much should you pay him?

When is Alf entitled to pay in lieu of notice?

12.5   When you dismiss Alf, he will be entitled to a notice period unless the dismissal is for gross misconduct (see 4.25). If he is dismissed for gross misconduct you should *not* give him any pay in lieu of notice – to do so would indicate that he was *entitled* to a notice period, which is inconsistent with your defence that you *had* to dismiss him immediately without giving notice.

When dismissing Alf you have a choice. If his notice period is, say, six weeks, you can adopt any of the following options:

a   Require Alf to work for you for during the notice period and pay him in the ordinary way (e.g. weekly in arrears).

b   Tell Alf that his employment ends immediately and pay him the six weeks' pay in lieu of notice as a lump sum.

c   Tell Alf that he need not come into work, but that you want him to be at home and available for work at your discretion (this is commonly known as 'garden leave'). In this case you should continue paying him in the ordinary way during the notice period.

d   A combination of the above, for example requiring Alf to work for a further two weeks and then giving him the final four weeks' pay as a lump sum.

12.6   The obligation to pay monies in lieu of notice is exactly what it says. If you do not allow Alf to work out his notice period, you should pay him the wages that he would have received if you *had* allowed him to work out the notice period.

12.7   If you dismiss Alf without notice, and do not require him to work out the notice period, then you are technically acting in breach of contract (your obligation being to give him a certain number of weeks' notice during which he can work). This will be the case unless Alf has a written contract that specifically states that you are entitled to pay him money in lieu of notice, and you state in your dismissal letter that you are doing so.

If you are technically in breach of contract, as you usually will be, then any pay in lieu you make to him is taken to be as compensation for this breach of contract. There is, however, a curious legal quirk. The law says that when you are in breach of contract, you compensate Alf only for his actual financial losses. If he were to find another job, his income from this job would be set-off against what you should pay him as compensation for your breach of your obligation to give him a working notice period. Thus, if Alf was entitled to six weeks' notice at £250 per week (i.e. £1,500), you breached the contract by not permitting him to work for those six weeks, and after two weeks Alf obtained another job for £275 per week, you would only have to pay him £400 (i.e. the £1,500 less the £1,100 he actually earned during those six weeks).

12.8   Very few employers take advantage of this loophole, unless Alf is entitled to a particularly long notice period (e.g. six months or more), and it would be very expensive *not* to take advantage. In practice, only company directors and football players customarily have lengthy notice periods. This is for several reasons: many employers are unaware of the loophole, many regard it as immoral to take advantage of it in this way, and again it may prompt Alf to initiate litigation against you.

If Alf does have a long notice period, and you believe that he is likely to obtain employment during the notice period, you may be better off adopting this route and *not* paying him any monies in lieu of notice at the time of dismissal. If the amount of notice money at stake is small, you may be best simply paying it up front.

Note that if you dismiss Alf due to long-term illness or similar incapacity, you will have difficulty justifying a belief that Alf is likely to obtain employment elsewhere during his notice period. Adopting this route might be perceived by a tribunal (should Alf claim for unfair dismissal) as an indicator that you are deliberately attempting to avoid paying monies that are lawfully due to Alf. The associated stigma will not assist in defending any unfair dismissal claim.

How much should you pay Alf?

12.9   This section is based on the assumption that you are not taking advantage of the loophole set out at 12.7. To do so, whilst legally justifiable, is regarded by many as poor industrial relations (other than in cases of very long notice periods).

12.10   When paying Alf in lieu of notice you pay him only his net, not gross, salary. If you paid him his gross salary, he would in fact be recovering more than if he had continued working throughout his notice period (since deductions would have been made for tax and national insurance contributions). You therefore pay him his net salary, plus other usual benefits, for such amount of the notice period during which you do not require him to work.

How much notice should you give?

12.11   If Alf has a written contract, it should stipulate the number of weeks' notice that you are obliged to give him. If there is no written contract, but you have agreed with Alf that he would be entitled to a certain amount of notice, this will be binding on you.

If nothing has been agreed as to the length of the notice period, then you are obliged to give Alf a 'reasonable' notice period. The length of a reasonable notice period will depend largely on the nature of the work he does. Thus a reasonable notice period for somebody who has been working as a receptionist for four years may only be one month, whereas a reasonable notice period for somebody who has been an executive sales director for a similar period may be, say, three months. Unless there has been express agreement to the contrary, three months is the maximum that the law will usually assess as a reasonable notice period.

12.12 The above is subject to one exception. The law lays down minimum periods of notice depending on the length of employment. If this minimum is longer than the notice period in Alf's contract of employment (or the period that was agreed between you) then it takes precedence. There is no minimum notice that must be given by you if Alf has been employed for less than one month. After this, the minimum notice periods are as follows:

- One month to two years – one week;

- Two to 12 years – one week for every complete year of employment;

- Over twelve years – 12 weeks.

Thus, for example, if Alf had been working for one day less than eight years and his contract stated that he was entitled to one month's notice, you would have to give him seven weeks' notice. This is because the minimum notice period is one week for each *complete* year (of which Alf had only completed seven) and this minimum period takes precedence over the shorter notice period in Alf's contract.

12.13 If you are paying Alf for seven weeks in lieu of notice, you should work out his *net* pay during this period. You do not need to give extra for holiday pay which he would have earned during those seven weeks. This is because holiday pay is, in reality, no more than a right not to work on certain days yet be paid normal wages. Since this is exactly what Alf is doing when he is paid in lieu, he is not entitled to be paid twice for the same loss.

If you make pension contributions on behalf of Alf, you should take these into account.

What is the position with overtime and bonuses? If Alf was contractually entitled to overtime then you must pay him the net equivalent of the overtime he would have earned during those seven weeks. If you awarded overtime at your discretion then you do not have to pay Alf for it. Likewise, if Alf would have received a bonus (such as a Christmas bonus) during those seven weeks, you remain obliged to pay it to him if he was contractually entitled to it. Contractual entitlement can be inferred, if there is nothing in writing, from the fact that you had regularly paid such a bonus over the years.

(b) Associated entitlements

12.14   In addition to pay in lieu of notice, you must also pay Alf any monies to which he has already accrued entitlement. Most commonly, this will be untaken holiday pay. Note that you can require Alf to *take* the holiday during his notice period. If he is entitled to seven weeks' notice and he has one week's holiday accrued, you could state in the letter where you set out his final payments that you are giving him seven weeks' notice, of which you are requiring him to take the first week as accrued holiday and you will pay him for the remaining six weeks. Note that you should not adopt this approach when you are dismissing Alf for gross misconduct, when an immediate dismissal is necessary.

12.15   An area which often causes difficulty is where Alf is given a periodic bonus, but the notice period does not take him to a date which triggers this bonus. Alf may argue that he has worked through *some* of the period which would have resulted in a bonus, and thus should be entitled to a proportion of the bonus on a *pro rata* basis. The true position will depend on the terms of the contract between you and Alf. If there is a lot of money at stake, seek legal advice. If it is not cost-effective to seek legal advice, either take the risk of Alf taking you to court successfully, or negotiate a settlement with him. Any legitimate dispute over bonus payments will have no bearing on whether a dismissal is fair or unfair.

12.16 Some contracts of employment provide for certain other events to be triggered on dismissal, unless the dismissal is for a specified reason (such as gross misconduct). This is common where Alf has invested money in the company, or where he has a share option agreement. This falls outside the scope of this book and you should consider seeking specific legal advice if this situation arises.

(c) Redundancy payment

12.17 If you have dismissed Alf due to redundancy, you must pay him a redundancy payment. Remember the definition of redundancy set out at 7.3 – if Alf's dismissal does not fall within this definition, then you do *not* need to make a redundancy payment. Many employers make the mistake of labelling a dismissal as being due to redundancy when it is not. It is often the case, however, that the incorrect labelling of a dismissal as redundancy coupled with a prompt redundancy payment deflects many employees from bringing unfair dismissal claims.

12.18 If Alf has been working for less than two years, or if he is under 18 or over 65, he is not entitled to a redundancy payment. If the usual retirement age at your company is less than 65, and Alf is over that age, he will likewise not be entitled to a redundancy payment.

In addition, if Alf is 64 years old (but has not yet reached 65, at which point his right to a redundancy payment ceases) then for each complete month that Alf is over 64, his redundancy award is reduced by one-twelfth. Thus if Alf is made redundancy three months before his 65th birthday, he will only be entitled to one-quarter of the normal redundancy pay (since it would have been reduced by nine-twelfths).

Remember that if Alf has unreasonably refused an offer of suitable alternative employment, he will not be entitled to a redundancy payment – see 7.39.

12.19 The formula for calculating a redundancy payment is as follows:
Redundancy payment = L × P × F

where 'L' is the length of Alf's employment with you, 'P' is Alf's weekly pay (subject to a weekly maximum – currently £220) and 'F' is a multiplication factor which takes account of Alf's age. Each of these is addressed below.

'L' – length of employment

12.20   The first factor is the number of complete years which Alf has been continuously employed by you or any associated employers (i.e. subsidiary or parent companies, or another subsidiary of your parent company). Bear in mind the following points:

- If Alf has been employed under different fixed term contracts then the length of these contracts should be combined to give a total length of employment. Periods whilst Alf is on holiday or temporarily absent will count if he remains employed by you during such periods.

- If Alf was absent through sickness or injury, his period of continuous employment will continue accruing provided he remained employed by you. If you had dismissed him whilst he was ill (whether due to his illness or not) but rehired him when he recovered, then up to 26 weeks can be counted towards continuous employment if he was incapable of doing his usual kind of work during this period. As soon as the absence extends beyond 26 weeks, his continuity of employment will be broken and the counter re-sets to zero when he is rehired by you.

- Female employees may also count weeks during which they are absent due to pregnancy or maternity leave – the former is limited, however, to 26 weeks.

- You do not count any period during which Alf worked for you when he was under 18 years old.

- If, during any part of a week, Alf was on strike then the *entire* week will be discounted for the purpose of calculating the total length of employment. The fact that he was on strike will not, however, re-set the counter to zero.

If you have bought your business from another employer and Alf worked for the old employer, then his continuity of employment will transfer and you should take into account his length of service before you bought the business.

Once you have calculated Alf's total length of employment, and made any necessary adjustments as set out above, the figure 'L' will be the number of *complete* years employment that Alf has achieved. As mentioned above, if Alf has been working for less than two complete years, he is not entitled to any redundancy payment.

'P' – weekly pay

12.21   The rules relating to the date on which you calculate Alf's weekly pay are complicated and depend on the manner of termination and the length of the notice period. In general, if you have not required Alf to work out all of his notice period then you calculate a week's pay as of the date that Alf's employment finished. If you *did* allow Alf to work out his full notice period (which is common in cases of redundancy) then you calculate Alf's weekly pay as of the date that you *would* have given Alf notice of dismissal if you had given precisely the minimum amount of notice required by law (see 12.12).

What is a normal week's pay? You should work out what Alf was earning in a normal week at the above date. This is calculated by reference to the number of hours he was obliged to work. Either this will be stated expressly in his contract, or will have arisen by custom and practice (for example, a normal working week might be 37 hours even if there is no written contract setting this out). Overtime is ignored, even if it is regular, unless you are contractually obliged to provide Alf with overtime *and* he is contractually obliged to do it.

Example

An employee's contract provided for a 40 hour week. He regularly worked a 58 hour week which, it was said, was necessary for the employer's business. Nevertheless, the court held that the normal week's work was 40 hours since he was not obliged to work for longer than this under his contract – **Lynch v Dartmouth Auto Casings** *[1969] 4 ITR 273*

You should work out what Alf's contractual wage would have been during the week in which the above date falls. This will usually exclude overtime, as stated above, but will include any regular bonuses or commissions which he would have received *provided* that he was contractually entitled to them. If the bonus is in respect of a longer period, it should be calculated on a *pro rata* basis.

12.22   Unlike pay in lieu of notice, you use Alf's gross, not net, pay. This will yield the figure 'P' for the redundancy payment, subject to one caveat. If his weekly pay, 'P', is greater than a set maximum amount, 'P' is *limited* to the maximum amount. The maximum is currently £220 per week. This limit is reviewed annually in April. Thus if Alf is earning over £11,440 per annum (on the basis of a normal working week, excluding overtime) he will exceed the maximum figure and you will simply calculate his redundancy payment on the basis of a weekly wage of £220.

'F' – multiplication factor

12.23   For every year of continuous employment (i.e. 'L'), working backwards from the date of dismissal, you adjust Alf's redundancy payment by a factor depending on his age during the year in question. You do this by calculating the factor 'F' as follows:

- for every year during the whole of which Alf was 41 or over, F is 1.5;

- for every year during the whole of which he between 22 and 41, F is 1.0; and,

- for every earlier year, i.e. during the whole of which he is between 18 and 22 (since years under 18 do not count), F is 0.5.

Examples of calculating redundancy payment

12.24   The above formula appears complex when set out on paper. In reality, it is quite simple. The following hypothetical examples demonstrate how a redundancy payment is calculated in practice.

Scenario 1

Alf is 35 years old. He has been working for you, without a break, for seven and a half years. His gross annual salary at the date of dismissal is £7,280, i.e. £140 per week. He usually earns an extra £40 to £50 per week doing overtime, although he has no right to the overtime work.

Redundancy payment = L × P × F.
L = 7 (Alf has worked for seven complete years – you do not include parts of years);
P = £140 (i.e. Alf's weekly gross wage. You do not include his overtime since he is not entitled to it under his contract);
F = 1.0 for all of his employment (since, during each of the seven full years he has been working, he has been aged between 22 and 41).
Accordingly his redundancy payment is £980, i.e. 7 × £140 × 1.0

> ### Scenario 2
>
> Alf is 45 years old. He has worked for ten years and two months, although he was absent through illness for four months (during which he remained employed by you and received statutory sick pay). His basic salary at the time of leaving was £14,300. He received commission on top of this.
>
> Redundancy payment = L × P × F.
> L = 10 (since Alf has been working for ten complete years. You count the period of his absence since he remained employed by you);
> P = £220 (although Alf's actual weekly gross wage was £275, and was in fact even higher due to commission payments, 'P' is capped at the weekly maximum of £220);
> F = 1.5 for four years (since he was 41 or over for four complete years) and 1.0 for the remaining six years.
> Accordingly his redundancy payment is £2,640. This is calculated on the basis of the four years when Alf was over 41, i.e. 4 × £220 × 1.5 *plus* six years when Alf was under 41, i.e. 6 × £220 × 1.0.

Ex Gratia payments

12.25   Some employers choose to give an extra sum to Alf as gratuitous compensation for being dismissed. You should not do this in cases of gross misconduct. If you do make an *ex gratia* payment, you should make it clear in writing that it is being made on an *ex gratia* basis. This is because, in certain circumstances, an *ex gratia* payment can be used to reduce the amount of any compensation if the dismissal is later found to be unfair – see 13.21.

Do not write in a letter that the *ex gratia* payment is being made on the basis that Alf does not bring a claim for unfair dismissal. Legally, this is of no effect and will only cause a tribunal to take a dim view of you. If you genuinely want to head off any potential claim, it must be done on the basis of a formal settlement – see Chapter 15.

13. WHAT DO YOU PAY IF YOU GET IT WRONG?

13.1   What happens if you get it wrong? If you dismiss Alf without going through the proper procedures? If another manager at your company sacks Alf when he was not authorised to do so?

Even if you think that you have dismissed Alf fairly, you may want to know how much you may be liable to pay so that you can make a sensible attempt at settling the claim.

There are three separate elements in what you have to pay Alf, namely:

a   Contractual monies – notice period, or pay in lieu of notice.

b   A 'basic award' – this is a fixed sum depending on Alf's age and length of service. It is calculated according to a precise formula.

c   A 'compensatory award' – this is usually the biggest section of any award. It reflects the loss of earnings that Alf has suffered due to being dismissed.

13.2   A tribunal might also order that Alf be reinstated or re-engaged (see 13.34). If this happens, and you refuse to comply with the order, you may also have to pay an 'additional award'. This is a discretionary sum, and will be between 13 and 52 weeks' pay depending on the circumstances of the dismissal. If you can persuade a tribunal that it was not practicable to comply with an order for reinstatement or re-engagement then you will not have to pay the additional award. This will not be an easy task, since before making the order the tribunal would have considered that it *was* practicable for you to comply.

Contractual monies

13.3   If you dismissed Alf for gross misconduct, you do not have to pay him any contractual sums reflecting a notice period. In all other cases, you do. If you did not do so at the time of dismissal, the tribunal *may* order you to do so. It can only do so, however, if Alf has specifically claimed notice money or breach of contract in his Originating Application. If he has not done so, the tribunal is not permitted to make a separate award reflecting the monies that Alf would have earned during his notice period.

If the tribunal does not make an award for contractual notice pay, it will usually include the same sum in the compensatory award, and thus Alf gets the benefit of notice monies in any event. The one exception is if Alf received more than £12,000 to reflect his loss of earnings as the compensatory award. As set out below, this sum is the maximum that the tribunal can award as a compensatory award, but it can award damages for a contractual notice period *on top* of this.

13.4   The method of calculation for contractual monies is set out in Chapter 12. If you paid notice monies to Alf at the time you dismissed him, you will not have to pay the same sums again.

Basic award

13.5   The basic award is an anachronistic lump sum theoretically intended to compensate for loss of a job. It depends on pre-dismissal salary, length of service and age. The maximum that can be awarded is £6,600. The basic award is calculated according to a standard formula which is almost identical to calculation of a redundancy payment – the difference being that, unlike for a redundancy payment, Alf is entitled to half a week's wage for each year he worked whilst he was under 18. See 12.19 for the method of calculating this.

13.6   If you dismissed Alf for redundancy, and paid him a redundancy payment, then any redundancy sum paid will be set-off against any unfair dismissal compensation. In other words, if you paid a redundancy payment (calculated according to the formula set out at 12.17) then you will not have to pay a basic award if you are found to have unfairly dismissed Alf.

Sometimes a tribunal might find that Alf had contributed to, or caused, his own dismissal. Say, for example, Alf had been stealing from your company but you dismissed him without going through a proper procedure. The tribunal might find that the dismissal was technically unfair, but reduce any theoretical compensation by up to 100%. If it does this, it will usually reduce the basic award by this percentage as well as the compensatory award. Contributory fault is addressed in more detail at paragraph 13.24.

13.7   If Alf is within one year of the normal retirement age for his job (or, if there is no normal retirement age, within one year of 65 years old), the basic award is reduced by one-twelfth for each month of that year. If, therefore, Alf was dismissed two months before his 65th birthday, he would only be entitled to two-twelfths of his basic award.

Compensatory award

13.8   The compensatory award can be difficult to estimate, and this chapter gives only an overview as to how tribunals calculate compensatory awards. As stated above, the purpose of the compensatory award is to compensate Alf for being without a wage. The overall test is that the award should be 'just and equitable': however, tribunals now calculate the award according to clearly laid down guidelines.

If, immediately after his dismissal, Alf obtained a better paid job, then he would have suffered no financial loss and will usually receive no compensatory award (except for a small award discussed at paragraphs 13.17 and 13.18). If Alf is at fault and is found to have contributed to his dismissal, an award will be reduced (or extinguished) to reflect this fault. If you gave Alf an *ex gratia* payment when dismissing him, you will usually get credit for this when the award is calculated. If the dismissal was unfair on technical grounds only, and Alf's dismissal was inevitable, he will receive little or nothing as a compensatory award.

When calculating the compensatory award, a tribunal will go through, in order, the following four stages:

a   calculate the financial loss that Alf has suffered;

b   give credit for any payments made by you;

c   make an appropriate deduction for contributory fault; and,

d   impose a total limit on the compensatory award. At the time of writing, this limit is £12,000, although the government intends to increase it to £50,000.

It is important to follow the above steps in the correct order since this may make a significant difference to the end result.

Step 1: calculate the financial loss that Alf has suffered

13.9   There is a standard method followed by courts when assessing the financial loss flowing from a dismissal. Essentially, a tribunal looks at what Alf would have earned if he had remained in employment, and deducts what he actually did earn (or, if he could have earned money by making reasonable efforts, what he should have earned).

A tribunal will usually consider the following items when calculating Alf's financial loss.

Loss of earnings up to date of tribunal hearing

13.10   The tribunal will calculate Alf's loss of wages up until the date of the hearing. This calculation is based on his net, not gross, wage. The starting point will be from the date up to which you paid him – i.e. the later of the date of dismissal or the expiry of his notice period.

If Alf would have received a wage rise during the period between dismissal and the hearing, his net wage will be based, for the appropriate period, on the theoretical increased wage.

If he has obtained a new job, the loss of earnings will be the difference between his old net earnings and his new net earnings. If he earns more in the new job, he would have suffered no loss of earnings. If he has been dismissed from a subsequent job, the loss of earnings will usually be calculated on the assumption that he had *not* been dismissed a second time, since the second dismissal would not be attributable to your dismissal of him.

> **Hypothetical calculation**
>
> Alf earns £200 per week net at the date of his dismissal. He finds a new job after ten weeks, paying £150 per week net. The tribunal hearing is five weeks later. Alf's loss of earning up to the tribunal hearing is £2,250, namely:
> 10 weeks × £200 = £2,000, plus
> 5 weeks × £50 (i.e. £200 − £150) = £250

13.11 When calculating Alf's net loss of earnings, you should also take into account the value of any benefits that he received. These might include:

a Tips – curiously, tribunals will take tips into account when calculating the compensatory award, but not when calculating the basic award. It is usual to work out Alf's total tips over, say, one or three months prior to dismissal and then take the average weekly figure.

b Bonuses – if Alf would have received a bonus (such as a Christmas bonus or a performance related bonus), the tribunal will usually compensate him for this loss. The question is one of fact – had he remained employed, would he have received the bonus? If he was entitled to the bonus under his contract, or if all other employees received a bonus, you will have great difficulty persuading a tribunal that Alf would not have received it.

c BUPA or PPP benefits – this will normally be valued on the basis of the cost to Alf if he were to take out the same medical cover himself.

d Use of a company car (although if the car was provided for business purposes only, there is no personal loss to Alf if he no longer has use of the car).

e Loss of pension rights – if your company makes pension contributions on Alf's behalf, and he is unfairly dismissed, he will lose out on pension contributions and the tribunal will attempt to assess this loss. Pension losses are extremely difficult to calculate and, usually, a tribunal will adopt a very rough-and-ready approach rather than attempting complex actuarial calculations.

(i)   Money Purchase Scheme: With a money-purchase scheme (i.e. where contributions are placed in a 'pot' reserved for Alf, and the money in the pot is used to buy an annuity when Alf retires) the loss is simply the value of the contributions that you would have made. This will be calculated for pension contributions both up until the date of the hearing and for a period into the future – see 13.16. Note that Alf's contributions are *not* included, since he will receive the money into his own pocket and is free to continue to make contributions should he so wish.

(ii)   Final Salary Scheme: A final salary scheme is one where Alf is entitled to a pension of up to two-thirds of his final salary on retirement, depending on the number of years for which contributions have been made on his behalf. His loss is therefore the difference between his final pension (given he has been dismissed and you are no longer making contributions) and what his final pension *would* have been if you had continued making contributions. The loss of enhancement of accrued rights then has to be calculated – this is because the pension that Alf will eventually receive will be based on a lower salary (i.e. his leaving salary) than that which he would have had if he had remained employed by you (since he probably would have received a salary increase every year). This sum then has to be adjusted to take account of the fact that Alf is receiving the money now rather than in, say, 20 years' time. The method of calculating final salary pension losses is outside the scope of this book. Traditionally, these calculations (which can involve large sums of money) have not been taken as seriously as they might, due to the overall limit on a compensatory award of £12,000. If, as seems likely, the government increases the cap on compensatory awards to £50,000, the pension loss can become a very substantial sum of money. If pension losses are significant in your case, seek professional advice from a specialist employment lawyer. Check that the solicitor is experienced in calculating pension losses, since pension loss cases are one of the most misunderstood areas of law.

13.12 You are not able to set-off unemployment benefit or income support against Alf's earnings. Thus you cannot try to argue that, because Alf is in receipt of £50 per week income support, his net loss is not the £200 per week that he was earning before the dismissal, but is only £150 per week. This is because *you* are responsible for paying the DSS back any social security benefits received by Alf and then deducting them from his total award *after* the award has been assessed. This is explained further at 15.1.

13.13 If Alf was close to retirement then, in addition to facing a reduction in his basic award (see 13.7), his loss of earnings would only be calculated up until the date that he would have retired. This is on the basis that if he had not been unfairly dismissed, he would have ceased earning a wage at that point in any event.

13.14 Sometimes the tribunal might find that your dismissal of Alf was unfair because you did not follow appropriate procedures. It might consider, however, that if you *had* followed an appropriate procedure, you would still have dismissed Alf. This happens most often in redundancy and gross misconduct cases. In such a case, the tribunal might decide that if you had followed a proper procedure, Alf would have been employed for a further, say, two weeks. Accordingly the tribunal would award only two weeks' loss of earnings and there would be no further compensatory award given.

13.15 If Alf is offered a job and refuses it, or if he fails to look for new employment, the tribunal may say that he has failed to 'mitigate his loss'. This means, in practical terms, that his ongoing loss of earnings will be attributable to *his* failure to take reasonable steps to minimise his financial loss, and not to *your* unfair dismissal of him. Since you are not required to pay for his failure to look after his own interests, any loss of earnings claim will stop at the point where a tribunal believes Alf could or should have obtained new employment.

> **Hint**
>
> It is completely open to you, in a compensation hearing, to suggest that Alf has failed to mitigate his loss. It may therefore be a sensible option, if Alf was dismissed for redundancy or some other similar reason, to offer him his job back. If he refuses to accept his old job back, there is often a chance that a tribunal will find that he failed to mitigate his loss. This will prevent a large loss of earnings claim from accruing.

Future loss of earnings

13.16   If, by the date of the tribunal hearing, Alf remains unemployed or on a lower wage than before, the tribunal will usually award an element of future earnings to compensate him for the ongoing loss of earnings.

The weekly loss of earnings is calculated the same way, i.e. if Alf has no job, it will be his net earnings (plus benefits) before dismissal, whereas if he has a new job but on a lower wage, his loss of earnings will be the difference between the two.

How far into the future will a tribunal look? There is no set rule; however, the majority of tribunals follow a similar practice. When Alf remains out of employment at the date of the hearing, a tribunal will usually award between three and six months' future loss of earnings. If Alf is employed but on a lower wage, a tribunal will often award between six and 12 months' loss of salary. There is no logical reason for these figures – it is merely a question of practice that has arisen over time.

Loss of statutory protection

13.17   Employees are not entitled to certain rights, such as unfair dismissal or redundancy rights, until they have been working for a new employer for two years. Accordingly, when you dismiss Alf, he will have a two-year period in his new employment during which he will lack employment rights. This is reflected in an unfair dismissal award by giving a small sum for loss of statutory protection. Conventionally, this figure is between £150 and £250.

Somewhat curiously, tribunals will always give this sum if it is requested, but will rarely give it if it is not requested. In practice, therefore, an unrepresented employee (who would not know about this element) will often receive £150 to £250 less than a represented employee.

The government is considering reducing the two-year qualifying period to one year. If this occurs, the standard £150 to £250 figure may be reduced slightly.

Expenses in finding new employment

13.18   The compensatory award will also include a sum to compensate or reimburse Alf for any out of pocket expenses to which he has been put because of having been dismissed. This may include the cost of looking for new employment, for example the cost of buying newspapers (for job adverts), cost of postage, stationery and telephone calls, and the cost of transport to and from job interviews.

In exceptional cases, tribunals have awarded substantial sums for expenses associated with changing jobs. This has even gone as far as, in one case, ordering the ex-employer to pay Alf's costs of moving house to change jobs! In practice, however, the value of an award for these expenses is usually modest.

Step 2: give credit for any payments made by you

13.19   It would be unfair if you voluntarily paid Alf a leaving bonus and then were not given credit for having given this payment. Likewise, it would be wholly lacking in common sense if you paid Alf a month's pay in lieu of notice, but a tribunal did not give you credit for such payment.

Pay in lieu of notice

13.20   Theoretically, there are two methods of factoring in sums paid by you in lieu of notice:

i   work out Alf's loss, and then give credit for the sums that you paid in lieu of notice; or,

ii   calculate Alf's loss from the time that the pay in lieu of notice expired.

On first glance, there would not seem to be any practical difference between the two. However, the effect of taxation means that the first method is more favourable to employers. Indeed, it is this method that tribunals adopt. The difference between the two approaches is shown in the following example:

Example

An employee was given three months' pay in lieu of notice (although, in fact, he was only entitled to one month). The tribunal assessed his loss of earnings as seven months. It followed method (ii) and awarded him four months' net loss of earnings (i.e. seven months, less the three months paid). The Employment Appeal Tribunal held that this was wrong. It said that the correct approach was to calculate the full loss of earnings, which would be calculated as seven months' net earnings, and then deduct the sum actually paid (i.e. method (i)). Since the three months' salary paid by the employer had been gross, not net, a greater sum was deducted and the employer ended up paying less to the employee than he would otherwise have done – *MBS v Calo [1983] IRLR 189*

Other sums paid

13.21   Sometimes employers will pay a voluntary bonus upon dismissal. This might occur if you were dismissing Alf due to ill-health after many years of service, or if you were paying him an enhanced redundancy payment.

The general rule is this: if you pay a voluntary, or *ex gratia*, sum to Alf at the time of his dismissal, the tribunal will try to decide whether or not you would have paid it in any event if Alf had been dismissed fairly at a later date. If you *would* have made the *ex gratia* payment in any event, then you will not be given credit for it when the compensatory award is calculated. This might happen if you are paying a leaving bonus to employees selected for redundancy, but get the redundancy selection procedure wrong. If a tribunal decides that you would have paid a £1,000 bonus to each employee if you had got the procedure correct, it will not allow you to have a windfall of that £1,000 (by deducting from the unfair dismissal compensation) because you got the procedure wrong.

Usually, however, tribunals will readily accept that *ex gratia* payments made by you can be deducted from any compensatory award.

13.22 Note that, when giving credit for *ex gratia* payments, if the reason for dismissal is redundancy then the *ex gratia* payment will first be set-off against the basic award, and the excess (if any) set-off against the compensatory award. In all other cases, i.e. where the reason for dismissal is *not* redundancy, the entire *ex gratia* award will be set-off against the compensatory award. This will make a difference where further reductions are made to the compensatory award because of fault by Alf (see 13.24) or because of the effect of the cap on the compensatory award (see 13.30).

13.23 Do not be misled into thinking that, because credit is usually given for *ex gratia* payments, you will be guaranteed the full benefit of the *ex gratia* payment if Alf is found to be unfairly dismissed. There are two crucial factors which can significantly diminish, or extinguish, the benefit to you of an *ex gratia* payment. In particular:

a Where the compensatory award is reduced because Alf contributed to his own dismissal through his own fault. This percentage reduction, which is discussed at 13.24 below, is applied to the compensatory award *after* credit has been given for your *ex gratia* payment. The effect of the *ex gratia* payment is therefore reduced. This is best demonstrated by way of a hypothetical example:

> **Hypothetical**
>
> A tribunal assesses Alf's loss of earnings at £6,000. You gave him an *ex gratia* payment of £1,500. The tribunal also finds that he was 50% to blame for his own dismissal, and thus reduces his compensatory award by 50%. If the reduction by 50% occurred first, you would have to pay £1,500 only, i.e. £3,000 (being £6,000 x 50%) less the £1,500 *ex gratia* payment. However, the correct method is for the *ex gratia* payment to be deducted first. When this is done, Alf's award is £2,250, i.e. £4,500 (being £6,000 - £1,500) × 50%. Thus you would, in practice, only get credit for 50% of your *ex gratia* payment.
>
> Ironically, the greater the reduction for Alf's contributory fault, the less credit you get from your *ex gratia* payment. Thus if Alf's award were reduced by 80% because of his fault, you would only get credit for 20% of your *ex gratia* payment.

b   Where the statutory cap on the compensatory award is reached (currently £12,000). This cap is imposed as the very last stage of calculating the unfair dismissal award. Therefore if Alf's loss of earnings is £20,000 and you paid him £5,000 as an *ex gratia* payment, the fact that you are credited with £5,000 (so as to make the loss of earnings only £15,000) is irrelevant since you will not have to pay more than the £12,000 statutory cap in any event. The statutory cap is discussed further at 13.30.

Step 3: make an appropriate deduction for contributory fault

13.24   The importance of procedural correctness when dismissing Alf cannot be understated. Dismissals are frequently held to be unfair, even in cases where Alf's conduct warranted immediate dismissal, simply because the employer had not engaged in sufficient investigation or consultation to satisfy the tribunal.

When inadequate investigation or consultation has occurred,

and the employer is consequently deemed to have acted unreasonably, Alf's dismissal will be unfair.

However, the tribunal is entitled to reduce the compensatory award in circumstances where Alf has been guilty of improper and blameworthy conduct which caused or contributed to his dismissal. This reduction is usually applied on a percentage basis: thus where the tribunal thinks that Alf is 75% responsible for the dismissal, the award will be reduced by 75%. The reduction should be applied against both the basic and the compensatory award, although the tribunal can reduce the compensatory award only, or reduce the two awards by different percentages. Although there would seem to be no logical reason for treating the two awards differently, the courts have made it clear that it is not improper to do so.

Hypothetical

Somebody is stealing tyres from your factory. Circumstantial evidence points to Alf, and you dismiss him without holding a proper investigation. After the dismissal, Alf is investigated by the police and convicted by the criminal courts of theft. Although the tribunal would find that the dismissal was unfair, because you failed to hold a proper investigation, it would significantly reduce Alf's award (quite possibly by 100%). Note that an alternative approach would be for the tribunal to say that although the dismissal was unfair, if a proper investigation had taken place a fair dismissal would have occurred, say, two weeks later – thus Alf is entitled to his basic award and two weeks' salary as the compensatory award. An employer would prefer the former approach since, if Alf was a longstanding employee, the basic award could be quite substantial. Both approaches are equally viable.

What amounts to blameworthy conduct?

13.25   An inability to do the job properly will rarely amount to blameworthy conduct. The fact that somebody does not measure up to the job cannot be something that disentitles them from receiving compensation when you dismiss them unfairly – you appointed them to the position in the first place, and if you appointed an inappropriate person or failed to train them properly, the fault is yours and not theirs.

The harshness of this rule is mitigated to some extent, in cases of procedural unfairness, by the fact that you will often be able to demonstrate that if you had operated the correct procedures, you would have dismissed Alf anyway within a few weeks – thus his compensatory award would be limited to these few weeks' pay. This is discussed further at 13.14.

The one exception to this rule is where a tribunal is satisfied that Alf's inabilities are due to his own fault in the sense of indifference or idleness (rather than simply lacking the intelligence or experience for the job). In this case, his conduct will be blameworthy and a reduction for contributory fault will be made. However, such reductions tend to be at the lower end of the scale, and rarely exceed 50%.

13.26 Blameworthy conduct will usually exist where Alf commits an act which is morally or legally wrong. The mere fact that he refuses to obey your instructions will not necessarily amount to blameworthy conduct.

Example

An employee was dismissed because he refused to obey an instruction which would have involved illegally falsifying records. The employer argued that any compensation should be reduced because he contributed to his own dismissal by refusing to obey instructions. The National Industrial Relations Court (the predecessor of industrial tribunals) held that there should be no reduction in his award because his conduct was not blameworthy – *Morrish v Henleys (Folkestone) Ltd [1973] 2 All ER 137*

The need for blameworthiness is important. If Alf is in breach of an express term of his contract of employment, this will usually be sufficient to amount to contributory fault. It has even been said by the Court of Appeal in one case that if Alf is merely 'bloodyminded' this may be sufficient to amount to blameworthy conduct (*Nelson v British Broadcasting Corporation (No 2) [1979] IRLR 346*). However, a morally or legally culpable act, such as theft, violence or provocative conduct is usually required before a reduction can be made for contributory fault.

13.27 There are three things which legally cannot amount to blameworthy conduct:

a   When Alf joins, or refuses to join, a trade union. The law gives trade union membership (or non-membership) certain privileges, and one of these is an immunity from being found to have been contributorily at fault in a dismissal. This is to prevent an employer from arguing that Alf caused his own dismissal by refusing to join a trade union in a closed-shop situation (closed-shops are, in any event, no longer lawful).

b   When Alf is involved in industrial action (such as a strike or a work-to-rule), the fact that he is involved in the industrial action cannot amount to contributory fault. If, whilst participating in the industrial action, he engages in conduct which goes *beyond* mere participation (such as throwing stones), then this may amount to contributory fault.

c   When the blameworthy conduct is discovered after the dismissal. This is because the blameworthy conduct must cause or contribute to the dismissal and, if it was not known about, it could not have caused or contributed to it. This is different from the hypothetical example set out at 13.24 above because, in that example, the employer dismissed Alf because of the theft of tyres, even if he lacked sufficient proof at the time, and thus the dismissal *was* caused because of Alf's conduct.

13.28 What if Alf fails to exercise his right to an internal appeal against your decision to dismiss? Although this is technically a question of failing to mitigate his loss, rather than an issue of contributory fault, it is convenient to deal with it here. Until recently, the law was unclear as to whether Alf's award could be reduced if he failed to exercise a right of appeal. However, the law has recently been changed (*Employment Rights Act 1996 s127A*). If Alf has been given written notice of his right to appeal, but fails to do so, his award can be reduced by up to two weeks' pay. Likewise, if the employer prevents Alf from appealing against his dismissal under an organised procedure, a supplementary award of up to two weeks' pay can be granted.

What percentage reduction should be applied?

13.29   Guidance from the Employment Appeal Tribunal indicates that a finding of 100% contributory fault (so that Alf receives no compensation whatsoever) should be rare. This is because, by the very fact that dismissal is unfair, it follows that the employer is at fault in some way (even if only through failing to follow proper procedures). Accordingly Alf cannot be said to be the sole cause of his dismissal, since some fault lies with the employer – thus a finding of 100% fault is inappropriate.

However, the Employment Appeal Tribunal has shown a marked reluctance to reverse the decisions of employment tribunals when they *do* find Alf to be 100% responsible. In practice, such a finding is not as rare as academics might wish. Situations when a finding of 100% contributory fault is made will usually be situations involving substantial violence (i.e. something more than throwing a few punches in a fight), theft involving large sums of money or long-term dishonesty.

A common scenario is where dismissal was not a reasonable response to Alf's actions, i.e. where Alf was technically at fault but you have gone over the top in dismissing him. Examples include peripheral involvement in a minor fracas by a long-standing employee, the use of postage stamps for personal mail or minor intoxication at work. In such a scenario, Alf will usually be found to be contributorily at fault; however, the percentage reduction will be small – perhaps around 25%. However, tribunals vary enormously in the reductions they apply, and there are no real guidelines so as to enable a prediction of the likely degree of contributory fault found in any given case.

Step 4: imposing the statutory cap

13.30   It is important to go through the above three stages in the correct order since, as demonstrated, the order of applying the reductions can make a difference as to the final sum arrived at.

13.31   Once the above three steps have been gone through by the employment tribunal, it will apply the statutory cap to the total compensatory award. At the time of writing, this cap is £12,000. This sum is the top limit which a tribunal can award as the compensatory award. This does *not* include the basic award (which has a current maximum of £6,600 – see 13.5). The very large awards, in the tens or hundreds of thousands of pounds that are sometimes seen reported by journalists, are in sex or race discrimination cases where no upper limit for the award exists.

Thus if Alf's net salary is £2,000 per month, the hearing is nine months after the dismissal and the tribunal decides to award him a further six months' future loss of salary, his loss of earnings would be £30,000. Even if you had given him a £5,000 *ex gratia* payment (bringing the award down to £25,000) and he was found to be 25% responsible for the dismissal (bringing the award down to £18,750), the tribunal could only award a maximum of £12,000 for the compensatory award.

13.32   There is currently one exception to the £12,000 statutory cap. Where the tribunal has ordered the reinstatement or re-engagement of Alf (see 13.34), this will usually include an Order for back pay. There is no limit of £12,000 on the Order for back pay. If you do not comply with the Order for reinstatement/re-engagement, the tribunal will order compensation in the ordinary way and order you to pay an additional sum (known as the 'additional award' – see 13.42). Therefore where the compensatory award comes about because of the employer's failure to comply with an Order for reinstatement/re-engagement, the limit of £12,000 does not apply (because otherwise the employer might be in a better position financially by refusing to comply with a tribunal Order to reinstate than by complying with it).

13.33   At the time of writing, the government is proposing to increase the statutory cap to £50,000. Although the majority of cases do not exceed the current £12,000 cap, the increase of the limit will mean that some employers may be ordered to pay very significant sums of money for unfair dismissal. It is also likely, when larger sums of money are at stake, that the number of cases taken to appeal will increase – thus increasing the demands on employers both in terms of legal costs and time-management.

Reinstatement and re-engagement

13.34   The tribunal is empowered to order that you reinstate or re-engage Alf and pay him back-pay to put him back in the position he would have been in had he never been dismissed. There is a box on the Originating Application (the form that he fills in to start his claim) in which Alf can tick a box stating whether he is seeking reinstatement, re-engagement or just compensation.

If Alf has ticked either of the first two boxes, or if he has told you that he wishes to be reinstated or re-engaged at least seven days before the hearing, you must come to the tribunal prepared to give evidence on whether reinstatement/re-engagement is practicable. If you fail to do so, the tribunal will adjourn and *must* order you to pay Alf's legal costs unless you can establish a 'special reason' for your failure to adduce reasonable evidence.

13.35   What is the difference between reinstatement and re-engagement? Reinstatement involves replacing Alf into the job he had before you dismissed him. Re-engagement will involve the tribunal specifying the nature of the employment that Alf is suited for, the amount payable to him (including benefits) and any other rights and privileges (including seniority). It is then up to you, or an associated employer, to re-engage him before a specified date in a job of your choice provided it complies with the specifications laid down by the tribunal.

When the tribunal order reinstatement or re-engagement, it will always make an order requiring that Alf receives all back-pay between the date of dismissal and the date of reinstatement or re-engagement.

When will the tribunal order reinstatement or re-engagement?

13.36   A tribunal will never order reinstatement or re-engagement unless Alf asks for it. If he does ask to be reinstated or re-engaged, he can indicate a preference (although the tribunal will not be bound by it).

13.37   The crucial question for the tribunal to decide when determining whether to order reinstatement or re-engagement is the practicability of such an Order. This will involve you providing evidence on, and the tribunal considering, the nature of the jobs that are available for Alf (including his old job). If there is a job which is fairly suitable for Alf, even if it is dissimilar to his old job, the tribunal may consider re-engagement in this post. The tribunal will not, however, expect you to create a job for Alf or dismiss existing employees in order to make room for Alf.

There is one exception: if you have replaced Alf, the tribunal may expect you to engage Alf in addition to the replacement (or dismiss the replacement) *unless* you can satisfy the tribunal that:

a   it was not practicable for you to arrange for Alf's work to be done without engaging a permanent replacement (i.e. it was not practicable to engage a temp pending the outcome of the employment tribunal hearing); or,

b   you hired the permanent replacement after a reasonable time had elapsed and Alf had not told you that he wished to be reinstated or re-engaged *and* that when you engaged the permanent replacement, it was no longer reasonable for you to expect Alf's work to be done except by a permanent replacement.

Unless you can satisfy one of these two tests, the tribunal will consider reinstatement/re-engagement *as if* you had not hired the permanent replacement and Alf's job was still being done by a temp.

13.38   How can you resist an Order for reinstatement / re-engagement? An important factor in whether it is practicable to order reinstatement or re-engagement is whether such an Order will cause disharmony amongst other members of staff. If Alf is no longer trusted by other members of staff, the tribunal is unlikely to order you to re-employ him (unless he can be moved to a different department or an associated employer). If his job involves contact with the public and his conduct, whilst not warranting dismissal, makes his continuing contact with the public undesirable, then the tribunal is unlikely to order reinstatement. Likewise, if yours is a small business and you would be in day-to-day contact with Alf, and there has been a breakdown in your personal relationship caused by the litigation, the tribunal is unlikely to order that you continue working together.

A mere assertion by you that one of the above reasons applies is unlikely to satisfy a tribunal. You should obtain written evidence that employees are unhappy about continuing to work with Alf, or get Alf to admit when he gives evidence that he would be uncomfortable returning to work. If, as suggested at 13.15, you offered Alf his job back and he refused, this might be a good reason for arguing against reinstatement (since it shows that he no longer has confidence in working for you).

What if you do not comply with an Order for reinstatement or re-engagement?

13.39   If you do not comply with an Order for reinstatement or re-engagement, Alf can take you back to the tribunal. Likewise if you offer Alf a job, purporting to comply with an Order for re-engagement, but the new job is not suitable, he can take you back to the tribunal. The tribunal will consider the same question as before, namely whether it was practicable for you to comply with the Order. This time, however, you have the benefit of hindsight (so that you can say *why* it was not practicable) rather than providing speculative forecasts.

Again, in considering practicability, the tribunal will not take into account the fact that you have hired a replacement for Alf unless you can bring yourself within one of the two limbs of the test set out at 13.37.

13.40   If the tribunal agrees, second time around, that it was not practicable for you to reinstate or re-engage Alf, then it will assess the basic and compensatory award as if the Order for reinstatement/re-engagement had never been made.

13.41   If, however, the tribunal considers that it *would* have been practicable to comply with its Order, it will:

a   calculate the basic and compensatory award as if the Order for reinstatement/re-engagement had never been made *with the exception* that the £12,000 cap on the compensatory award will not be applied – see 13.32; *and,*

b   it will order you to pay an 'additional award' as punishment. To complicate matters, this is called a 'special award' if the reason for dismissal was connected with trade union activities or health and safety. The calculation of the 'special award', when the dismissal is for trade union activities or is health and safety related, is outside the scope of this book.

13.42   How is the 'additional' award calculated? The additional award is calculated on the basis of between 13 and 26 weeks' pay, unless the reason for the original dismissal was also discriminatory on grounds of sex or race, in which case it will be calculated on the basis of between 13 and 52 weeks' pay.

For the purpose of calculating a weeks' pay, the tribunal will take Alf's gross weekly wage but apply a maximum of £220 per week – thus the calculation is similar to that performed when calculating the basic award (see 13.5).

How will the tribunal decide where to place the award within the scale (i.e. should it award at the bottom of the scale, being 13 weeks' pay, or towards the top of the scale, being either 26 or 52 weeks' pay)? This is very much a matter for the tribunal's discretion: however, an employer who deliberately flouts the tribunal's order will generally have to pay at the higher end of the scale, whereas an employer who genuinely believes that reinstatement is not practicable (even if the tribunal disagrees) is more likely to pay at the lower end of the scale.

14. TACTICS BEFORE THE TRIBUNAL HEARING

Introduction

14.1 This chapter is concerned with procedural steps you can take once you discover that Alf is contemplating a claim for unfair dismissal. There are two purposes to taking these procedural steps:

a   you will often be able to obtain additional information about his case, which will enable you to be better prepared at a hearing; and,

b   you can place pressure on him and force him to undertake additional work, which may expose weaknesses in his case and may make him inclined to accept a lower settlement offer than he would otherwise do.

Not all of the following steps will be appropriate in any given case. However, you should familiarise yourself with the procedural applications available which can be used to place pressure on Alf.

Basic outline of procedure

14.2 The first you will hear about a claim of unfair dismissal, unless Alf has informed you in advance of his claim, will be the claim form arriving on your doorstep. This is called an 'Originating Application', and is often referred to as an 'IT1' (which is the HMSO reference number of the standard claim form).

In order to claim, Alf will have sent an Originating Application to his local employment tribunal. The tribunal will then forward a copy to you, with your response form enclosed for you to complete and return. The response form is called a 'Respondent's Notice of Appearance', and is likewise often referred to as an 'IT3'.

You should complete the Notice of Appearance, which contains space for you to set out the reasons why you dispute Alf's claim. You have 21 days in which to complete and return the form.

Until recently it used to be the case that the tribunal would always allow an extension of time, but a recent change in the rules provides that they will not allow extra time unless you have a good reason for the delay. Do not ignore this form – if you do not return it you may not be allowed to defend the proceedings. If you think you may not be able to comply with the 21 day limit, write to the tribunal earlier (rather than later) explaining your reasons for seeking further time and asking for an additional, say, 14 days.

14.3   Employees have often been known to get the name of the employer wrong on their IT1 forms! If Alf is employed by a small company, it is not uncommon for him to state the name of the managing director (rather than the name of the limited company) as his employer. Provided you are not misled by this (for example, if you operate several similarly named companies and Alf has named the wrong one as his employer) a tribunal is likely to allow Alf to amend his claim form – accordingly there is little point in making an issue out of this.

If, however, Alf really has claimed against the wrong company, you may wish to include this as one of your grounds of defence on the IT3. If the tribunal does *not* allow Alf to amend his IT1, and it is found that he has claimed unfair dismissal against the wrong person or company, his claim will fail. Further, by the time of the hearing the three months for presenting a claim will have elapsed, and thus it will be too late for Alf to start a new claim against the *right* employer.

14.4   Unless you or Alf make any of the applications set out below, the next document you will receive will be the Notice of Hearing. This is simply a form which tells you where and when the hearing will take place. If you cannot attend on the date stated, or if you do not think enough time has been allocated to the hearing, you must write to the tribunal *immediately* stating your reasons for seeking an adjournment. If you wait until a few days before the actual hearing date to request an adjournment, it is likely that your request will be refused. See 16.3 for a more detailed discussion of adjournments.

Procedure at the hearing itself is addressed in Chapter 16. However, before the hearing there are various steps that are often taken, known as 'interlocutory' steps. These include exchanging documents and witness statements with the other side, and procedures for formally requesting documents or answers to questions. Methods of doing these, and the tactical advantages and disadvantages of doing so, are addressed below.

Using a lawyer

14.5   This is not, strictly speaking, a procedural step! However, it may place you at a significant psychological and tactical advantage if Alf is unrepresented. If he *is* represented, then you may find yourself positively disadvantaged unless you are also taking legal advice. Chapter 16, and the remainder of this chapter, deal with procedure if you choose to represent yourself; however, it is unwise to do so if Alf is using a lawyer.

One advantage of engaging a lawyer is that Alf may be intimidated by one or two carefully drafted letters from a solicitor. Many employees will feel guilty at claiming against an employer, particularly if yours is a small, friendly company. They will also feel that they cannot put up a proper fight in a tribunal against a barrister or solicitor.

Accordingly, receipt of a letter from a solicitor which points out the weaknesses in Alf's case and offers a nuisance value settlement of, say, £500 or £1,000 (to be withdrawn if not accepted within seven days) may put sufficient pressure on him to cause him to accept the offer. Settlement is considered in more detail in Chapter 15.

It may be galling to have to pay Alf £1,000 as a nuisance settlement. However, the alternative is losing *at least* one day's productivity for yourself and, possibly, a number of other employees who would be called as witnesses at a tribunal hearing. In addition, you would be saving the cost of engaging lawyers (if you were planning to do so). This is a commercial decision for you to make, but when balancing these factors against the additional risk of having to pay Alf thousands of pounds in compensation should you lose your case, it might seem foolish to refuse to pay a token sum in order to get rid of Alf's claim.

14.6   The disadvantage of using a lawyer at an early stage, if you do not intend to do so throughout, is that disinstructing the lawyer would appear weak from a tactical point of view.

At the end of the day, if you are willing to spend a few thousand pounds on a lawyer, you should also be willing to offer that sum to Alf in order to make his claim go away. However, if Alf is not prepared to settle (or if you are not prepared to settle), you will usually be better off engaging the services of lawyers rather than placing larger sums of money at risk and conducting the case yourself.

You may choose to engage an employment consultant. These are people who are (usually) not legally qualified but who have set themselves up in business representing companies at employment tribunals. Some employment consultants are very good and will do an excellent job. Others are not so good. Employment consultants are not regulated by any professional body and may not be insured if they are negligent in the preparation of your case. It is unwise to use an employment consultant unless you have seen him in action or have a personal recommendation from someone whose judgment you trust.

There is one potential disadvantage in using an employment consultant. Any correspondence between you and a solicitor is regarded as 'privileged'. This means that it is confidential and the tribunal cannot order you to produce it. There is some doubt concerning whether correspondence with an employment consultant is privileged, or whether the tribunal is entitled to demand copies of letters from and to the consultant. This could be dangerous since your letters may contain damaging admissions, or the consultant's letters could contain unfavourable advice. The Employment Appeal Tribunal has decided (*New Victoria Hospital v Ryan [1993] IRLR 202*) that tribunals *should* be allowed to look at correspondence between an employer and an employment consultant, on the basis that litigants were only entitled to protection from disclosure of advice given by qualified lawyers. After the end of the case, it gave permission to the employer to appeal, but the employer did not do so. Take this risk into account when deciding whether to engage a lawyer, an employment consultant or, indeed, nobody at all.

What will a lawyer cost?

14.7 How long is a piece of string? Some lawyers will agree to represent you for a fixed fee (although this is not common). Others will be willing to represent you for a percentage of money that they may save you – although you are at their mercy when they tell you what Alf's claim might have been worth and thus how much you have saved. Most frequently, however, you will be charged at an hourly rate.

Do ensure that your solicitor has experience of employment matters. Employment law and procedure can be complex, and there is little purpose in paying large fees to someone who is simply working out of a book like this one!

A broad average for engaging a high street solicitor to manage a basic one-day unfair dismissal claim would be around £2,000 to £3,000. Many solicitors will recommend that you engage a barrister for the tribunal appearance. A junior barrister, who has been practising for three or four years, is likely to charge up to £750 for one day's hearing (this includes all necessary preparation before the hearing) and up to £500 for subsequent days. For a more senior barrister you will be looking at higher figures. Remember you will probably be unable to recover these fees from Alf even if you win the hearing. Having your 'day in court' can cost much more than principles.

Spin out negotiations and internal appeals

14.8   An unfair dismissal claim must be lodged with the tribunal within three months of a dismissal. Extensions of time are only granted in limited circumstances – see 18.9. If, therefore, Alf fails to lodge his application within three months, his claim is likely to be automatically dismissed.

Extensions are only granted where it is 'not reasonably practicable' for Alf to lodge his claim within three months. This means 'not reasonably feasible' and tribunals interpret it fairly strictly. In general, an extension will only be granted if Alf was incapable of lodging his claim within the prescribed period (through illness or other incapacity) or if he was unaware of the facts which would give rise to his claim. If he has received erroneous legal advice he will not normally be entitled to an extension of time (his remedy being to sue his advisers).

The onus is very firmly on Alf to present his claim within the time limit. There is no obligation on you to assist him in doing this, or to inform him of the applicable time limits. In this situation, delay in negotiations is very much to your advantage since it increases the chance of Alf failing to lodge his claim within time. The one thing you must not do is mislead Alf in any way – if you tell him that time runs from the date of an internal appeal hearing (rather than the dismissal) or that he actually has *six* months to present his claim, many tribunals would grant an extension of time. If no extension was granted, Alf might have a claim against you for negligent (or fraudulent) misstatement or for the legal 'tort' of deceit. Legal aid may be available for Alf for these claims (it is not available for unfair dismissal) and you may find yourself in a substantially worse position as a result.

14.9   It is obviously in your interest if Alf does not present his claim within the three-month period. If he has threatened to lodge a claim of unfair dismissal unless you 'compensate' him, you may be able to drag out negotiations beyond the three-month period. If you do, provided you have not actually agreed to settle, you can then break off negotiations and there is little that Alf will be able to do.

Likewise, if an internal appeal procedure takes the full three months, Alf may think that he does not have to present a claim until after the appeal has been turned down. This is wrong. The three-month time limit starts running from the actual date of dismissal, not the date that the appeal is turned down. If he fails to present a claim within three months whilst awaiting the result of an appeal hearing, he will be prohibited from claiming against you.

14.10   This tactic will probably not work if Alf is represented by a solicitor, or if he is being advised by a trade union or Citizens' Advice Bureau. However, even professional advisors sometimes miss the deadlines for lodging a claim, and if they do so Alf will find that he suddenly has to sue them instead of you!

14.11   If Alf *does* lodge his claim outside the three-month limit, the tribunal will send both of you a notice stating that it appears that Alf is out of time for presenting his claim and that you are required to attend a preliminary hearing to determine whether or not the tribunal has jurisdiction to hear the matter. In order to be allowed to continue with his claim, Alf will have to show *both* that it was not reasonably practicable for him to present his claim within the three months, *and* that he has presented it within a reasonable time of it becoming practicable.

The tribunal may deplore your conduct if it decides that you were dragging out events in the hope that Alf would miss the time limit. However, in the absence of fraud or deceit on your part it is powerless to do anything about it, provided it was reasonably practicable for Alf to present the claim within three months, and it will have to dismiss Alf's claim without a hearing on the merits.

Offering a job back

14.12   As you have seen in Chapter 13, the bulk of any award Alf receives for unfair dismissal will be the salary that he has lost as the result of being unemployed. He is under a duty to mitigate this loss by accepting any reasonable job that is offered to him. If you are prepared to have him back (which might be the case if you dismissed him for redundancy or because of a business relocation), and you are not confident about your chances of success at the hearing, you should offer him his old (or an alternative) job.

Although he is not obliged to take the job, there is a chance that you will be able to persuade a tribunal that Alf should not be entitled to any compensation for loss of salary from the date that you offered it to him. A tribunal will reject this argument if it decides that your job offer was not realistic, in that Alf's dismissal took place in such circumstances that he could not reasonably be expected to re-start work (due to the acrimony of dismissal or the nature of the allegations made against him indicating that your new job offer is a sham).

However, if you would consider taking Alf on again, you cannot lose anything by offering him a job. If he accepts, he may well agree to drop his claim (although you should not insist on this, or, indeed, suggest it prior to him recommencing work). In any event, his claim for loss of earnings will be frozen at the date that he re-started work, and will not continue on into the future.

What you must *not* do is make an offer to Alf and then, if he accepts it, dismiss him again. He would be entitled to claim unfair dismissal for the *second* dismissal as well as the first one, and, in those circumstances, the second dismissal would undoubtedly be unfair. You would not be able to argue that Alf lacked two years' employment in respect of the second dismissal (assuming he had it for the first). This is because the 'two years employment' rule has an exception, namely if Alf had been working previously and there had been a 'temporary cessation of work' (which would be the case if you had dismissed and then re-hired him), his continuity of employment would continue running.

Pre-hearing review – getting Alf to pay a deposit

14.13   This is one of the best ways of putting pressure on Alf if his claim is weak. In essence, you can ask the chairman to look at the IT1 and decide whether Alf's case has a reasonable prospect of success. If he decides that Alf's case, based on the IT1, does not have a reasonable prospect of success, he can order Alf to pay a small deposit as a condition of continuing to bring his claim.

The test which a chairman applies, i.e. 'no reasonable prospect of success', is not an easy one to satisfy. The chairman holds a hearing, looks at both the IT1 and IT3, and reads (or listens to) any written (or oral) submissions made by yourself and Alf.

It is important to note, however, that evidence is *not* permitted at a pre-hearing review. It is not a mini-trial – rather it is an attempt to weed out cases which appear hopeless simply on reading the claim form. If you and Alf are in dispute over the circumstances leading up to his dismissal, a pre-hearing review will not be appropriate. If, however, Alf states in his claim form that 'I was drunk on duty when operating dangerous machinery and, just because I hit somebody after having received three warnings for violence, I was sacked' then a pre-hearing review would be a wise tactical move since, on the face of his application, he would have no reasonable prospect of success at a full tribunal hearing.

14.14   If a chairman accepts that Alf's claim has no reasonable prospect of success, he will order Alf to pay a deposit before he is allowed to continue with his claim. This deposit is small, usually being £150 (which is the maximum) but sometimes being reduced if Alf is of limited means.

The tribunal which actually hears the full case will not be told, and is not permitted to know, about the requirement that

Alf pay a deposit. If Alf is particularly belligerent about his claim, and is able to risk a small deposit, winning a pre-hearing review may be a pyrrhic victory. However, sometimes it can do a remarkable job of focusing Alf's mind on the weaknesses of his case – statistically, about two-thirds of claims where the employee has been ordered to pay a deposit are struck out because he fails to come up with the money.

14.15 If a chairman is not persuaded that Alf's claim has no reasonable prospect of success, he will permit Alf to continue with his claim unfettered by the need to put down a deposit. This is a result which should be avoided. Firstly, it means that you have wasted your own time – particularly if you attended the hearing rather than making written representations.

Secondly, and more fundamentally, it will boost Alf's opinion of the merits of his claim and increase his determination to proceed. He may misunderstand the nature of the pre-hearing review, and believe that a chairman has told him he is likely to succeed at the full hearing. This makes him less likely to accept a nuisance value settlement of his claim at a later date.

It follows that this tactic, although potentially rewarding, should not be used unless Alf's case comes across as lacking in merit on paper. Do not be tempted by the thought that you can persuade the chairman that Alf is lying or mistaken – the chairman will not be interested in hearing evidence or testing the relative strengths of each side's claims. It is only if Alf appears to have no reasonable prospect of success on a plain reading of his Originating Application that this procedure should be utilised.

Obtaining further details of Alf's case

14.16 Sometimes Alf's claim form will be a bare assertion that you dismissed him unfairly. Sometimes he will give a long, rambling account of every perceived discourtesy to him which occurred over the last five years. Sometimes Alf will set out the details of his complaint on the form in reasonable detail. It is often the case, however, that you will want to know more about exactly what he is alleging, in order to enable you to prepare a defence properly.

You should write to Alf and ask him for further details of his case. This letter should take the form of short questions. For example, if Alf asserts that 'I was told that I could use the machine without engaging the guard', you might ask 'Who told you you could use the machine without engaging the guard?', 'On how many occasions were you told this?' and 'Please state the date and location of each occasion and the gist of the words used.'

Send a copy of this letter to the tribunal at the same time. This is so that, if Alf later denies having received the letter, you can prove that you had written it on the date you claim.

If Alf fails to provide a reply (or satisfactory answers) within 14 days, you should write to the tribunal and ask them to make an Order requiring Alf to answer the questions. Enclose another copy of the original letter, state the date it was first sent and either that you have not received a reply, or that the reply was unsatisfactory (and enclose a copy of the unsatisfactory reply). The tribunal will then make an Order, if it considers it appropriate, that Alf should answer the questions (usually within a further 14 days).

What questions will a tribunal consider appropriate?

14.17   A tribunal will not allow you to ask a long list of questions which are of marginal relevance only, oppressive (in that they require unreasonable time or expense to provide answers) or that ask for evidence.

Whether or not your questions are asking for evidence is not always obvious. If you ask Alf for the grounds on which he says, for example, he was not fairly selected for redundancy, then this is asking for further details of his claim. If, by contrast, you ask Alf which witnesses he is going to call in support of his claim, or how a particular document assists his case, then this is asking for evidence. If in doubt, ask the question! The worst that can happen is that the tribunal will decline to make an Order forcing Alf to answer.

A common ground for ordering further details is when an employee states that the points supporting his case *include* certain matters. In such a situation you should ask whether there are any other points on which he relies. A tribunal should support you and make an Order if Alf fails to respond.

Example

An employee, who was dismissed for making fraudulent expense claims, alleged that he was only doing what had been done by other employees over a long period of time and that it had been condoned by management. The Employment Appeal Tribunal ordered that the employee should give more details concerning the allegation that other employees had been permitted to steal – *International Computers Ltd v Whitley [1978] IRLR 318*

Example

An employee claimed he had been dismissed for 'redundancy/victimisation'. The tribunal ordered him to give further details about the redundancy and victimisation, and state the name of the person who he said had been victimising him – *Colonial Mutual Life Assurance Society v Clinch [1981] ICR 752.*

One area in which tribunals discourage questions about is the financial loss suffered by an employee. As you will see in Chapter 13, the amount of money you have to pay to a successful claimant is governed, in part, by his loss of earnings: however, tribunals will usually not permit you to ask questions about his financial losses in advance of the hearing.

It is probably best to avoid asking questions about whether Alf has applied for other jobs (again, this is relevant to how much you might have to pay). A tribunal is unlikely to order that Alf answers such questions, and you run the risk of making Alf aware that he may disentitle himself to some of the financial award if he has not been taking reasonable steps to find alternative employment.

What if Alf disobeys a tribunal's Order to answer questions?

14.18   If Alf fails to comply with an Order of the tribunal within the time allowed, you should immediately write to the tribunal and tell it. You can suggest an appropriate penalty, although the tribunal is entirely free to do as it chooses.

There are two possible penalties for non-compliance with a tribunal's Order to answer questions. The first is extremely rare. A tribunal is entitled to impose a fine of up to £1,000 for failure to obey its Orders. You should avoid asking for this since it will make you appear retributive. Further, the other sanction is much more effective and is far more in your interests.

The second penalty is that the tribunal can strike out all, or some, of Alf's claim. In other words, the tribunal can either throw out the entire claim, or the part of it which he has failed to give further details of. This is, needless to say, a particularly satisfying way for an employer to avoid having to go to a full tribunal hearing and risk paying large sums of money. However, before a tribunal is allowed to strike out any, or all, of Alf's claim, it must first write to him asking him why he has failed to comply with the Order. This requirement takes much of the sting out of the striking out provisions because, in reality, if Alf offers an excuse and provides the answers a tribunal will always give him the benefit of the doubt and not strike out his claim.

14.19   Asking for further details is a particularly useful tactic to adopt whilst waiting for a hearing date. Unless your requests are wholly irrelevant, at the very least you will get a clearer idea of the case Alf intends to bring against you. This is beneficial for three reasons:

a   You are better able to investigate his complaints, obtain all relevant documents and evidence, and ensure that yourself and other witnesses are prepared to be cross-examined on the points he raises.

b   You can often tell as much about Alf's case from what he does *not* say as from what he *does* say. If there is a particularly damaging fact, of which you do not know if he is aware, the fact that he does *not* mention it when supplying further details will be a strong indicator that he is not aware of it. Since there is no duty on you to volunteer information (unless a tribunal orders you to do so), you can negotiate and plan your defence on the basis that both Alf and the tribunal will remain ignorant of such matters. Be aware, however, that you may face cross-examination on this point and you must not mislead the tribunal in answers to direct questions.

c   The more information Alf provides in writing, the more scope you have for discovering an inconsistency when cross-examining him at the tribunal hearing.

d   There is a chance that Alf will decide he simply cannot be bothered to answer the questions and continue his claim, thus giving you the opportunity to have his claim struck out.

Obtaining copies of Alf's documents

14.20   Unlike cases in civil courts, Alf is entitled to turn up to the tribunal hearing clutching reams of documents that you have never seen before. In an extreme case, you may be permitted an adjournment – however, it is usually preferable to know what documents he has well in advance of the hearing. Accordingly you can ask to see copies of any documents Alf intends to use before the tribunal date.

This is a procedure that is more frequently used by an employee, who will wish to have copies of all documents relevant to his dismissal. Nevertheless, there is no reason why you should be placed at a disadvantage at a hearing by being surprised by Alf's evidence.

As with requests for further details of Alf's case (see 14.16 above), the first thing you should do is write to Alf, asking for copies of all documents on which he relies. Send a copy of this letter to the tribunal. If Alf does actually have incriminating documents, which he believes you are unaware of, he is likely to ignore your letter.

If he fails to respond within, say, 14 days, you should write to the tribunal and ask them to make an Order requiring Alf to produce copies of the documents. This will usually be permitted if you are simply asking for the documents Alf is going to produce at the hearing.

14.21   There may be situations when you believe Alf has documents, which you have not seen, which might help your case. An example would be if you have dismissed Alf for breaking (or preparing to break) confidentiality clauses or restraint of trade clauses in his contract of employment. Another example would be if you dismissed Alf for theft of large sums of money – you may wish to see his bank account to see whether large deposits, which cannot be his salary, have been made.

Again, you should first write to Alf asking for voluntary disclosure of the documents. Be specific in what you want. If you simply ask for 'all relevant documents' you are unlikely to receive any sympathy from a tribunal when seeking an Order to enforce the request. Your request should state precisely which documents you seek.

As above, if Alf fails to produce the documents within 14 days of your request, you should write to the tribunal asking for an Order that Alf produce copies. Enclose a copy of your earlier letter to Alf and confirm that he has not responded (or, if he has responded inadequately, enclose a copy of his reply).

You then need to set out the reasons why the tribunal should order Alf to supply the documents. This is not always straightforward. You must justify your request by proving that production of the documents is necessary for disposing fairly of the proceedings. To do this, you will need to show that you are doing more than simply fishing for evidence. Set out your reasons for suspecting that Alf has relevant documents in his possession.

The tribunal will either decide upon your application or, if it wants to hear Alf's argument as to why he should *not* have to supply the documents, it may call both sides for a 'directions' hearing. This is a hearing where the chairman, who is legally qualified, listens to submissions from both sides and decides whether or not to order Alf to produce the documents.

Unless the point being argued is complex, and lawyers are involved, these hearings will usually be fairly short (no more than ten minutes). Nevertheless, before attending such a hearing you should weigh up the advantages of getting copies of the documents you have requested against the cost involved (and time wasted) in attending the tribunal hearing. If you decide not to proceed with the application, you should write as soon as possible to both the tribunal and to Alf stating that you are withdrawing your application and asking that the directions hearing be 'vacated' (this means cancelled!). It is, however, up to the tribunal whether they cancel the hearing – it may be that the chairman thinks it would be unjust *not* to consider whether you are entitled to the documents, and thus insists on having the hearing anyway.

14.22   The penalties for non-compliance with an Order are as set out in 14.18 above and, again, the tribunal must write to Alf seeking an explanation for failure to comply with an Order before it is allowed to strike out his claim (or part of it). Alternatively, the tribunal (when hearing the actual case) can refuse to allow Alf to rely on any documents that he has failed to supply in advance in breach of an Order.

What if Alf tries to obtain your documents?

14.23   Alf will frequently ask to see a copy of his personnel file or of any notes you made during the dismissal process. He is entitled to these documents (unless documents in his personnel file are so old they cannot conceivably be of any use) and it is sensible to release these on request without the additional burden of a directions hearing.

However, sometimes Alf will ask to see documents that you do not want him to have access to. Your reluctance to provide copies can be for several reasons. He may be asking for an oppressive amount of documentation, so that the time and cost involved in collating the documents is unreasonable. He may want to see confidential information. Sometimes you may wish to stop him seeing documents because they harm your case!

You are under no obligation to give Alf copies of documents simply because he asks for them! You are only obliged to give Alf copies of documents if a tribunal orders you to. If Alf is unrepresented and unadvised, he may not be aware that he can apply to the tribunal for an order requiring you to produce documents. Accordingly it is often tactically wise to wait to see if Alf applies to the tribunal, and only then to consider whether a tribunal is likely to order you to provide Alf with copies.

14.24   In order to persuade the chairman that he is entitled to see the documents, Alf must show that production is necessary to dispose fairly of the proceedings. Once he has overcome this hurdle (and, if you can show that the documents are not relevant, that is the end of the matter), it is for you to show that it would be oppressive for you to be ordered to produce them. This will frequently depend on the attitude of the individual chairman – some consider it to be oppressive to produce anything other than the most vital documents, whereas others will allow Alf to have copies of a whole range of company documents.

You should note that the fact that a document is confidential will *not* be a defence if it is necessary to produce it to dispose fairly of the proceedings (although confidentiality may be a factor in deciding whether production would be oppressive). Some chairmen will ask to look at the document themselves, without showing it to Alf, so that they can weigh up the relevance against the confidentiality factor.

Remember that any correspondence with your legal advisers, or with witnesses in connection with Alf's claim, will be 'privileged' and the tribunal cannot order you to produce copies – see 14.6.

Forcing witnesses to the hearing

14.25 You can ask the tribunal to issue a witness summons (better known by its name in the criminal courts as a subpoena), which compels a named individual to come to the tribunal hearing and bring any specified documents.

This is more usually done by an employee (if, for example, Alf is alleging that you treated another employee less severely, he may wish to compel that employee to give evidence). If you wish to rely on another employee's evidence, you can simply tell them to attend. However, the need for you to issue a witness summons may arise if persons *other* than your own employees are relevant witnesses. Examples would include a customer against whom Alf used violence, or a competitor whom you suspect Alf has approached with an offer to pass on confidential information.

If you compel a witness to attend against his will it can be a double-edged sword. He may resent being forced to spend a day at the tribunal, and may not cooperate in the witness box. If you call a witness yourself (rather than if he is called by Alf), you are deemed to be putting him forward as an honest and credible witness and thus are not usually allowed to cross-examine him. Accordingly you may end up in a worse position than if you had not called him at all.

Note that the power to compel a witness to attend a tribunal hearing is limited to people in the United Kingdom. If the potential witness lives overseas, the tribunal is not permitted to issue a witness summons against him.

14.26   You need to know the name and address of any witness you want to summon to the tribunal hearing. If you do not have their name and address, a witness summons cannot be issued. Sometimes you may be able to ask Alf for a potential witnesses's details – see 14.16 above.

Before applying to the tribunal for a witness summons, you must ask the witness if he will attend voluntarily. If he agrees to do so, you will not be entitled to a witness summons (unless you can show that there is a good reason why his agreement should not be taken at face value).

If he fails to answer your letters, if his agreement is ambivalent (such as, 'I'll try to turn up, but I might have to be away on business') or if his own employer will not release him for the day without a witness summons, you should write to the tribunal, asking for a witness summons. The letter must include the following points:

- The witness's name and address.

- The gist of the evidence that you expect the witness will give. If you do not explain the reason *why* you think his evidence is relevant, the tribunal will not issue a summons.

- The reason why it is necessary to issue a summons (i.e. why the witness will not attend voluntarily). Attach any reply from the witness, or the letters which you wrote to him to which he failed to reply.

- Identify any documents that you want the witness to bring with him.

14.27   On receipt of your letter, a chairman will consider it. He has three options:

    a   Your request can be refused. This will usually be on the basis that the chairman thinks that the witness will not be of much help, or that he is willing to attend voluntarily (i.e. without an order). You are able to re-apply if additional evidence turns up.

b   Your request can be granted. The tribunal will send a witness summons directly to the witness by recorded delivery and will send a copy to you. It will *not* inform Alf of the witness summons.

c   A copy of your application can be sent to Alf, and his comments invited on whether a witness summons should be issued. The tribunal will give Alf a set number of days within which to respond, after which the chairman will reconsider the matter.

What if the witness does not want to attend?

14.28   If a witness does not want to attend the hearing, he can write to the tribunal and ask to have the witness summons discharged. The chairman will send you a copy of his letter and allow you to comment on it before making a decision. Usually the witness will seek to have a summons discharged on one of the following three grounds:

a   he is not able to offer any useful evidence (since, for example, he did not actually see Alf stealing the company's property);

b   the evidence that he can give is not disputed by Alf, and thus his evidence can be presented in writing rather than by personal attendance; or,

c   he is unable to attend the hearing. Unless he gives a good reason, the chairman is unlikely to discharge a witness summons on this ground. Mere inconvenience is not sufficient, and since the Department of Education and Employment will reimburse any travel expenses or loss of earnings (up to a set maximum), cost of travel or loss of earnings will not be valid reasons either. If he *does* have a good reason for not being able to attend the hearing, the chairman will consider whether to adjourn the hearing and fix a new date or whether to release the witness completely. You should indicate your preference, and the reasons for it, in any letter you write to the tribunal commenting on the witness's application.

15. SETTLING CLAIMS

15.1   Settlement should be encouraged. If you are going to pay money
to a lawyer to represent you, you should ordinarily be willing to
pay that amount directly to Alf as a nuisance settlement. Many
employees, if not properly advised, have little idea of how tribunals
assess compensation. Accordingly, if Alf is prepared to accept
£1,000 plus an apology or a reference (irrespective of whether
you feel an apology is deserved) it would be peculiar to, instead,
pay £2,000 to lawyers and still risk having to pay Alf considerably more should he win the tribunal hearing.

There are other advantages to settling a claim. These include:

- You will not lose the time entailed in preparing for a hearing and your employees will not have to lose a day's work
attending the tribunal.

- When you settle a claim, you can do so on any terms you
think appropriate. These can include agreeing to provide a
carefully worded reference for Alf. Often this can be a vital
incentive to Alf to settle at a sum considerably lower than
he might achieve if he went to a tribunal since tribunals are
not empowered to order you to provide a reference.

- The DSS does not claw back from a settlement any benefits,
such as income support, received by Alf whilst he was
unemployed (as happens when the tribunal makes an award).
Thus, if Alf's claim was worth £10,000 and he won this amount
in a tribunal, but he had received £2,000 in social security
benefits whilst waiting for the tribunal hearing, you would
have to pay Alf £8,000 and pay the DSS £2,000. If Alf's claim
is settled before a hearing, the DSS does not get to recoup
benefits. It is common practice to split the recoupment between
the parties – thus you might pay £9,000 to Alf – which means
you save £1,000 and Alf gets an extra £1,000.

15.2   With most legal disputes, such as disputes between you and a
supplier, you can settle a claim at any time simply by agreeing
the terms of settlement (whether by word of mouth or in writing). With employment disputes and, in particular, prospective
or pending unfair dismissal claims, you cannot do this. Parlia-
ment has provided two specific mechanisms for settling unfair

dismissal claims. If you do not adopt one of these two mechanisms, the settlement will not be binding and Alf can continue with his claim even if he has taken the settlement monies.

The two methods of settling unfair dismissal claims are by going through a conciliation officer at ACAS, or entering into a formal compromise agreement (which is a written contract of settlement, containing certain formalities, in connection with which Alf needs to obtain specific independent advice for it to be binding).

Settlement through ACAS

15.3   You can settle a claim through ACAS both before or after Alf's claim has been issued. Copies of the IT1 and IT3 will automatically be sent to an ACAS conciliation officer, who will contact you and Alf at some point before the hearing to see whether he can help you come to a settlement. Alf may also invoke the assistance of a conciliation officer, before he issues the claim, simply by contacting ACAS. Although, technically, you can do the same, there is little advantage for employers in taking steps that will focus Alf's attention on a claim before he has issued it. Further, an ACAS officer might remind Alf of the three-month time limit for presenting a claim which, if he is unaware of it, he might otherwise miss (and thus be prevented from claiming unfair dismissal, subject to an extension of time – see 18.9).

An ACAS officer will not try to force settlement on you. He will encourage you and Alf to discuss your case, through him, and will act as a conduit for any offers. He will take offers back and forth until agreement is reached (or it becomes clear that no settlement is possible). Not only is this service of great assistance where there is animosity between you and Alf (which might escalate if you negotiated with each other directly), but you are given 'thinking' time when an offer is made in either direction.

When negotiating through ACAS, you are able to settle a claim on any terms that you want, including a reference or confidentiality clauses. The conciliation officer will offer both sides general advice, but will not give specific advice to either of you. They are meant to be neutral and should not favour either employer or employee. Although they are not meant to disclose to Alf any information you reveal to them without your permission (or vice versa), mistakes sometimes happen – thus it is prudent not to mention anything to the conciliation officer which may be damaging to your case and of which Alf is unaware. Anything said to the conciliation officer, even if you have given him permission to pass the information onto Alf, is regarded as 'without prejudice' (i.e. confidential) and should not be revealed to a tribunal by Alf without your consent.

15.4   Usually, once a settlement is reached, the conciliation officer will produce a standard form (known as a 'COT3'). He will assist you in ensuring that the agreement is clearly worded. Technically, however, it is not necessary for the settlement to be set out in writing – if both sides have agreed the terms through the conciliation officer, it will be binding.

Example

An employee and employer agreed a settlement through the ACAS conciliation officer. The officer then sent a COT3 form to the employee for signature. He refused to sign it and tried to continue with his claim in the tribunal. Both the industrial tribunal and, on appeal, the Employment Appeal Tribunal, held that the oral agreement through the conciliation officer was binding and that the tribunal claim was not allowed to proceed – *Gilbert v Kembridge Fibres Ltd [1984] ICR 188*

15.5   The wording on the COT3 is important. You want to make sure that you limit Alf from bringing as many claims as you possibly can. It is no good settling an unfair dismissal claim if he can issue a claim the following day for breach of contract or sex discrimination. It used to be traditional to use the following wording in a COT3 agreement:

'. . . in full and final settlement of all claims which Alf might have against us arising out of his employment or out of its termination.'

This was fairly bland wording and many employees did not realise that it precluded them from bringing any further claims against their employers of any nature (unless unrelated to employment).

Recently the courts have stated that such wording, although effective to prevent an unfair dismissal claim continuing (or other linked claims, such as a claim for unpaid wages or redundancy pay), will not be effective to exclude all claims. In order to do that, more stringent wording will be needed. The following is suggested:

'. . . in full and final settlement of all claims which Alf might have against us under the *Employment Rights Act 1996*, the *Trade Union and Labour Relations (Consolidation) Act 1992*, the *Sexual Discrimination Act 1975*, the *Race Relations Act 1976*, the *Disability Discrimination Act 1996* or European Law.'

The difficulty with this is that most employees will take one look at the wording and refuse to agree to it on the basis that they do not understand what rights they are giving up. You therefore have to choose between the risk of not settling at all, or not being able to exclude all potential claims Alf might bring.

If a claim has already been issued, a sensible alternative form of words might be:

'. . . in full and final settlement of all claims which arise under the Originating Application number _____ or such claims as may be brought on the basis of the facts alleged therein.'

15.6   One limitation on the use of ACAS is that the conciliation officer must be actively involved in bringing about the settlement. ACAS will not 'rubber-stamp' an agreement which you and Alf have come to without its assistance. The alternative method, therefore, of making a settlement binding on Alf is to enter into a formal compromise agreement.

Compromise agreements

15.7   In order for a settlement to be binding, unless it is done through ACAS, the following requirements *must* be met:

a   The agreement must be in writing.

b   It must relate to the particular complaint, or claim, that Alf is bringing (or proposes to bring) against you. Accordingly the written agreement must specifically mention each claim that is being settled, for example an unfair dismissal claim together with claims for unpaid pay in lieu of notice and holiday pay.

c   Alf must have received advice from an independent adviser, who is covered by a policy of insurance, as to the terms and effects of the agreement and, in particular, on its effect on his ability to pursue his rights before an employment tribunal.

d   The written agreement must identify the adviser and state that all the relevant conditions required for compromise agreements are satisfied.

A sample compromise agreement is set out at Appendix II.

15.8   Until recently, it was necessary for Alf to seek independent advice from a qualified solicitor or barrister. This requirement has now been relaxed, so that a compromise agreement is binding if Alf has received advice from a 'relevant independent adviser' who is covered by an insurance policy. This covers lawyers, certain trade union officials and certain Citizens' Advice Bureau workers.

Before entering into a compromise contract, therefore, you should ensure that Alf has consulted a Citizens' Advice Bureau or a solicitor. It used to be common practice for employers to pay for Alf to obtain independent legal advice (up to a limit of, say, £150 or £250). Now that Citizens' Advice Bureaux advisers are capable of ratifying an agreement, this will no longer be necessary.

16. PREPARING FOR AND CONDUCTING THE HEARING

16.1   This chapter is concerned with the presentation of your case, should you decide not to have legal representation for the tribunal hearing. It contains general advice about how to prepare for the hearing and the procedure which will be followed in tribunals.

Preparation for the hearing

Hearing dates

16.2   You should be given at least 14 days' notice of the hearing (although, in practice, considerably more notice will be given). Many tribunals now contact the parties before fixing a hearing and set out a range of possible hearing dates. They then invite both sides to respond with their dates to avoid, after receipt of which a mutually convenient date will be allocated.

All tribunal cases are allocated one day for the hearing. This is enough time for the majority of standard unfair dismissal cases which involve about two to four witnesses. If your case is particularly complex, or there are a large number of witnesses and the case is likely to take longer than one day, you should write to the tribunal as soon as possible – ideally, before the hearing date is fixed. If a case is not concluded on the day of the hearing, it will not continue the following day but will be adjourned, part-heard, to a day which may be several months away. This inevitably means that the parties' and, more importantly, the tribunal members' recollections of the evidence dims. Since you, as the employer, usually give your evidence first (see 16.21) it means that the tribunal may have forgotten much of what you had to say. Avoid this by ensuring that you have told the tribunal that your case might take longer than the allocated day.

Adjournments of the hearing date

16.3   If you need to apply for an adjournment (for example, because a witness is unavailable), you must do this as soon as possible in advance of the hearing. Some tribunals now refuse any requests for an adjournment made less than 14 days before the hearing and require both parties to attend and explain to the full tribunal why the adjournment is needed. Clearly this wastes both time and money – thus if an application to adjourn can be made earlier, it should be.

You can make an application in writing. Address your letter to the Clerk to the Employment Tribunal, and ask him to place your letter in front of the duty chairman. State the case reference number, the hearing date and set out your reasons for an adjournment. If a witness is out of the country on the date set for the hearing, try to obtain a short letter addressed to you from the witness and enclose a copy with your letter to the tribunal.

If the application is on the grounds of ill-health of a witness, ask the witness for a certificate from his doctor. Many tribunals have had experience of employers who seek repeated adjournments with the intention of delaying the date that they may be ordered to pay compensation – thus unsupported applications for adjournments are sometimes viewed with scepticism.

16.4   An occasional ground for an adjournment is that there are proceedings being taken simultaneously in the County Court or High Court. This will usually occur if Alf is claiming large sums for breach of contract (rather than unfair dismissal) which exceed the employment tribunal limit of £25,000. It may also occur if you are seeking to rely on a restraint-of-trade clause and are seeking an injunction in the courts. It is neither cost effective nor desirable to have the same issues tried in both an employment tribunal and in other courts. Since cases in the courts invariably take longer to bring to trial than cases in the employment tribunal, it is usual to apply for the employment tribunal proceedings to be adjourned, or 'stayed', pending a decision in the courts.

A tribunal is likely to grant a stay if the issues before the High Court or County Court are similar to those which the tribunal will have to decide. In particular, if the issues are complex or there is a large amount of money at stake, a tribunal will be reluctant to hear the case before the other court (since it might bind the other court by its decision). Frequently employees will be able to obtain legal aid to bring or defend proceedings in the ordinary courts, and the availability of legal representation is a factor which disposes tribunals to allow a trial to take place elsewhere.

If, however, the issues for the courts and tribunal are very different, the tribunal is unlikely to grant a stay. This might happen if Alf claimed compensation, or 'damages', for a long notice period in the High Court (where the only issue might be whether he had failed to seek employment elsewhere so as to minimise his financial losses) and unfair dismissal in the employment tribunal (where the issue might be whether he had been fairly selected for redundancy).

Likewise you might want to apply for a stay if you have dismissed Alf for misconduct and he is being prosecuted in the Crown or Magistrates' Court for the relevant offence. If Alf is convicted, it will clearly assist your case in the employment tribunal proceedings (note: an acquittal will not necessarily damage your case since the issue for the employment tribunal is not whether Alf was guilty, but whether you had reasonable grounds to believe he was guilty). In this scenario you would again write to the tribunal, as set out above, and ask for a stay pending resolution of the criminal proceedings.

16.5   Tribunals are free to award costs against any party in the event of an adjournment. They are not fettered by the rules which apply at the conclusion of a case, when they can only award costs in certain circumstances. If Alf applies for an adjournment on the day of a hearing, in circumstances where he could have applied earlier in writing and saved you the cost of attending, you may wish to ask the tribunal for the costs wasted by the hearing. The costs that can be awarded are governed by strict rules – see 16.40.

Witness statements

16.6   If a case goes as far as the tribunal, you should always make attempts to settle it (unless you are wary of setting a precedent which might encourage others to claim). The advantages, and formalities, of settlement are set out at in Chapter 15. If, however, settlement does not appear likely then you will need to commence detailed preparation for the hearing itself.

Prepare witness statements for every witness you intend to call. Although witness statements are not strictly necessary, tribunals like them (since they shorten proceedings) and they generate an image of efficiency. The statements should be carefully drafted and must include everything that you would want your witnesses (yourself included) to say if they were giving evidence in the witness box. This is because the tribunal will often expect the statements to stand as your entire evidence (subject to other matters which may come to light during and after cross-examination).

The witness statements should state at the beginning whose witness statement it is. It should be set out in short, numbered paragraphs, and each paragraph should deal with one point only. This makes it easy to cite a particular section of the statement when referring to a specific item of evidence. The statement should start in a standard way by describing yourself, the company, and then move on to the specifics of the claim.

Hypothetical statement

Statement of Stephen Isaacson

1. I am the managing director of Special Clothing Limited, and I make this statement in connection with the unfair dismissal claim brought against the company by Alf. The contents of this statement are true to the best of my knowledge, information and belief.

2. The company is a small company which has been trading for seven years. It deals in distributing 'seconds', i.e. clothes carrying brand-names which do not meet the manufacturers' standards, to wholesale outlets. We employ 15 people in total.

3. Alf has been employed by us since 12th September 1992. He was employed as a telephone negotiator. He was dismissed on 17th December 1997 for misconduct. . .

You should ensure that your statement (or statements, if more than one witness is to be called) deals with the procedural steps you have taken as well as the substantive reasons for Alf's dismissal. The statement should be signed and dated at the end.

16.7   It is not obligatory to send copies of the statements to Alf before the hearing (unless the tribunal instructs you to do so or you agree with Alf to exchange statements in advance), but you should hand them to him on the morning of the hearing before you are called into the tribunal.

Documents

16.8   You should arrange a bundle of documents for the tribunal's use. This bundle should contain all relevant documents which might be referred to during the proceedings. You should ask Alf, a week or two before the hearing, if there are any additional documents that he wants in the bundle. Any documents he supplies should be incorporated into the bundle or, if he does not cooperate, the bundle should be clearly labelled with the words 'Respondent's Bundle' to indicate that it contains your documents only.

It is not obligatory to send copies of the statements to Alf before

The bundle should be paginated and arranged in a sensible order. Although this sounds obvious, make sure that all the bundles have the pages in identical order with the same numbering – it is remarkable how frequently bundles have pages in different orders. This causes confusion and is frustrating for the tribunal.

It is often convenient to divide the bundle into sections as follows:

a   The Originating Application ('IT1') and Respondent's Notice of Appearance ('IT3'). Although the tribunal will already have copies of these, their inclusion in the bundle makes it easier to refer to them.

b   Witness statements – both your witnesses and Alf's.

c   All documents which are relevant to the decision to dismiss, such as written warnings, complaints by customers, notes of investigative and disciplinary meetings, details of how you selected Alf for redundancy, any statements produced at the time of the dismissal (rather than for the tribunal hearing itself after the unfair dismissal claim was lodged), the letter of dismissal and any documents relating to appeals. Arrange these, as far as possible, in chronological order.

d   Other relevant sections from Alf's personnel file, including his contract of employment (if one exists) and job appraisals.

e   Correspondence arising in connection with the unfair dismissal claim, again arranged in chronological order.

16.9   Note that certain documents must not be included in the bundle or produced to the tribunal. These are letters between you and Alf (or his advisers) in which you or he try to settle the claim. These letters are known as 'without prejudice' and cannot be shown to the tribunal unless both sides agree. Note that a letter does not have to be marked 'without prejudice' in order to attract this immunity from production – if it is part of a series of correspondence which is a genuine attempt to settle any issues in the claim, it automatically attracts that immunity. Conversely, any letters labelled 'without prejudice' do *not* automatically attract immunity from production *unless* they are part of a series of correspondence which is genuinely intended to settle the claim – thus they can be produced to the tribunal.

16.10   You should ensure that the front page of the bundle contains a proper index of the documents. Describe the documents in as short and neutral a form as possible – thus the index should state 'p7 – Letter from Alf dated 15th January 1998' rather than 'p7 – Letter from Alf in which he lies about his reasons for not attending work'.

You should prepare at least six copies of the bundle for the tribunal – one for each of the three members of the tribunal, one for you, one for Alf and one for the witness box. If you are able to, you should send a copy to Alf a week before the hearing.

The day before – trial preparation

16.11   Ensure that the trial bundles are in good order. Contact each of your witnesses and remind them of the time and place of the hearing.

As employer, you will usually present your case to the tribunal first (see 16.21). As such, you are entitled to an opening speech. In practice, some tribunals do not require unrepresented parties to make an opening speech, and they ask you to launch straight into presenting the evidence. You should, however, prepare one. The opening speech is a valuable opportunity to set out the issues to the tribunal and explain the gist of the evidence on which you will be relying. Practise it a couple of times before a mirror – this is the only part of the hearing where what is said is wholly within your control. See 16.22 for what you should include in your opening speech.

The next thing to do is decide exactly what evidence each of your witnesses will give (including yourself). If you have already prepared witness statements, you should already have done this. If not, prepare a list of the main points which each witness must give evidence on. Although hearsay evidence is allowed in an employment tribunal, it is best to limit each witness to giving evidence on matters which they personally saw or heard. This list, if no witnesses' statements are available, will form the basis of your examination of your witnesses.

You must also consider what documents you want the tribunal to see. It is *your* responsibility to check that the tribunal is shown all relevant documentation. If you do not introduce the documents yourself, the tribunal may not see them. The mere fact a document is in the bundle does not mean that it will be read. The documents should be identified by one of your witnesses during their evidence.

16.12   Next, consider the evidence that Alf is likely to call. Think about how he is likely to try to establish that you have unfairly dismissed him. You will have his Originating Application, and possibly other documents, which set out his case. Anticipate the ways in which he might try to cross-examine you, and think about your responses.

You will also need to prepare your cross-examination of Alf's witnesses. The content of an effective cross-examination is considered at 16.29. Whilst preparing, try to make a list of any inconsistencies within Alf's case (for example, where his account is inconsistent with a document) so that you can challenge him on these points.

You will have seen on the Originating Application that there is a box which Alf would have ticked requesting reinstatement, re-engagement or compensation only. If he has ticked either of the first two, or told you at least seven days before the hearing that he wishes the tribunal to consider ordering that he be reinstated or re-engaged by you, then you *must* be prepared to give evidence to the tribunal on the practicability of reinstatement or re-engagement (or you will probably be required to pay

Alf's legal costs, if any, caused by an adjournment). This is discussed further at 13.34.

16.13   An experienced advocate, working efficiently, can prepare a straightforward employment tribunal claim in a couple of hours. A difficult case can take a day or more to prepare. Do not underestimate the amount of work it takes to prepare a case thoroughly – it is wise to allow a full day even if the case is straightforward.

16.14   You may wish to make one last attempt to settle the claim. Alf's feelings of resentment at being dismissed have probably been replaced with nerves by the day before the hearing. He may be seeking a way to avoid the hearing without being seen to surrender. A sensible offer, possibly even coupled with an apology (thereby allowing Alf to save face), may encourage him to withdraw his claim.

Any settlement at this stage will have to go through ACAS (see Chapter 15 on settlement) – there will be insufficient time for Alf to obtain independent advice so as to render any non-ACAS settlement binding. If your case is weak, there may be very sound commercial reasons for settling the case for a few hundred or thousand pounds.

The hearing

16.15   Take a book for you to read to the hearing. This may sound absurd, but there can sometimes be long waits (for example, if your case is 'floating' or if the tribunal takes a long time to make up its mind).

Before you go in

16.16   Get to the tribunal early. Most tribunals start sitting at 10.00am, and open their doors at 9.00am. Check in at reception and tell the receptionist that you will be representing yourself. You will be asked for the names of your witnesses (and their job titles) so that the tribunal has a list of the evidence you are calling.

There will be a list, somewhere in reception, of all the cases that the tribunal is hearing that day. Check that your case is on the list and make a note of the name of the chairman and the clerk (in case there are any queries afterwards). Your case may be floating, which means that you have not been allocated to a particular tribunal. This happens because tribunals know that many cases settle shortly before the hearing, and therefore they list too many cases on the assumption that some of them will settle. If you are floating, you may have a long wait (and, indeed, you may not get called on at all – if this happens, it is extremely frustrating but there is nothing that can be done about it).

You will be directed to the Respondent's waiting room – the tribunals have separate waiting rooms for employees and employers. At some point, the clerk will come and introduce himself to you. He will ask you for four copies of your bundles (one for each of the three tribunal members and one for the witness box). He will also ask you whether each of your witnesses prefers to swear on the Bible or affirm. If you have any questions about procedure, ask the clerk before you go into the hearing.

The Department of Trade and Industry will repay all your witnesses' expenses. Ask the clerk before you go in for witness expense repayment forms – you will not be told about the witness expense procedure and you must ask for the forms. Your witnesses will be entitled to reclaim their travel expenses and loss of earnings, up to a certain limit, irrespective of whether you win or lose.

You should also, about 20 minutes before the hearing, go into the Applicant's (employee's) waiting room and speak to Alf. You do not need permission to go in there – simply walk in. Give Alf a copy of the bundle (assuming you have not sent it to him earlier) and check whether he will be relying on any other documents. If he tells you that he has no other documents, and then produces some during the hearing, you are quite entitled to complain to the chairman that Alf has misled you. Although the chairman is unlikely to do anything about it, it may affect Alf's credibility.

16.17   It is quite common to be approached by the press whilst waiting to go into the tribunal. They will ask you what your case is about – there is no obligation to talk to them and you are quite entitled to decline to comment. Publicity tends to be a bad thing for employers, since reporters tend to be interested in the more salacious details of a case. The press are also likely to approach Alf and ask him what the case is about. Even if you both decline to comment, they are usually entitled to sit in the tribunal to find (and report) any interesting cases.

16.18   If Alf does not attend, the clerk will try to contact him by telephone. If he appears to have a genuine reason for not attending, the tribunal will usually adjourn the case. If he does not have a good reason, the tribunal is likely to dismiss his claim. If the clerk is unable to speak to Alf, the tribunal may either dismiss the claim or adjourn it. If the claim is dismissed and it transpires that Alf has a good reason for not attending (for example, he was stuck on a broken down train), he can apply for a 'review' (which, in practice, means a rehearing) – see 16.47.

Going in

16.19   The clerk will come and collect you when the tribunal is ready to start the hearing. They will normally have read (or, at least, skimmed through) the bundles – accordingly if there is a lot of documentation you may not start promptly at 10.00am.

Your witnesses will go into the tribunal at the same time as you: they are entitled to watch the entire hearing and are not required to wait outside until it is their turn to give evidence.

Wait outside the tribunal door until the clerk tells you to go in. When you go in, you will see the three tribunal members sitting at a long desk (often on a slightly raised platform). You will also see a long table facing the tribunal (at which the parties sit), a chair and table for the witness and rows of chairs at the back of the room for observers (which includes witnesses when they are not giving evidence). The public and press are usually allowed into tribunals to watch. The employer always sits on the tribunal's right-hand side (i.e. on the left-hand side of the long table as you walk to them). Walk straight to your chair and sit down – you do not need to wait to be invited to sit.

The chairman, who sits in the middle, will be a lawyer specialising in employment law. The two wing members provide a balanced view of employment relations from a practical perspective – one will have been appointed by a trade union, and the other by an employer's association. You will not be told which is which.

16.20   All questions and remarks are addressed to the chairman. Unless being asked a question by one of the wing members, do not speak directly to them. You address the chairman as 'Sir' or 'Madam'. Unlike an ordinary court, you do not stand to address the tribunal but remain seated.

16.21   As employer, you will usually present your case first (since it is up to you to establish the reason for Alf's dismissal). If, however, you deny dismissing Alf (for example, if he resigned and is claiming constructive dismissal) then he will present his case first. Occasionally, if Alf is claiming discrimination (on grounds of sex, race or disability) as well as unfair dismissal, the tribunal may ask him to present his claim first. In such a case, the procedural order in the following sections will be reversed.

Opening speech

16.22   If you are unrepresented, the chairman will usually introduce himself and explain the order of proceedings. If he has read the bundle, he may ask you to present your evidence without making an opening speech – there is no right for you to have one. More usually, however, you will have the opportunity to address the tribunal (briefly) on the issues for the tribunal and how you intend to prove that Alf's dismissal was fair.

You opening speech, which you ought to have prepared the day before, should contain the following points:

- A brief summary of Alf's employment history; namely his job description, salary and length of employment.

- The reason for his dismissal.

- The reason Alf alleges his dismissal was unfair. Be neutral – the tribunal will realise if you are trying to score points at this stage, and an impartial opening will impress upon them that you are an unbiased and reasonable employer.

- Your main two or three points rebutting Alf's allegations. Try to refer to the evidence you will be producing rather than merely asserting that Alf is wrong. Also, be careful not to embellish your evidence – if you do, your case will inevitably appear weaker than it should do once the evidence has been heard. It is more impressive to say 'we will be calling Justin Donn, who will give evidence that he smelt alcohol on Alf's breath on at least four occasions in May' than to say 'He came in drunk most days'.

- Explain, briefly, any investigative meetings and disciplinary hearings that you held.

- If applicable, refer the tribunal to the two or three most important documents in the bundle. This will usually include the letter of dismissal.

An important point to bear in mind is that if your opening speech is too long, you will probably be doing nothing more than lecturing the tribunal on the same points that you are going to make when giving evidence. If they have heard all your points during the opening speech, they will be bored when you give evidence. Try to limit your opening speech to about five minutes.

Presenting your case

16.23   It is for you, and only you, to decide what evidence you wish to call and the order in which you wish to call it. If there is a person whose evidence will be central, such as a person with whom Alf was fighting, it is customary to call him first. Likewise, it is customary to call the person who actually took the decision to dismiss as early on as possible.

If you are the witness, you will not have anybody asking you questions but will have to rely on your memory (or a witness statement).

To call a witness to the stand, simply say 'I call *name* to give evidence' or 'my next witness will be *name*'. The clerk (or, if no clerk is present, a tribunal member) will deal with administering the oath.

16.24   If the witness has provided a statement which you wish to rely on, your opening questions will follow a standard format. This is set out in the following example:

Q. Please state your name and address.
A. Justin Donn, 8 Landsdown Court, Hendon NW4.
Q. What is your job title and for whom do you work, Mr Donn?
A. Assistant manager at Special Clothing Ltd.
Q. Please turn to page 22 of the bundle. . .Is that document your witness statement?
A. Yes.

Q. If you turn over the page, you will see a signature. Is that your signature?

A. Yes.

Q. Have you recently read the contents of your witness statement?

A. Yes.

Q. Are its contents true?

A. Yes.

You would then ask the chairman if the witness statement can 'stand as' the witness's evidence. The tribunal members will usually agree and read the statement themselves, although many tribunals prefer the witness to read the statement aloud.

If you have any additional questions, concerning matters which are not covered in the witness statement, you can ask them at this stage.

16.25 If the witness does not have a witness statement, or if you do not want to rely on it, you will need to take him through the events in question carefully (so as not to miss anything out).

Start, as above, by asking for the witness's name, address and job details. You should already have prepared a list, for each witness, of the points which you wish them to give evidence on. Go through this list, asking them as many questions as are necessary in order to bring out the necessary points.

When asking questions of your own witnesses, you are not normally allowed to ask 'leading questions'. A leading question is not, as is commonly believed, a question where the person answering does not like the answer. Rather, it is a question where the answer you are seeking appears *within* the question, such as 'did you then see Alf take some money out of the till?' or 'did you then tell Alf to go home for the rest of the day'. Instead, you should ask questions such as 'what happened next?' or 'what did you then say?' This method of questioning has the advantage that the tribunal is less likely to think that you, as employer, are influencing the testimony of your witnesses by the way you phrase your questions.

There are two main exceptions to the prohibition on asking leading questions, namely:

a   Where the answer is not contentious, for example 'are you

Alf's line manager?' or 'were you in the office at about 4.00pm on Monday, 21st September 1998?'

b   Where you are seeking to elicit a negative response, such as 'Q. Was Peter acting at all aggressively before Alf punched him?' A. 'No.' This is an exception because if you had to ask the question in a non-leading way, i.e. 'what was Peter not doing before Alf hit him?', it would be almost impossible to elicit the answer you are looking for.

16.26   When you have finished your examination, the witness will be cross-examined by Alf. To formally conclude the examination, say 'no further questions' or 'please wait there whilst Alf asks you some questions'.

Alf is then given an opportunity to cross-examine the witness. Normally the chairman will stop him (as he would stop you) if Alf asks inappropriate or irrelevant questions. Do not object to Alf's questions unless there is a very good reason (such as Alf is referring to 'without prejudice' offers). Tribunals are not like television courtroom dramas, where objections are common, and parties are usually entitled to cross-examine on any relevant matters.

After Alf has finished cross-examining, the chairman will ask the two wing members if they have any questions. Next, the chairman may ask some questions. Finally, you will be offered a chance to clarify any matters which have arisen during cross-examination. Do not use this opportunity to procure a complete rehash of the evidence. Limit it to one or two central points which require further questioning. If you do not ask any questions in re-examination, it can give a favourable impression that the evidence completely supports your case.

16.27   Go through this routine with each witness you want to call. Remember that each of the documents in the bundle has to be identified by a witness – if you forget to do this, the tribunal may disregard the document or not give it much weight.

After your last witness, you can show the tribunal statements from any witnesses who were unable to attend. Although this evidence is hearsay, because the witness is not available to confirm the truth of what is being said, it is admissible in tribunal hearings. If you rely on a hearsay witness statement, the chairman will probably tell you that the tribunal will consider it, but will not be able to give as much weight to it as to the evidence of 'live' witnesses because the witness was not available to be cross-examined.

16.28   When you have finished presenting your evidence, you must formally close your case. This is done simply by saying 'that is the Respondent's case' or 'I have no further evidence'.

Challenging Alf's case

16.29   It will then be Alf's turn to give evidence. Although there is no reason why Alf should not have witnesses to support his case, in practice it is more common for employees to be the only person giving evidence on their own behalf.

Alf (and his witnesses, in turn) will go into the witness box and give their version of events. As they give evidence, you should make a careful note of what they are saying (so that you have a record of their evidence when you cross-examine them).

Sometimes Alf will agree with the gist of your evidence, but go further than your evidence or simply challenge your decision to dismiss. This might occur, for example, when you have dismissed Alf due to persistent absence through illness. He may agree that he was ill for 12 weeks prior to the dismissal, but say that you failed to investigate whether he was likely to be able to return to work and, therefore, the dismissal was unfair.

More commonly, particularly in cases relating to his conduct, Alf's evidence may be wholly different from yours. You may have called witnesses who said that Alf was asleep on duty. Alf denies it. You may have called witnesses who said that Alf attacked a customer without provocation. Alf says that the customer hit him and he was acting in self-defence. The tribunal will be faced with making a decision as to whose evidence is the more reliable.

The purposes of cross-examination are two-fold:

i   to elicit additional information from Alf which assists your case; and,

ii   to attack Alf's credibility, so as to make the tribunal more inclined to prefer your evidence to that of Alf.

(i) Eliciting additional information

16.30   If you feel that there is additional information which Alf has
not revealed to the tribunal, or additional information which
can be used to make Alf look bad, use cross-examination as the
opportunity to elicit this evidence. This method of cross-
examination is useful where both sides agree the basic facts, but
put a different interpretation on them. An example may assist
in understanding how effective this type of cross-examination
can be:

Scenario: Alf works in a music shop. He has been dismissed for
selling CDs to friends, but not charging for all of them. He
agreed in his evidence that he had sold CDs to friends, but said
that he had rung all the transactions into the till properly.

Q. The store has a rule against employees serving its friends,
doesn't it?
A. Yes – but everyone does it.
Q. Were you aware of the rule?
A. Yes.
Q. Had you ever been told by your manager that the rule had
been revoked?
A. No.
Q. Had you ever been told by your manager that the rule was
not to be taken seriously?
A. No.
Q. What do you think the purpose of the rule is?
A. Well, I suppose to stop fiddling going on.
Q. Do you accept that, when you served your friends, you
were in breach of the rule?
A. I suppose so.
Q. And you knew that what you were doing wasn't allowed.
A. I suppose so.
Q. Why did you breach the rule?
A. I didn't think it mattered.
Q. Knowing it was wrong, presumably you didn't advertise
what you were doing to Mr Smith [the manager]?
A. What do you mean?
Q. You didn't call out a greeting to your friends when they
approached you, or introduce them to any of the other staff.

A. No.

Q. So your manner at the till was designed to conceal the fact that they were your friends.

A. Not really – I just didn't say anything to anyone.

Q. If you met your friends on the street, would you greet them?

A. Of course.

Q. Would you introduce them to whoever you were with?

A. Normally yes.

Q. So the fact you didn't greet them on this occasion, or introduce them to your colleagues, indicates that you didn't want anybody to know they were your friends.

A. It wasn't like that.

It is important to keep questions short and simple. Also, remember to ask questions and not make statements. Long rambling sentences can confuse the tribunal and the witness, leading in turn to further confusion as the witness gives an answer to a question which was perceived differently by the tribunal.

(ii) Attacking Alf's credibility

16.31   If Alf has given a very different account of events, it will be necessary for you to persuade the tribunal that your evidence is more believable than that of Alf. There are two main ways of attacking credibility.

16.32   Firstly, you can put inconsistent statements to Alf. These may be statements in writing or something he has said earlier in the witness box. Inconsistent statements are most effective when Alf produced the statements himself, as the following example shows:

Scenario: Alf is dismissed for incapability. He complains that the allegations have been made up, and that he is extremely good at his job. He also says that he had never been warned that his job performance was unsatisfactory.

Q. Do you remember complaining in February 1999 that you were being given too much work?

A. Yes.

Q. And, as you were asked to do, you put your grievance in writing to James Arney [the managing director].

A. Yes.

Q. Please turn to page 12 of the bundle. . .is that your letter?

A. Yes.

Q. Is it in your writing?

A. Yes.

Q. And it has your signature at the bottom?

A. Yes.

Q. Please read out the letter.

A. [Reads out letter, which includes the sentence 'It's not fair when I get told off for not working fast enough – Peter [the line manager] expects too much from everyone.']

Q. Do you accept that you were regularly told off for poor job performance during early 1999?

A. All right.

Q. Why did you tell the tribunal that you had never been told off?

A. Don't know.

Q. Did you take the warnings seriously?

A. Yes [note: an answer of 'no' would be even better from the employer's point of view!]

Q. You didn't just forget about them?

A. No.

Q. If you didn't forget about them, why did you tell the tribunal that you had never been warned about job performance?

A. I didn't think they counted!

16.33   This approach can also be effective when the inconsistent documents are prepared by other people. Thus, in the same scenario as above, Alf might allege that he was not given the opportunity to argue against dismissal. You can show notes made during the disciplinary interview to Alf and ask him questions such as 'has the person who made these notes got anything against you? Then why would he make it up?'.

16.34   Secondly, you can attack Alf's credibility by questioning him on why he did or did not do any particular act. This, again, is best demonstrated using an example:

Scenario: Alf is made redundant. He says that, as an alternative to dismissal, he should have been offered a transfer to another part of the company. You say that he was offered the job, but he turned it down. There is nothing in writing (which, ordinarily, would cause you difficulties since a tribunal would expect a job offer to be in writing).

> Q. How did you know about the other job?
> A. I heard about it from a colleague.
> Q. Who?
> A. I can't remember now – it was ages ago.
> Q. When did you hear about it?
> A. The week I was sacked.
> Q. Was this before or after our meeting?
> A. Before – so you must have known about it.
> Q. None of that is true, is it? You heard about the other job because I told you about it when we met.
> A. It is true. You never mentioned it.
> Q. What exactly did you hear?
> A. I heard the job was going and that it had not been filled.
> Q. Did you approach anybody and ask if you could be considered for the job?
> A. No.
> Q. Did you not think you were capable of doing it?
> A. No – I was quite capable of doing it.
> Q. Then why did you not approach anyone and ask to be considered for the job?
> A. Well, I assumed that I'd be offered it.
> Q. You say I didn't offer it to you during our meeting?
> A. That's right.
> Q. Then, if you knew about the existence of the job and you knew you were capable of doing it, why didn't you raise it?
> A. I can't remember.

16.35   When cross-examining, do not get into an argument with Alf. Exchanges such as 'oh yes you did' – 'oh no I didn't' are of very little assistance to the tribunal. If you do not score with a particular line of questioning, move on. Repetition gets tedious very quickly, and if the tribunal gets bored with your cross-examination they may miss important points that you make later.

16.36   After you finish cross-examining, the tribunal will ask questions and, as with your witnesses, Alf will be given the opportunity to clarify any matters he thinks fit. This procedure is gone through with all of Alf's witnesses.

Closing speeches

16.37   After all the evidence has been heard, both sides are given the opportunity to make a closing speech. The purpose of the closing speech is to allow each side to highlight their best two or three points and submit why their evidence should be preferred to the other side. It is also the opportunity each party has to make submissions on any relevant law.

Alf will make his speech first, and you are then given the final word (again, this is reversed in the circumstances set out at paragraph 16.21). This places you at two very distinct advantages, namely:

a   you get the last word and are able to comment on anything Alf has said during his closing; and,

b   whilst Alf is closing, you have a couple of minutes to make notes on what you want to say during your speech.

16.38   What should you say when closing? There is no golden rule, although you should avoid repeating the evidence that the tribunal has just heard. Remember that, in cases of misconduct, the tribunal is *not* concerned with whether Alf actually committed the act in question, but is concerned with whether you undertook reasonable investigations and whether *your* decision that he committed the act was reasonable. Often the best closing argument will be a short list of bullet-points indicating why your evidence should be preferred. This can be done by listing inconsistencies in Alf's evidence and identifying places where, if what he said was true, one would have expected him to act differently.

The decision and afterwards

16.39   After your closing speech, both sides will usually be asked to leave the room whilst the tribunal comes to a decision. Sometimes, if it is late in the afternoon, the tribunal might decide to 'reserve' its decision – this means that everyone goes home, and the tribunal will put its decision in writing and send it to both sides. If any further hearing is then necessary (such as to determine compensation for Alf), the parties will be required to return on another day.

Once the tribunal has made its decision, you will be called back into the room. The chairman will give a brief speech and announce whether the dismissal is fair or unfair. He will also tell you whether their decision was unanimous or by a majority (i.e. two to one).

16.40   If the tribunal has decided that the dismissal was fair, you are theoretically entitled to make an application for your legal costs. Tribunals will only award costs up to a maximum of £500 (unless the parties wish to go through a complicated, and expensive, assessment process known as taxation). More significantly, however, tribunals only award you costs if they consider that Alf has acted unreasonably, frivolously, vexatiously, abusively or disruptively in bringing or conducting the proceedings. In practice, it is quite unusual for an employment tribunal to award costs. The main exception to this is where either side has asked for an adjournment: in such a case, the tribunal will consider whether any additional costs are caused by the adjournment, and if so, may order the party responsible to pay them (irrespective of whether their conduct was unreasonable or frivolous etc.). The only other exception is where the employer is aware that Alf is seeking reinstatement or re-engagement, but fails to have evidence ready – in such a case, costs will almost always be awarded – see 13.34.

In any event, since you will not have used any lawyers in the conduct of your case, you would not actually have incurred any legal costs.

16.41   Unless you request otherwise, the tribunal will send out summary written reasons only for their decision. These reasons are extremely sparse and usually give little indication of the tribunal's thought process. Either side is entitled to ask for extended written reasons – i.e. a fully reasoned decision. If you want extended reasons, ask the chairman at the end of the hearing (or, alternatively, you are entitled to ask at any time in writing up to 21 days after you obtain the summary written reasons).

16.42   If the tribunal has decided that the dismissal was unfair, they will proceed immediately to a remedies hearing. This is to determine whether they are going to order that Alf be reinstated or re-engaged, and to decide how much compensation Alf will get. Sometimes, if you ask the tribunal or if it is close to 4.00pm (when the tribunal stops sitting for the day), the tribunal will adjourn the remedies hearing so as to enable negotiation to take place.

The remedies hearing

16.43   In the Originating Application (the form that Alf filled in to start his unfair dismissal claim), Alf would have ticked a box saying whether he wanted reinstatement (going back in his old job on the same terms, as if he had never been dismissed), re-engagement (coming back to work for you on different terms, i.e. in another job) or compensation only. The majority of employees seek compensation only.

Even if Alf seeks reinstatement or re-engagement, it is uncommon for tribunals to order it unless you are a large organisation or there is little animosity. In circumstances where there is bad feeling between you and Alf, or between Alf and other employees, it is rare for tribunals to make an order that you re-employ him. Reinstatement and re-engagement are discussed in more detail at 13.34.

16.44   The method of calculation of Alf's compensation is discussed in Chapter 13. The remedies hearing is a short hearing when Alf gives evidence as to his earnings pre- and post- dismissal, so as to enable the tribunal to calculate what his compensatory award should be.

If you have evidence that Alf has been working since his dismissal, but he tells the tribunal that he has been unemployed throughout (so as to increase his compensation), you should ask the tribunal for permission to give evidence yourself.

16.45   After having heard the evidence, you and Alf will then be given the chance to make any submissions on the calculation of an award. The tribunal will afterwards ask you again to withdraw whilst they decide the amount of compensation. Once you are called back in, they will explain to both sides how they have calculated the compensation.

Appeals and reviews

Appeals

16.46   You are only allowed to appeal from an employment tribunal decision if the tribunal has made a legal, rather than a factual mistake. You cannot appeal simply because you disagree with their decision – they, not you, are the judges. You need to obtain extended written reasons for the decision before an appeal can be considered, so you should ask for them at the hearing if you are considering an appeal.

Whether the tribunal has gone wrong on a question of law is outside the scope of this book – you should consult an employment law solicitor if you wish to consider appealing against a tribunal decision. Note that any appeal must be received by the Employment Appeal Tribunal within 42 days of the employment tribunal's written decision being sent out.

Reviews

16.47   A review, which is very different from an appeal, is a much underused procedure. Either party has the right, either at the hearing or within 14 days of receiving the written decision, to ask the tribunal for a review of its decision. Equally, the tribunal can review a decision of its own volition (this may happen if there is a change in the law between the oral hearing and sending out the decision).

A review will normally involve a re-examination of part of the decision, or an entire re-hearing, depending on the reason for the review. It can be heard by the same or a different panel of employment tribunal members.

A review may be granted in the following circumstances (each of which is similarly applicable to Alf):

a   If you did not receive notice of the proceedings, i.e. you did not receive notice of the hearing date and so did not turn up to the hearing. This is difficult to establish because there is a presumption that you would have received anything properly posted (and it is rare to find that the Notice was improperly addressed). Tribunals often have great difficulty accepting somebody's assertion that they did not receive a properly addressed and posted document.

b   If the decision was made in your absence, you may be entitled to a review if you can show a good and genuine reason for failing to attend. Examples of this might be a car accident on the way to the tribunal, a death in your close family or sudden illness. Tribunals are unlikely to be forgiving of a failure to attend if they think it would have been possible for you to telephone on the morning of the hearing to explain your absence, but you failed to do so.

c   If new evidence has become available. Note that tribunals do not like re-opening cases on the basis of new evidence – ordinarily you are entitled to one bite at the cherry only and you cannot continue litigating cases indefinitely. In order to persuade the tribunal to re-open the case, you will have to show that the new evidence was not available at the time of the earlier hearing and that there were no reasonable grounds for knowing of or foreseeing the existence of the new evidence. If the evidence could have been obtained for the original hearing, a review will not be granted.

d   The decision was wrongly made as the result of an error by the tribunal staff. This relates to administrative errors only. You cannot apply for a review because you think the tribunal members made an error in their decision – the correct approach if this happens is to appeal to the Employment Appeal Tribunal.

e   If a review is necessary in the interests of justice. This may occur if there have been *substantial* procedural irregularities, such as bias by a tribunal member or if one side was not given a proper opportunity to examine witnesses or address the tribunal on a relevant point. The other occasion on which this might happen is where, after the decision, events have occurred which show an assumption of the tribunal to have been wholly wrong. For example, if compensation for a long period of future loss is awarded, but Alf obtains new employment shortly after the hearing, an application for a review might succeed (although, if only a small amount of money is involved, the tribunal will be reluctant to re-open proceedings). Similarly if Alf is convicted by the criminal courts of an offence for which he was dismissed, and of which the tribunal thought him not guilty, the case might be re-opened to reassess the fairness of the decision on the level of contributory fault.

17. COMMON PITFALLS I – SITUATIONS DEEMED TO BE DISMISSALS

17.1   Before Alf can show he was unfairly dismissed, he needs to establish that he was dismissed in the first place. The law recognises that employers are often in an advantageous position over employees when it comes to the circumstances of terminating employment. Accordingly certain circumstances are regarded as dismissals by tribunals even if you have not actually uttered words such as 'you are sacked'.

The following circumstances, each of which is addressed below, are situations where the law may regard Alf as having been dismissed – thus allowing him to claim unfair dismissal:

a   where you are in breach of Alf's contract of employment and Alf resigns as a result – this is known as 'constructive dismissal';

b   where Alf resigns in the heat of the moment but reconsiders and asks for his job back within a short period;

c   pressuring Alf to resign ('resign or be sacked') or agreeing a termination payment if he resigns;

d   where Alf is on a fixed-term contract and you do not renew the contract at the end of the term;

e   where Alf is on short-time or where he has been temporarily laid off for a certain number of weeks;

f   where you refuse to allow a female employee to return to work after her maternity period.

(a) Constructive dismissal

17.2   Constructive dismissal is merely a legal phrase meaning that Alf has resigned in circumstances where he is legally entitled to resign because of your breach of his employment contract. The phrase is often incorrectly used to suggest that the dismissal was unfair. Constructive dismissals can be fair or unfair, depending on the circumstances surrounding them.

Alf is entitled to claim constructive dismissal when you are in 'repudiatory' breach of his contract of employment and he resigns because of it.

When will you be in 'repudiatory' breach of contract?

17.3   Not every breach of contract by you will amount to a repudiatory breach which allows Alf to claim constructive dismissal. It must either be a significant breach of an important term, or the last straw following a series of minor breaches.

It is not necessary for there to be a written contract of employment in order for Alf to claim constructive dismissal. A contract can be oral, and certain terms are deemed to be included even if they are not written down (such as a term that you have to pay Alf his wages).

Some examples of breaches of important terms which would entitle Alf to resign and claim constructive dismissal are:

- Reducing his wages – *Industrial Rubber Products v Gillon [1977] IRLR 389;*

- Failing to pay wages when they fall due – *Hanlon v Allied Breweries [1975] IRLR 321;*

- Suspending him without pay (unless Alf's contract of employment specifically states that you can do this);

- Changes to his working hours – this can be a major change, such as from a day-shift to a night-shift (*Simmonds v Dowty Seals [1978] IRLR 211*), or lesser changes such as requiring Alf to work from 9.00am to 6.00pm when he previously worked from 8.00am till 5.00pm (*Muggridge v East Anglia Plastics [1973] IRLR 163*);

- Changing Alf's place of work and expecting him to travel further each day. Unless there is a 'mobility clause' in Alf's contract of employment stating that you can require him to work anywhere (or, say, anywhere within 60 miles of Birmingham), then he cannot be obliged to travel anything more than a 'reasonable distance' to work each day. There is no definition of what amounts to a 'reasonable distance': however, if you require him to work somewhere that entails a significant increase in journey time or cost, then he will probably be entitled to resign and claim constructive dismissal;

- Changing Alf's duties so as to involve a loss of prestige (*Coleman v Baldwins [1977] IRLR 342*) or changing his status within the company (*Stephenson v Austin [1990] ICR 609*).

17.4 It must be emphasised that the fact you may be in repudiatory breach of contract, meaning that Alf is entitled to resign and claim he has been constructively dismissed, does *not* mean that the dismissal will be unfair. Sometimes such a dismissal can be justified on the basis of a business reorganisation, provided you have acted reasonably. For example, you may reorganise your business so that employees are expected to work eight hour, rather than seven hour, days. This would be a breach of contract and entitle Alf to resign and claim that he has been constructively dismissed. However, if you gave all employees reasonable notice of the change and offered them a *pro rata* pay rise then the dismissal is likely to be found fair.

17.5 Asking Alf to do something which he does not usually do is not necessarily a breach of contract – you are entitled to issue Alf with any reasonable instructions (provided they are lawful). This is addressed in Chapter 6.

Example

A Health Authority introduced a no-smoking rule for employees. An employee who smoked, and could not obey the rule, resigned and claimed constructive dismissal. The Employment Appeal Tribunal held that the employer was entitled to introduce such a rule and was not in breach of contract in so doing, since there was no contract term that the employees should be *allowed* to smoke – **Dryden v Greater Glasgow Health Board *[1992] IRLR 469***

17.6 *Can being 'horrible' to Alf be a repudiatory breach of contract?* Yes. The law presumes a relationship of trust and confidence between employees and employers, and if you act in a way which is intended (or likely) to destroy this relationship, you will be in breach of contract. Although this is not quite the same as saying you have to act nicely or reasonably towards Alf, if you persistently act unreasonably and Alf resigns as a result a tribunal might decide you were in breach of the duty of mutual trust and confidence.

Although small breaches of trust and confidence will not be enough to entitle Alf to resign and claim constructive dismissal, many such breaches can be added together so that the final breach can be viewed as the 'last straw'.

The following are examples of cases where an employer has been found to be in breach of the term of mutual trust and confidence:

- Failure to investigate staff's complaints properly. Likewise, failure to redress grievances promptly is also a breach of contract entitling an employee to resign and claim constructive dismissal (*Goolds v McConnell [1995] IRLR 516*).

- Verbal abuse of employees. In one case a nightclub manager called an employee 'a big bastard, a big cunt, you are pigheaded' (*Palmanor v Cedron [1978] IRLR 303*). In another case, an assistant manager told an employee who had been in the job 18 years, 'You can't do the bloody job anyway'. It was held that this was in breach of the term of trust and confidence – *Cortaulds v Andrew [1979] IRLR 85*. Likewise, constructive dismissals occurred when a female assistant was called 'a bloody fat cow and stupid stuck-up bitch' (*MacNeilage v Arthur Roye [1976] IRLR 88*) or referred to as 'an intolerable bitch on a Monday morning' (*Isle of Wight Tourist Board v Coombes [1976] IRLR 413*).

- Arbitrarily refusing to give pay rises to a particular employee when giving pay rises to others (*Gardner v Beresford [1978] IRLR 63*).

- Unjustifiably criticising a manager in front of her subordinates, thereby undermining her position (*Hilton Hotels v Protopapa [1990] IRLR 316*).

- Failing to provide proper support for staff (e.g. a hairdresser who was given no assistance when her junior resigned, despite complaints and requests for help – *Seligman v McHugh*

*[1979] **IRLR** 130*). In order for this to amount to a breach of trust and confidence, the overworking of staff would have to be significant and inappropriate – employers are entitled to expect their staff to work reasonably hard.

Alf's resignation

17.7   In order to establish constructive dismissal, Alf must prove that he resigned *because* of your repudiatory breach of contract. If he had been intending to resign anyway, there will be no constructive dismissal.

> **Hint**
>
> If Alf claims constructive dismissal, but he obtained a job soon after resigning from your company, see if you can discover the dates he applied for the job and attended interview (by telephoning his new employer). If it transpires that he applied for the new job whilst still working for you, you will have a good chance of persuading a tribunal that he was intending to resign in any event, and is simply trying it on with his claim.

17.8   It is also important that Alf resigns reasonably promptly after your breach of contract. If he waits six months after you change his working hours, and then resigns, he can be said to have waived his right to resign. Unfortunately, tribunals are not always consistent in determining what a reasonable period is. Some tribunals will expect Alf to resign within days of becoming aware of the breach of contract, whereas some will allow several months to elapse if Alf makes it clear he is reserving his position whilst searching for another job.

(b) 'Heat of the moment' resignations

17.9   If Alf resigns, using clear words of resignation, one would think that you were entitled to rely on the resignation and that he could not retract it (in the same way that you cannot retract a dismissal, once the words of dismissal are uttered or the letter sent).

However, in the last 15 years the law has introduced an exception to this for 'heat of the moment' resignations. Although you are normally entitled to take a resignation at face-value, if 'special circumstances' exist that alert the reasonable employer that a resignation might not be genuinely intended, then Alf is entitled to a short cooling-off period during which he can ask for his job back. If you refuse to give him the job back during this cooling-off period, you are deemed to have dismissed him.

Example

A mentally handicapped employee resigned after an argument with his managers. He appeared for work the next day, indicating that he had changed his mind, but the employers made him sign a blank payslip (which indicated his employment had terminated). The Employment Appeal Tribunal held that, in all the circumstances, the employers ought to have known the resignation might not have been genuine. Their refusal to have him back amounted to a dismissal – **Barclay v City of Glasgow District Council [1983] IRLR 313**

17.10   What amounts to 'special circumstances'? The few cases dealing with this point have generally dealt with resignations uttered in the heat of the moment whilst arguing with the employer. They have involved shouting, losses of temper and acting in an uncontrolled and emotional manner.

Example

Mr Lineham was the manager of a Kwik-Fit depot. In breach of company rules, he entered the premises one night to use the toilet. This was discovered by security staff and he was given a written warning. Whilst being given the warning, an argument ensued and Mr Lineham threw his keys down on the table and walked out. The Employment Appeal Tribunal treated this as a 'heat of the moment' resignation and stated that the employers ought to have allowed a cooling-off period before taking the resignation at face value – **_Kwik-Fit v Lineham [1992] IRLR 156_**

In addition, the _Barclay_ case (above) dealt with a mentally handicapped employee where the employers ought to have known he did not understand the significance or effect of a resignation. If Alf is calm and rational, a resignation can safely be accepted at face value and no cooling-off period need be allowed.

17.11   What is a reasonable cooling-off period? The courts have given little guidance over what amounts to a reasonable cooling-off period. It seems, however, that a cooling-off period need only be very short – perhaps a day or a weekend. Certainly if Alf returns after a week and asks for his job, you are quite entitled to refuse.

17.12   Do you need to offer the job back, or can you sit back and wait for Alf to approach you? At present, the courts have said that you are entitled to sit back and wait to see if Alf approaches you to ask for his job back. Nevertheless, in order to be safe, if Alf has resigned in the heat of the moment (and you are prepared to have him back), you should write to him immediately and ask him to contact you within 24 hours if he wishes to withdraw his resignation. If you do this, you will be protected before any tribunal if Alf then claims dismissal (subject to him bringing a claim for constructive dismissal, and alleging that you were in breach of contract in getting into an argument with him in the first place).

Remember that if Alf does ask for his job back, you are quite entitled to adopt disciplinary sanctions (such as a written warning, or such sanction as you consider appropriate) for both the loss of temper and the conduct which led to the argument (and loss of temper) in the first place.

(c) Pressuring Alf to resign or offering a 'resignation' package

17.13   Subject to the three exceptions below, never deliver an ultimatum to Alf to resign or be dismissed. Such an ultimatum, should Alf resign in response, is *always* regarded by the courts as a dismissal. This is because, in reality, it is your action and not Alf's which has caused the employment to terminate.

Many employers consider that the mere fact of Alf agreeing to resign will pre-empt him from bringing an unfair dismissal claim. However, it only takes a casual conversation with a friend to trigger a visit to Alf's local Citizens' Advice Bureau or a solicitor. Should this occur, you will shortly find a claim for unfair dismissal being brought against you.

It may be that any such dismissal is fair. If you said, 'if you don't resign, I'll sack you' after Alf has admitted stealing company property, the dismissal will probably be fair. However, in a borderline case, the use of such tactics will predispose a tribunal against you.

17.14   There are three exceptions to the rule that an ultimatum will amount to a dismissal:

a   Where the dismissal is not absolutely guaranteed. If Alf commits an act of gross misconduct, and you tell him that he will have to go through the disciplinary procedure and 'there is a good chance you will be dismissed', but you offer him the opportunity to resign, this will *not* be a deemed dismissal.

b   Where the ultimatum is not 'resign or be dismissed', but is 'perform or resign or be dismissed', i.e. an ultimatum to do the job properly. This is perfectly proper because you are quite entitled to demand that Alf carries out his duties properly even when his failures to perform do not justify immediate dismissal.

c   Where there is a genuine inducement to resign. If you say to Alf, 'I'll give you £5,000 if you resign – if you don't accept it, you're dismissed without a penny', this may amount to a genuine resignation (and not dismissal) if Alf accepts the money. The issue the tribunal have to decide is precisely what caused Alf's decision to resign. If it was the money, and he would have resigned without the threat, then it will be a genuine resignation. If the principal reason for his resignation was the threat, and he would not have taken the money if he had not been threatened with dismissal, then the tribunal will treat his resignation as a dismissal by you. Common sense suggests that the more money you offer in this scenario, the more chance you have of persuading a tribunal that it was the offer of money that triggered Alf's resignation.

(d) Failing to renew a fixed-term contract

17.15   One of the more surprising situations in which the law deems there to be a dismissal (and thus the potential for an unfair dismissal) is if Alf is on a fixed-term contract and you fail to renew it at the end of the term.

There is a very good reason for this: if employers could avoid unfair dismissal claims by placing employees on fixed-term contracts, then unscrupulous employers (being the ones against whom the law is meant to protect employees) could insist that *all* employees be employed only on short fixed-term contracts, which they might renew (or not renew) at their pleasure.

Accordingly, if Alf is on a fixed-term contract which you do not renew, the law treats it in the same way as if he had been on a normal ongoing contract and you dismissed him on the date that the fixed term expired. Remember that, at present, employees need two years' continuous employment before they can claim unfair dismissal – thus, at present, if you fail to renew a fixed-term contract after any period of less than two years, Alf cannot claim for unfair dismissal in any event. As stated elsewhere, however, the two-year rule is under challenge at the moment and the government has indicated an intention to reduce it to one year.

17.16   There is one exception to the rule that Alf is deemed to be dismissed on expiry of a fixed-term contract. If the fixed term is for one year or more, and the contract contains a provision that the employee agrees to forego his right to claim unfair dismissal, then he will be disentitled from claiming unfair dismissal. This is the only situation in which an employee is allowed to sign away his right to claim unfair dismissal.

(e) Placing Alf on short-time or laying him off

17.17   Sometimes laying Alf off, or placing him on short-time, will amount to a dismissal even if you are contractually entitled to do so. This occurs when specific criteria are fulfilled. In such a scenario, the reason for dismissal is deemed to be redundancy and Alf will be entitled to claim a redundancy payment from you.

In order for this to occur, Alf has to bring himself within some fairly complex rules. In practice, unless Alf is being advised by a trade union, he is unlikely to be familiar with this procedure and will not claim under it.

17.18   What do 'lay-off' and 'short-time' mean? The terms 'lay-off' and 'short-time' have very specific legal meanings. In order to qualify, Alf must work for you on terms that his right to be paid depends on being provided with work, i.e. he has no fixed wage. This situation is often found with temporary workers or workers in the building trade. He is laid-off in any given week if, during that week, he is provided with no work (and thus entitled to no remuneration). He is on short-time in any given week if, during that week, he is provided with a reduced amount of work so that his remuneration falls below half a normal weeks' pay.

If Alf works in a normal job for a fixed salary (e.g. £250 per week plus overtime) then you are not permitted to place him on short-time or lay him off unless there is a specific provision in his contract of employment entitling you to do so. If there is no such provision, and you lay him off for a week, he is entitled to resign and claim constructive dismissal on the grounds that you have not paid him the salary to which he is entitled.

When is Alf deemed to be redundant?

17.19   This procedure only applies if Alf has been employed by you for two years or more (although the two-year qualifying period may soon be reduced to one year). When calculating whether he has been working for two years or more, you do *not* count any period during which Alf was under 18 years old. However, weeks in which Alf has been laid-off, or placed on short-time, do count towards the two-year period.

Alf is deemed to be made redundant if the following criteria are satisfied:

a   he must have been laid-off, or kept on short-time, for *either* four consecutive weeks *or* six non-consecutive weeks within a period of 13 weeks;

b   within four weeks of fulfilling the above four-week or six-week period, he must have told you in writing that he intends to claim a redundancy payment;

c   within seven days of Alf telling you in writing that he intends to claim a redundancy payment, you do *not* tell him in writing that you will challenge his right to claim a redundancy payment; and,

d   he resigns within three weeks of the seven-day period in (c) expiring, giving you a proper notice period (either that which is set out in his contract of employment or, if there is nothing set out, one week).

17.20   When can you challenge Alf's right to a redundancy payment? If Alf has been laid-off, or placed on short-time, for the requisite periods (as set out above), he is entitled as of right to a redundancy payment *unless*:

a   on the date he wrote to you stating his intention to claim, it was reasonably to be expected that, within four weeks of his letter to you, he would start on a period of employment with you of at least 13 weeks during which period he would not be laid-off or kept on short-time for any week; and,

b   you give Alf notice of that in writing within seven days of his letter to you – see (c) above.

17.21   If you do challenge Alf's right to claim a redundancy payment on the grounds that work can soon be expected, he does not have to resign but is entitled to send in a claim to the employment tribunal *without* resigning, so that the tribunal can determine whether at the date of Alf's letter, the defence set out in (a) applied. If a tribunal rules in Alf's favour, and considers that as of the date of his letter it could not reasonably be expected that he would soon be provided with at least 13 weeks' work, then he has a further three weeks from the date of the tribunal's decision in which to resign and claim his redundancy payment.

(f) Failing to allow a female employee to return to work after maternity leave

Basic right to return

17.22   All female employees, irrespective of how long they have worked, are entitled to a maternity period of up to 14 weeks. During this period, which can be extended further if the baby is born late or the mother becomes ill with a pregnancy-related condition, an employee is entitled to return to work in her old job. In order to qualify, the employee must give written notice that she is pregnant and must give notice of the date that she wants her maternity leave to commence and the date that she wants to return to work.

If you refuse to allow an employee to return to work after her maternity period, you are deemed to have dismissed her. If the reason for the refusal is maternity-related (as it almost always will be, unless you can persuade a tribunal that she would have been dismissed anyway – for example, because of redundancies) then the dismissal will be automatically unfair. In such circumstances, the employee does not need two years' continuity of employment to qualify for an unfair dismissal claim, and she is entitled to bring a claim as of right.

Extended right to return

17.23   If, 11 weeks before an employee's expected date of childbirth, she has been employed for two years or longer then she is entitled to an extended period of a right to return to work. This additional period is 29 weeks after the beginning of the week in which childbirth occurs.

She is entitled to extend the 29-week period by four weeks if, and only if, before the notified date of return (or the last day of the 29-week period) she gives you a doctor's certificate stating that she will be incapable of working on the notified date of return (or the end of the 29-week period).

17.24   The right to return to work during this extended period, however, is *not* a right to return to the same job that she was doing at the time she went on maternity leave. The job must be similar, but not necessarily the same. In particular, she has to be offered terms and conditions which are not less favourable than those she worked under before.

If you fail to offer her similar (or better) employment, then you are deemed to have dismissed her.

What conditions must an employee fulfil before she obtains her extended right to return?

17.25   Before she is entitled to claim an extended right to return (i.e. so that you *must* re-employ her within 29 weeks from childbirth), an employee must fulfil the following conditions:

a   At least 21 days before her maternity period commences, she must inform you in writing of the fact she is pregnant, the expected date of childbirth *and* the fact that she intends to claim an extended right of return to work.

b   If, in the last three weeks of the basic 14 week maternity leave period (or after), you write to her asking her to confirm that she intends to return to work within 29 weeks of childbirth, she must confirm within 14 days of receiving the request (or, if it is not practicable for her to reply within 14 days, as soon as is reasonably practicable) that she does intend to return to work. Note that for your request to be valid (and thus prevent her from returning if she fails to respond), you must enclose a statement explaining that she will lose her right to return to work if she fails to reply within 14 days of receiving the letter (or, if not reasonably practicable, as soon as is reasonably practicable).

c   She gives you written notice at least 21 days before she intends to return to work. If she fails to do this, she will lose her right to return to work. Note that the notice must be given three weeks before the date of return, and that the right to return extends for 29 weeks from childbirth. Thus if the employee gives notice 27 weeks after childbirth, she will have lost her right to return to work since the right only lasts for 29 weeks and she will have failed to give three weeks' notice.

17.26   Once an employee has given notice of intention to return to work during the extended maternity period, you are entitled to postpone her return to work for up to four weeks from the date she has chosen. If, however, you fail to allow her to return then you are deemed to have dismissed her (and, unless you can satisfy the tribunal that the dismissal was not on grounds related to pregnancy – which will not be easy – the dismissal will be automatically unfair).

18. COMMON PITFALLS II – OPENING YOURSELF UP TO COMPENSATION CLAIMS

18.1 A number of situations amount to specific exceptions from the general rules set out in this book. For example, dismissals for certain reasons will *always* be unfair, no matter how good your justifications or how much consultation and discussion you went through. Likewise, although an unfair dismissal claim must ordinarily be started within three months of the dismissal, this time limit can sometimes be extended. Unless you are aware of these pitfalls, you may find yourself at the end of a claim which you might otherwise have avoided.

The following matters are discussed in this chapter:

a when the dismissal will automatically be unfair (irrespective of the number of years for which Alf has been employed or the procedure you follow);

b opening yourself up to claims of sex, race or disability discrimination;

c bringing an unfair dismissal claim more than three months after dismissal;

d dismissing because of pressure by other employees;

e dismissing after less than two years' continuous service.

(a) Automatically unfair dismissals

18.2 Certain dismissals will always be automatically unfair, irrespective of the business justification or the procedures which you adopt when carrying out the dismissal. Essentially, these dismissals are connected with trade union functions, health and safety matters, pregnancy or asserting a statutory right.

18.3 If a tribunal decides that the reason, or principal reason, for Alf's dismissal is one of the reasons set out below, it will find the dismissal to be unfair. It should be noted that these reasons are summarised and do not follow the exact wording set out in the relevant legislation.

Dismissals for the following reasons will always be unfair:

Trade union related dismissals

- If Alf is, or proposes to become, a member of a trade union.

- If Alf is not, or refuses to become, a member of a trade union.

- If Alf takes part in, or proposes to take part in, trade union activities.

Health and Safety related Dismissals

- Carrying out activities in connection with preventing or reducing risks to health and safety at work, if Alf been designated by you to carry out such activities

- Carrying out duties as a workers' representative (or committee member) on matters of health and safety at work, if Alf has been legally appointed or elected as a representative or committee member, or if you have recognised him as such.

- If Alf leaves (or refuses to return to) his place of work in circumstances where he believes there to be serious and imminent danger which he cannot reasonably avert, or if he takes steps to protect himself or others from that danger.

- If there is no health and safety representative or committee at work, or if Alf cannot practicably go through the representative/committee, bringing health and safety matters to your attention.

Pregnancy related dismissals

- Any reason connected with pregnancy.

Asserting a statutory right

- If Alf asserts you breached certain statutory (legal) employment rights, or brings a claim against you alleging such a breach, and you dismiss him as a result, the dismissal will be automatically unfair. The rights protected include claims to a minimum notice period, claims for itemised payslips or written terms and conditions of employment and rights connected with trade union membership or time off for trade union duties.

Other reasons

- If you dismiss Alf because of a transfer of undertakings – which may occur if you take over a business or a major contract – and you cannot establish an economic, technical or organisational reason entailing changes in the workforce, then the dismissal will be automatically unfair. This is considered further in Chapter 9.

- If you dismissed Alf because he failed to disclose a 'spent' conviction – see 5.4.

- If you dismiss Alf because he has told you or any other person (subject to certain conditions, such as he has told the other person in good faith, not for personal gain and when it was reasonable to tell that person) anything which suggests or proves:

  (i) a criminal offence has, or is likely to be, committed;

  (ii) you or any other person has failed to comply with a legal obligation;

  (iii) there is a significant risk to any person's health and safety;

  (iv) there is a risk of damage to the environment; or,

  (v) you are trying to conceal any of the above.

- If you dismiss Alf because he refuses to work more than 48-hours a week. This is a new law which states that all employees, subject to certain exceptions, cannot be forced to work more than a 48-hour week *unless* they have agreed in writing that they are willing to work more than a 48-hour week. The main exceptions are policemen, medical (and support) staff, family workers, or employees who set their own hours (such as senior managers). This is a complex area of law, and you should seek legal advice before considering dismissal on this ground.

- If you dismiss Alf because he insists on three weeks' paid holiday (increasing to four weeks in November 1999). Again, this is a new law and the same exceptions apply as to the item above, except that any written consent to waive paid holiday is invalid.

18.4 It is also important to bear in mind that if you select Alf for redundancy on one of the above grounds, the dismissal for redundancy will *also* automatically be unfair. It is crucial to ensure that the above reasons do not form any of your redundancy selection criteria.

Exception to the two years' employment rule

18.5 Ordinarily, Alf requires at least two years' employment with you in order to qualify to bring an unfair dismissal claim (although, as stated elsewhere, at the time of writing the government is considering reducing this period to one year).

However, if the reason for the dismissal was one of the above reasons, *other* than being due to a transfer of undertakings (first reason under 'other reasons' in the above list), it is not necessary for Alf to have worked for two years. Thus he will be entitled to claim for dismissal (and will succeed) if he has only worked for one month but you dismiss him because he wants to join a trade union.

More commonly, if a new employee announces that she is pregnant when she first arrives for work (not having told you at interview), and you dismiss her as a result, you will automatically be found to have unfairly dismissed her even though she has not been working for two years. She would also have a claim for sex discrimination (in which there is no upper limit for compensation), as she would have had if you refused her the job because she told you she was pregnant at interview.

(b) Claims of sex, race or disability discrimination

18.6 Employees are entitled to claim sex or race discrimination in addition to unfair dismissal. Since 1995 employees have also been able to claim that they have been discriminated against on grounds of physical or mental disabilities. Although it is not yet common to see disability discrimination claims tied with unfair dismissal claims, it is likely that the frequency of these claims will increase in the future.

The advantages to Alf of claiming sex or race (or disability) discrimination as well as unfair dismissal are three-fold:

a   The mere allegation of sex or race discrimination, as contrasted with unfair dismissal, can place greater pressure on an employer to settle because of the fear of adverse publicity.

b   Alf does not need two years' continuous employment to claim discrimination. Thus sex or race discrimination is often used as a way of claiming unfair dismissal by the back door when an employee lacks the requisite two years' employment. This is wholly improper, and such discrimination claims are often without merit (even if an unfair dismissal claim might have merit) – nevertheless you should be careful when dismissing to avoid allowing any opening for the employee to allege discrimination.

c   At present, unfair dismissal awards are limited to £18,600 (i.e. a maximum of £6,600 for the basic award and £12,000 for the compensatory award). There is no limit on discrimination claims, and thus employees sometimes claim sex or race discrimination in the hope of getting a higher award.

18.7   Resisting a claim for sex, race or disability discrimination is outside the scope of this book. As with an unfair dismissal claim, if Alf wishes, or is advised, to claim discrimination then you will be forced to fight the claim. Alf's ability to claim discrimination is something you should be aware of and have at the back of your mind so as to avoid saying or doing anything foolish. There are a few elementary steps you can take to show that your dismissal of Alf (or selection of him for redundancy) is not on grounds of sex or race. These steps include:

●   Be very cautious when dismissing any pregnant employee – unless your justification for dismissal is extremely clear, you may have difficulties persuading an employment tribunal that pregnancy was not the principal reason for dismissal.

- Ensure that all the steps you take in connection with the dismissal, including notes of meetings, interviews and consideration of alternative employment are fully documented.

- If you are selecting a large number of people for redundancy, ask a colleague to draw up a list showing peoples' sex and race *after* you have made your initial selection. Work out, as a percentage, whether the sex and ethnicity of the people you have selected for redundancy broadly matches the spread of sexes and races in your workforce. If there is a significant disparity, for example 20% of the people you employ are black, but 80% of those selected for redundancy are black, you will have difficulty persuading a tribunal that your selection was not affected by racial overtones and you may wish to reconsider your selection criteria. By contrast, if you can show that you monitored the race and sex of employees you selected for redundancy *after* the initial selection (not during), this will go some way to persuading a tribunal that you are not inadvertently discriminating.

18.8   If Alf does claim sex, race or disability discrimination, it is important to bear in mind that frequently the only way in which a tribunal can judge whether you were guilty of discrimination is by drawing inferences from your manner of giving evidence. Effective presentation at the hearing is particularly important, and if you end up facing an allegation of discrimination you may wish to give thought to engaging a lawyer.

(c) Bringing a claim more than three months after the dismissal

18.9   Claims for unfair dismissal must ordinarily be brought within three months of the dismissal (six months for an unpaid redundancy payment).

The three-month period starts running on the date of the dismissal, if it is a summary dismissal, or the date that the notice period expires if you dismiss with notice. Sometimes it is not always straightforward as to when the three-month period starts running: for example if you have paid Alf monies in lieu of notice, a tribunal will often have to construe the letter of dismissal to determine whether the employment ended on the date of the letter or the date that the notice period expired.

Ordinarily, if Alf fails to present his claim within three months, he will be prohibited from claiming. There are two things to note:

a   The three-month period includes the day of dismissal. Thus if Alf is dismissed on the 15th September 1998, his claim must be presented by 14th December 1998. If it is presented on the 15th December, it is a day too late and the claim will be dismissed (subject to the exception below).

b   The claim must be presented at the tribunal within three months. This means that it must have been delivered to the tribunal – proof of posting within the time period is insufficient. If Alf leaves it right until the end of the three-month period to post his claim, and it arrives late because of delays in the post, it will be regarded as too late and Alf will have to bring himself within the exception set out below.

What is the exception to the three-month limit?

18.10   If Alf can establish that it was 'not reasonably practicable' to present his claim within three months, then he will be permitted an extension of time. Tribunals tend to be fairly strict when applying this rule, and it is not easy for employees to satisfy a tribunal that it was not reasonably practicable to bring a claim within three months. Essentially Alf will have to prove that it was not reasonably feasible for him to present his claim within the expected time period.

18.11   Examples of when it would be 'not reasonably practicable' to bring a claim within three months: A tribunal would find that it was 'not reasonably practicable' to bring a claim within three months (and thus allow an extension of time) in the following circumstances:

- If there was a physical problem impeding Alf from claiming, for example he was in hospital with two broken wrists and incapable of writing for three months after dismissal. It is not easy to satisfy a tribunal that physical infirmities rendered it not reasonably practicable to claim.

- If Alf was actively misled by you as to his rights: this is a loose interpretation as to the meaning of practicability – however, if you have acted fraudulently and misled Alf as to the period in which he has to claim, a tribunal is likely to allow him an extension of time.

- If Alf is unaware of the right to claim unfair dismissal at all – although very few tribunals will accept Alf's word on this since very few employees have not heard of unfair dismissal claims.

- If Alf is unaware of the facts giving rise to the claim during the three-month period, but becomes aware of new facts which give rise to a claim subsequently, he will usually be granted an extension of time if it was reasonable for him to be unaware of those facts previously and the acquisition of the new facts is crucial in the decision to bring the claim. A classic example of this is where you have said Alf's job was redundant, but he discovers outside the three-month time limit that you hired somebody to replace him (thus indicating that no redundancy situation actually existed).

18.12   Examples of where it is *not* 'not reasonably practicable' to bring a claim within three months: A tribunal would not find that it was 'not reasonably practicable' to bring a claim within three months (and thus not allow an extension of time) in the following circumstances:

- Ignorance of the three-month time limit for bringing the claim. If Alf has engaged lawyers or advisers, and they do not tell him of the three-month limit, he is able to sue them for negligence but will be unable to proceed with a claim against you.

- Failure by his solicitors or other advisers to present the claim in time.

- Failures of the postal service when Alf leaves it to the last moment to present a claim. If Alf leaves it till the day before the time limit expires and thereby takes the risk of the claim not arriving in time, he will probably not be permitted an extension of time. If, however, he has posted the claim in good time and unexpected delays occur which could not ordinarily be anticipated then, subject to satisfying the tribunal that the claim form *was* posted on the date claimed (which may not be easy), Alf is likely to obtain an extension.

- Waiting for the outcome of other proceedings – if Alf was waiting for the outcome of criminal or other civil proceedings before presenting his unfair dismissal claim, this will *not* mean that it was not reasonably practicable to bring the unfair dismissal claim within three months of dismissal.

- If Alf has delayed bringing his claim whilst going through an internal appeal procedure against dismissal, this will *not* be sufficient to allow him an extension of time, since it would still have been 'reasonably practicable' to present the claim within three months from the original dismissal.

If it was not reasonably practicable for Alf to present his claim within three months, what extension of time will be given?

18.13   If Alf can persuade the tribunal that it was not reasonably practicable to present his claim within three months, he will be entitled to proceed with the claim *provided* he can satisfy the tribunal that the claim was presented within a reasonable time after the three-months expired. Accordingly Alf does not become entitled to bring his claim irrespective of how late the application was lodged.

There is no firm rule as to how long is allowed to elapse between Alf becoming aware of his right to bring a claim and actually presenting it once he has gone past the three-month limit. If he presents it within a week of becoming aware of all relevant facts, this is almost certain to be a reasonable period. A month may well be too long, depending on his reasons for taking a full four to five weeks to fill in a form. Anything over two months is likely to be regarded as going beyond a 'reasonable period' and thus Alf will not be permitted to proceed with the claim.

(d) Dismissing because of pressure by employees

18.14   Sometimes disharmony between employees can be a fair reason for dismissing Alf – see 10.4. However, the law provides that if other employees call or threaten a strike, or other industrial action, then any such pressure placed on you must be disregarded when determining whether Alf has been unfairly dismissed.

Accordingly, therefore, you can sometimes rely on tension in the workplace as a reason for dismissing Alf. However, as soon as things deteriorate and become more formal (due to threatened, or actual, industrial action), you cannot dismiss Alf unless you can show that you would have dismissed without the threatened or actual industrial action.

If you *do* dismiss Alf because of strikes or industrial action, and the tribunal decides that the dismissal was unfair, you may still be able to show that Alf's conduct contributed to the industrial action by triggering the enmity of his colleagues. This would lead to a reduction in his award – see 13.24.

(e) Dismissing Alf after less the two years' continuous service

18.15   At present, employees need to have been working for two years before they become entitled to certain employment rights, such as the right to claim unfair dismissal or a redundancy payment. There are, however, two exceptions to the need for Alf to have been working for two years before he can claim:

a   where the dismissal is for an automatically unfair reason (except when it arises out of a transfer of undertakings) – see 18.2;

b   where you did not give Alf his statutory minimum notice period (see 12.11 for how to calculate this period) and, if you *had* given it to him, he would have satisfied the two-year requirement. Note that it is the statutory minimum notice period, and not any notice period set out in Alf's contract, which you must add to the date of dismissal if he was dismissed without notice.

18.16   You should also be aware that, as mentioned elsewhere in this book, the two-year qualifying period is being considered by the European Court of Justice as being potentially contrary to European law. The government is, in any event, considering reducing the qualifying period to one year.

APPENDIX I
SAMPLE WRITTEN STATEMENT OF PARTICULARS OF EMPLOYMENT

Employer: Chequers' Alpacas and Dalmatians Limited

Employee:_____

This is the written statement of the Particulars of your Employment as required by the *Employment Rights Act 1996*.

1. Dates of Employment
   Your employment with us began on 12th January1997. You had not previously been employed by us or an associated company, and so your continuity of employment also started on 12th January 1997.

2. Job Title
   You are employed as an administrative assistant to Anita Alexander, manager of Chequers' Alpacas and Dalmatians Limited. Your duties include general administration, filing, dealing with customers' enquiries and general secretarial duties. You may, however, be required to undertake any reasonable tasks that are necessary in the interests of the business.

3. Place of Work
   Your normal place of work is Chequers' Farm, Redhill, Surrey, although you may be required to travel around Great Britain on an occasional basis. We reserve the right to change your normal place of work to any location within 50 miles of Redhill but will give you at least 28 days' notice before doing this.
   Chequers' Farm is a non-smoking environment.

4. Hours of Work
   Your normal working hours are 8.00am to 5.00pm Monday to Friday, although we may require you to work overtime on occasion. Any overtime will be paid at time-and-a-half. You are entitled to a one-hour break for lunch.

5. Remuneration
   As at 12th January 1997:

a   Your remuneration is £12,500 pa, payable monthly in arrears.

b   You are entitled to 20 days' paid holiday per year plus authorised bank holidays, which accrues on a *pro rata* basis. The holiday year runs from 1st May to 30th April. Up to five days' holiday may be carried over into the next holiday year. All holiday entitlements shall be taken entirely at our discretion, although we will not unreasonably refuse your requests for holiday. In the event of termination of employment you will forfeit any accrued entitlement to holiday.

c   Your remuneration does not include any pension contributions.

6. Termination of Employment

We reserve the right to terminate your employment immediately in cases of gross misconduct. In all other cases, periods of notice required are as follows:

a   If we dismiss you: you are entitled to one week's notice during your first two years of employment. After this, we will give you one week's notice for every complete year that you have worked, up to a maximum of 12 weeks.

b   If you resign: you must give us one weeks' notice during your first two years of employment. After this, you must give us one month's notice.

7. Sickness

a   In the event of sickness we will pay you full sick-pay for six weeks, after which you will be placed on statutory sick-pay. 'Qualifying days' for the purpose of statutory sick-pay are those days on which you normally work under this contract.

b   In order to qualify for sick-pay, you must inform us of the reason for your absence not later than midday on the first day of your absence and must complete a self-certification form if you return to work within seven days.

c   If you are sick for longer than seven days, you must provide a doctor's medical certificate by the eighth day of sick-leave, and must produce further certificates as necessary upon the expiry of each of the previous certificates.

d   We reserve the right to require you to undergo a medical examination in the event that you have been absent through sickness for over four weeks.

8. Confidentiality

Any information about the company, including any information about our customers and suppliers, of which you become aware due to your employment must be treated as confidential. It must not be disclosed to any third person, or used for your own advantage, either during your employment or after termination of your employment.

9. Disciplinary Procedure

We regard high standards of conduct as crucial. This disciplinary procedure sets out the procedure which we will follow, and the possible disciplinary sanctions that may be applied, if you fall short of the standard expected of you. Since we are a small, family business, the disciplinary procedure will usually be carried out by Anita or John Alexander.

a   In any case of misconduct, we will undertake a full investigation into the circumstances surrounding the misconduct before undertaking any disciplinary action. This will include a meeting with you (at which you may have a representative present) during which the allegations are discussed and you are given a full opportunity to put your case.

b   In cases of minor misconduct: you will either be given an oral warning or a written warning, depending on the seriousness of the misconduct. A record of the warning will be kept for two years, after which time it will be discarded.

c   In cases of gross (or very serious) misconduct, you will either be dismissed or, if there are extenuating circumstances, you will be given a written warning.

d   In the case of repetition of minor misconduct (whether of the same or a different nature) you may be dismissed.

e   The following are examples of minor misconduct which would warrant an oral or a written warning: poor job performance, absence from work, smoking, poor timekeeping, failure to comply with an instruction, mild intoxication due to alcohol, swearing, rudeness to colleagues. This list is not exhaustive.

f   The following are examples of gross misconduct which would warrant dismissal: intoxication at work in front of customers, illegal use of drugs, theft, actual or threatened violence, malicious damage to property, personal use of confidential information, falsification of records, negligence resulting in serious loss or injury, harassment of employees, customers or any other third parties on grounds of sex, race, age, sexual orientation or disability. This list is not exhaustive.

g   In the event of an allegation of gross misconduct, you may be suspended without pay whilst the allegation is being investigated and the disciplinary action considered. Any period of suspension without pay will not exceed four weeks.

h   You are entitled to appeal against any disciplinary decision with which you do not agree. An appeal should be sent in writing to John Alexander within seven days of the decision, stating your grounds for the appeal.

10. Grievances

In the event of any grievance arising out of your employment, you should firstly discuss the matter informally with Anita Alexander. If the matter cannot be resolved you should address your grievance in writing to John Alexander, who will respond in writing and take such action as is appropriate within 14 days (or such longer period as is reasonable).

I acknowledge receipt of this written statement of Particulars of Employment and confirm that this constitutes my understanding of my contract of employment. In particular, I confirm that I have read and understood the disciplinary procedure set out at section 9.

Signed.. Dated....................
[Employee]

Signed.. Dated....................
[Employer]

APPENDIX II
SAMPLE COMPROMISE AGREEMENT

This compromise agreement is made between Chequers' Alpacas and Dalmatians Limited ('Chequers') and Alf pursuant to the provisions of section 203 of the *Employment Rights Act 1996.*

WHEREAS:

1 Alf was employed by Chequers as an administrative assistant by a contract of employment dated 12th January 1997, and dismissed by a letter dated 14th March 1999;

2 Alf has received advice from a relevant independent advisor, namely Amanda Olins of the Radlett Citizens' Advice Bureau, as to the terms and effect of this agreement and, in particular, its effect on his ability to pursue his rights before an employment tribunal;

3 the conditions regulating compromise agreements under the *Employment Rights Act 1996, Sex Discrimination Act 1975, Race Relations Act 1976* and *Disability Discrimination Act 1995* are satisfied in relation to this agreement:

IT IS AGREED AS FOLLOWS:

1 Chequers will pay to Alf the sum of £2,000 within 28 days of this Agreement in full and final settlement of all claims which arise in case number _____ or such claims as may be brought on the basis of the facts alleged in the Originating Application therein;

2 Chequers will provide a reference to potential employers of Alf, upon request, in the following terms:

'Alf worked for this company as an administrative assistant between January 1997 and March 1999. He was a hard and diligent worker during his period of employment and his work was always of the highest standard. He was dismissed because of a misunderstanding between himself and another member of staff.'

Alf agrees not to discuss the details of this settlement with any persons apart from his wife and his legal advisors.

Signed.. Dated...................
[Chequers' Alpackars and Dalmatians Limited]

Signed.. Dated...................
[Alf]

APPENDIX III
USEFUL ADDRESSES AND
TELEPHONE NUMBERS

Essential addresses

- Central Office of the Employment Tribunals – 100 Southgate Street, Bury St. Edmunds, Suffolk IP33 2AQ (tel: 01284 762171)

- Employment Tribunal Helpline (free telephone helpline) – 0345 959775

- ACAS Head Office – Brandon House, 180 Borough High Street, London SE1 1LW (tel: 0171 396 5100)

Employment tribunals

- Ashford: Tufton House, Tufton Street, Ashford, Kent TN23 1RJ (tel: 01233 621346)

- Bedford: 8–10 Howard Street, Bedford MK40 3HS (tel: 01234 351306)

- Birmingham: Phoenix House, 1/3 Newhall Street, Birmingham B3 3NH (tel: 0121 236 6051)

- Bristol: The Crescent Centre, Temple Back, Bristol BS1 6EZ (tel: 0117 929 8262)

- Bury St. Edmunds: 100 Southgate Street, Bury St. Edmunds, Suffolk IP33 2AQ (tel: 01284 762171)

- Cardiff: Caradog House, 1–6 St. Andrews Place, Cardiff CF1 3BE (tel: 01222 372693)

- Exeter: Renslade House, Bonhay Road, Exeter EX4 3BX (tel: 01392 279665)

- Leeds: 4th Floor, Albion Tower, 11 Albion Street, Leeds LS1 5ES (tel: 0113 245 9741)

- Leicester: 5A New Walk, Leicester LE1 6TE (tel: 0116 255 0099)

- Liverpool: Union Court, Cook Street, Liverpool L2 4UJ (tel: 0151 236 9397)

- London (North): 19–29 Woburn Place, London WC1H 0LU (tel: 0171 273 8575)

- London (South): Montague Court, 101 London Road, West Croydon CR0 2RF (tel: 0181 667 9131)

- Manchester: Alexandra House, 14–22 The Parsonage, Manchester M3 2JA (tel: 0161 833 0581)

- Newcastle: Quayside House, 110 Quayside, Newcastle upon Tyne NE1 3DX (tel: 0191 232 8865)

- Nottingham: 3rd Floor, Byron House, 2A Maid Marian Way, Nottingham NG1 6HS (tel: 0115 9947 5703)

- Reading: 5th Floor, 30–31 Friar Street, Reading RG1 1DY (tel: 01734 594917)

- Sheffield: 14 East Parade, Sheffield S1 2ET (tel: 0114 276 0348)

- Shrewsbury: Prospect House, Belle Vue Road, Shrewsbury SY3 7NR (tel: 01743 358341)

- Southampton: 3rd Floor, Duke's Keep, Marsh Lane, Southampton SO1 3EX (tel: 01703 639555)

- Stratford: 44 The Broadway, Stratford, London E15 1XH (tel: 0181 221 0921)

INDEX